PHR Study Guide 2024-2025

Complete Review + 480 Questions and Detailed Answer Explanations for the Professional in Human Resources Certification (4 Full-Length Exams)

Printed in the United States of America

Access the Bonus Audiobook and Flash Cards!

Scan the QR code below with your phone and you will be given a link to google drive, where you can download the audiobook and flash cards.

If the QR code does not work for you, please contact us at info@newstonetestprep.com

Table of Contents

Introduction

Although there are a few different kinds of Professional in Human Resources tests, most of them follow a similar format. You will take exams on a computer at a Pearson VUE testing center.

The majority of tests feature multiple-choice questions. However, there may also be some brief scenario questions, fill-in-the-blank, drag-and-drop and multiple-choice questions with multiple correct answers.

Rules

1) You must arrive 15 minutes early for your exam. This will give you enough time to complete the required sign-in process before the exam starts.

2) If you do not arrive at the testing facility on time, you will be declared late and be unable to take the exam on that day. You will forfeit all fees.

3) You will need to bring a valid government-issued photo ID to the testing location. This must include your entire name as it appears on your application, a current and identifiable photo and your signature. IDs with missing or wrong information will not be accepted. You will be unable to take the exam and will be marked as a no-show.

How to Register for the Exam

You can apply for PHR certification and register for the exam at any time online. However, before you begin, spend a few minutes reviewing the most up-to-date information and qualifying criteria for the PHR. All HRCI (HR Certification Institute) certificates are based on academic and employment experience, geographical location and whether or not you work for a multinational corporation.

Create an HRCI Account and a Profile

If you have not already done so, create a user profile with HRCI on the official site. To begin, enter your email address and password, followed by your full legal name, country of residence and company.

Fill out the Application

On your user profile, go to the My Exam Applications section. Click the Apply button after you have found the certification you want to obtain.

The information needed is as follows:

1) Personal information: Your legal name, residence and any human resources affiliations or preparation courses you have taken. If you previously mentioned it in your HRCI profile, some of this information may be automatically entered for you already.

2) Professional and educational background: Indicate your educational qualifications and any relevant job experience. HRCI will analyze your application to confirm that you match the qualifying criteria.

3) Need for special arrangements: You must submit a Special Testing Accommodation Request with your exam registration and show documentation if you require alternate testing arrangements due to a handicap.

Submit your application and check out when you are finished. You can save your work and come back to it later if necessary.

Validation and Scheduling

You should receive an email confirmation within one business day of completing your application and payment. Allow for extra processing time as HRCI reviews your application.

This normally takes a day or two, with lengthier wait times for individuals who have requested accommodations or who have been selected at random for auditing.

What Students Can Do

It is best to register for your exam as soon as possible to ensure you get the time, date and venue of your choice. The number of seats available is restricted, and they are filled on a first-come, first-served basis.

What Students Cannot Do

No personal items are allowed within the testing facility.

This includes the following:

- Cell phones
- Food and beverages
- Jackets
- Jewelry and timepieces
- Any items for research or testing

During the exam, these materials will be kept in a secured locker.

Chapter 1: Business Objectives and Best Practices

Business management is a functional area of the PHR exam that covers the management of HR as well as organizational activities. The objective of a strategic business management process is to develop different business metrics to evaluate the effectiveness of business activities.

Strategic business management focuses on managerial tasks and activities to establish and maintain a qualified HR strategy. HR management contributes to the effectiveness of organizational goals. Thus, recognizing the link between HR and organizational strategies is essential for the success of a business.

Human Resource Management and Strategies

HR strategy pertains to the management of human capital and performance to meet an organization's mission, values and goals. It is also critical to the success of a business, as employee behavior and performance largely impact business goals.

An effective HR strategy helps departments, teams and individuals working in an organization perform more effectively. The HR strategy aligns the organizational goals with HR management.

There are seven main functions of HR:

- **Strategic Management** – Develop a proactive plan for the future that meets the organization's long- and short-term business objectives.
- **Employment and Workforce Planning** – Develop the organization's selection, recruitment, placement and resignation processes. It is the HR department's responsibility to establish the best candidate criteria for different roles. A workforce plan is critical to developing an effective HR strategy that sets goals for human capital.
- **HR Development** – Ensure that new candidates get appropriate training and assist the organization with change and performance management.
- **Total Rewards** – Develop and administer benefit and compensation packages.

- **Develop Policy** – Develop and ensure the implementation of the organization's policies and procedures.
- **Labor and Employee Relation** – Align employees' rights and needs with the organization's goals and objectives. For example, appropriately handle union and non-union problems.
- **Risk Management** – Identify risks that may threaten business goals. It is the HR department's responsibility to provide safety information and training to decrease risk.

Ensuring optimum management of staff, labor relations, compensation and the health and safety of employees is HR management's responsibility and objective. An emerging trend in HR strategies includes talent management, succession planning and capitalization of human potential.

Talent management helps attract, employ and retain employees with the highest productivity. Succession planning develops a system for the transfer of knowledge between teams and employees. Capitalization of human potential ensures that all teams are equipped with resources to deliver the highest performance standards.

Business Objectives

The first step in developing a strategy for HR is to examine the company's objectives and goals. Business objectives form the basis of HR strategy.

Jeffrey Gold and John Bratton's human resource management theory states that strategic HR management is the process that links HR policies and procedures with strategic business objectives. HR objectives set the foundation for various organizational goals, including business reputation, profitability, ethics and principles.

An HR strategy focuses on maximizing organizational performance to accomplish future goals. For the successful execution of HR strategies, all organizational functions must align with departmental strategy. So, the HR department needs to understand each department's decision-making tools and systems.

An effective way to accomplish this is by regularly conducting meetings with business leaders to discuss business strategy and goals. Aligning business objectives to an HR strategy requires that HR professionals:

- Understand business objectives
- Assess existing business conditions
- Develop and implement HR strategy
- Measure and analyze results

Best Practices

The role of the HR department is divided between transformational and transactional activities.

Transactional activities refer to routine tasks, including recruitment, payroll administration, performance management, maintaining records, etc. In comparison, transformational activities include determining the performance of employees based on their experience and needs.

Employee engagement and motivation toward the growth of the company are an HR department's key transformational responsibilities. In fact, measuring and evaluating an organization's transformational activities can directly impact the organization's growth and success.

Research shows that effective management of employee engagement and productivity can increase retention, profitability and growth. Organizations with effective HR practices see greater financial performance and customer satisfaction. Other studies also reveal that customers report higher levels of satisfaction if the organization's employees collaborate and the organization's environment is positive.

The following includes a strategic approach to align HR, business objectives and HR strategies:

1. Job Analysis

Encourage employee engagement to increase the performance of managerial initiatives, HR practices and teamwork to increase collaboration within the organization. Make decentralization and self-managed teams a basic component of the organization to reduce management layers and promote confidence. Develop strategies that increase employees' work-life balance.

2. Staffing

Identify and attract talent by using proactive methods of hiring, such as considering cultural fit, attitude, customer focus and the flexibility to learn.

3. Training

Develop organizational programs and training to increase skills that align with business objectives. Consider internal candidates for promotional priority to encourage them with growth and career opportunities within the organization. Growth opportunities allow employees to improve their skills and perform better.

4. Performance Management

Recognize employees' efforts by giving them nonmonetary and monetary rewards. Providing high compensation contingent on good performance minimizes turnover. Base team and individual compensation or benefits on results and remove status distinction. Eliminate barriers, such as office arrangement, wage differentials, dress code, language, parking and other status distinctions to promote equality and compensation based on goal-oriented results.

5. Employee Rights

Effectively communicate initiatives and organizational issues with employees. Share performance as well as financial and salary information to maintain trust. Offer employment security to high-performance employees in order to eliminate the fear of downsizing during economic downturns or management problems.

Other practices include:

- Assessing the organization's mission and environment
- Developing the organization's business strategy
- Recognizing HR requirements that align with the business strategy
- Measuring the existing HR inventory with future requirements
- Developing an HR strategy that meets future goals

- Implementing HR best practices to gain a competitive advantage and reinforce the business strategy

Although the above-mentioned HR practices positively impact an organization's performance, their effectiveness is measured against their alignment with the organization's mission, values and strategic goals.

Chapter 2: The Core Values of an Organization

Core values are guiding principles that represent an organization's beliefs, priorities and driving forces. Core values set the standard for how the organization interacts with stakeholders, partners and customers. The concept of core values was first coined in 1984 by Jim Collins and Jerry Porras in their book *Built to Last*. They argue that the most successful organizations stand on principles called "core values."

Core values are important to an organization's vision because they set the foundation of how an organization presents itself and how the world perceives it. Organizational values should be integrated with the business management process to ensure that all organizational interactions with vendors, clients and customers are aligned with the company's core and ethical values.

The mission, vision and values are the foundational attributes of a strategic planning process in an organization. They define the purpose and set the organizational direction and expectations for behavior and ethics.

HR practitioners are required to serve as role models for the company to reinforce and communicate guidelines for different behaviors. These guidelines are developed as vision, mission and core value statements.

Vision Statement

An organization's vision statement informs shareholders, partners and customers about the organization's driving force and the best practices to accomplish it. A vision statement should communicate what the organization wants to become and its long-term goals.

Mission Statement

A mission statement describes the company's motivation and purpose. It states the contribution an organization aims to make in society and what differentiates it from competitors within the same industry.

The mission statement directs the message toward the organization's workforce, informing them about the company's goals and direction. Strategic plans and objectives are based on a company's mission statement.

Core Values

Core values communicate the standard to which business will be conducted in an organization. The executive team communicates the core values within an organization, setting the foundation based on which the employees make decisions, interact in a professional capacity and plan strategies.

An organization's core values remain constant regardless of the changes in business processes or product lines. When developing core values, it is important to establish whether or not the values will hold true if an organization's focus and business processes change entirely.

Core values, such as teamwork, excellence, integrity, mutual respect and customer service, are constant regardless of modifications in business operations. An organization's culture reflects these beliefs.

It is important to establish values not only from a management perspective but also based on how they will be demonstrated in the company's everyday performance and activities. Discrepancies between written formal values and what is demonstrated by the employees can be aligned with the use of a strategic business plan.

Core Competencies

In addition to the vision, mission and values, an organization also has to identify its "core competencies." These are the organization's strengths that set it apart from the rest.

Core competencies help organizations focus on expanding their revenue through various methods. These competencies may include the use of technology in operations, manufacturing processes, the organization's culture, product characteristics, management of customer relationships, knowledge management and other aspects of an organization that are difficult to replicate.

Core competencies are an organization's unique standing points; they help the organization develop a strategy that focuses on areas of strength.

In most companies, HR is defined as the core competency that helps streamline the organization's processes. HR, embedded in operations—such as developing staff, fostering teamwork, supporting strategic planning and decision-making—is a core competency that leads to an organization's success.

Next to vision, mission and core values are corporate goals, which define how the organization will achieve all that is stated in the strategic planning process over the long term.

The SMART model is used to develop effective corporate goals:

- **Specific** – Goals should be concise and detailed enough to help department managers develop strategies to accomplish them.
- **Measurable** – All business objectives must have a method for assessing performance and determining when the goal is achieved.
- **Action** – The business objective should define the appropriate course of action needed to be taken in order to achieve the goal.
- **Realistic** – The business objective should challenge the abilities and capacity of the workforce but not be unachievable.
- **Time-based** – The objective must have a deadline for completion.

Once identified, the SMART model should be compiled in a strategic document called the business plan. A business plan should meet the purpose of the organization established in the strategic planning process.

The Importance of Core Values

An organization's core values are the foundation of its culture and principles. They run through the DNA of the organization, guiding its workforce and operations toward a shared goal.

There are many advantages of having strong corporate values in place, such as:

- **They support decision-making** – Core values set guiding principles that eliminate biased choices. For example, if an organization's core value is to sell the highest-quality sustainable cotton, the operation teams will automatically eliminate the choice of contacting vendors that supply unsustainable cotton.

- **They prevent conflicts from occurring** – In an organization that shares the same goals and values, there is less conflict and challenges are resolved based on common ground.

- **They make recruitment easier** – Defined principles and company standards help HR procure relevant talent. Individuals who share the same attitudes, beliefs and passions are more motivated and engaged with the organization.
- **They allow clear communication** – Core values help stakeholders, employees, customers and partners understand an organization's principles. For example, it will be easier to complain about bullying, biased decision-making or an unhealthy workplace environment if employees know that their complaints will be addressed.
- **They help build trust** – Organizations with high standard core values allow the management to make tough decisions even if those decisions cost the organization. This helps the organization, including leadership and management, gain the respect and trust of employees and customers.

Therefore, an organization that lives by its vision and core values has a higher competitive advantage over businesses that exhibit less transparency.

Chapter 3: The Role of Cross-Functional Stakeholders

Cross-functional stakeholders are a team of people from different departments of an organization working on a common objective. Cross-functional group members have complementary skills and bear the responsibility for:

- Developing new products
- Reevaluating different organizational processes
- Enhancing customer relationships
- Improving organizational performance

In a cross-functional collaboration, different teams from different departments work together on large or midsize projects. They collaborate and communicate regularly to accomplish the organization's short- and long-term goals.

A common example of cross-functional collaboration includes the procure-to-pay process in which the finance and procurement departments work together to pay for services and goods. Similarly, in a new product development project, research, legal, development and sales teams work together to deliver the desired results. Digital campaigns are also a great example of cross-functional collaboration in which marketing, production and IT teams work together.

A cross-functional partnership may involve a dedicated team or several teams with the aim of achieving several small or one large goal for the company. The number of members in a team varies from organization to organization.

Cross-functional teams form on their own in a startup formed of single-person departments working together toward growth. In comparison, in larger corporations, communication and collaboration have several forms, such as response to change (for example, remote teams during COVID-19) or launching a product, etc.

Regardless of the form, cross-functional work:

- Is critical to the success of a business
- Requires training, a strategic set of practices and tools that are different from single department policies

The Importance of Cross-Functional Collaboration

Effective collaboration allows organizations to capitalize on the diverse skill sets of their employees to achieve more goals. Teams working in collaboration deliver more than teams working in private silos.

Cross-functional teamwork builds buy-in and trust by promoting camaraderie and eliminating misconceptions within organizations. It enhances employee engagement as well as the capacity to innovate. A cross-functional setting also provides an excellent opportunity to promote learning and knowledge sharing, which adds diversity to skill sets.

These aspects play a critical role in the age of digital transformation that redefines how organizations streamline and measure their business practices. In a digitally driven organization communication system, cross-functional collaboration and shared goals boost the engagement of employees toward the company's goals. Competitive strength, growth, innovation and effective process management are key characteristics of cross-functional collaboration.

One of the key advantages of cross-functional stakeholders is their capacity to engage with an unexpected change of events, such as the recent pandemic. Working as a single unit within the organization helps the employee effectively maintain continuity even when policies, controls and workflows are modified. Transparency, shared purpose and engagement with the project help the team maintain interest in and understanding of the project in question.

Cross-functional teams are a great way of identifying inefficiencies and developing methods of improvement. With the help of cross-functional teams, organizations can greatly reduce cycle times for repetitive challenges. For example, instead of transferring customer feedback from one department to the other, all teams can work together collectively to quickly resolve the problem.

The Key Challenges of Cross-Functional Teams

Despite the value of cross-functional collaboration, effective management of teams and tasks remains a challenge for organizations. *Harvard Business Review* stated that "three-quarters of cross-functional teams" are dysfunctional. That is an astonishing amount!

While challenges vary from organization to organization, common challenges are:

Lack of Accountability and Commitment

Poor communication and interest in team building can cause problems between coworkers who may see each other as rivals instead of partners.

If leadership is missing and business objectives are poorly communicated, team members lose interest in the cross-functional project and continue to prioritize routine tasks, resulting in a performance-killing lack of accountability and commitment to the task.

Lack of Trust

In a cross-functional collaboration, a diverse group of people with different skill sets and personalities work together on a shared goal. A lack of familiarity and understanding of each other's capabilities may prevent the teams from building the connection required to work together. The team leader's inability to communicate and provide trust-building opportunities to coworkers also keeps team members from trusting each other with responsibilities.

Avoid Conflict

A critical analysis of a situation promotes collaboration and drives innovation. Teams that lack engagement, communication and transparency avoid feedback to prevent conflict. Lack of communication between teams results in failure or delay in the project.

Lack of Interest

Even a skilled and ambitious group of people may not show interest in a goal they do not understand. Lack of guidance and leadership may prevent teams from stepping out of their comfort zones and delivering expertise. Individuals keep working in their respective fields without indulging in the project, limiting productivity and hampering collaboration.

Best Practices for Cross-Functional Collaboration

Diverse viewpoints and personalities can drive productivity and innovation, as long as all the members involved have the information, guidance, tools and training required to achieve a goal.

The following best practices can ensure effective performance of cross-functional teams:

Create the Right Team

An effectively performing cross-functional team includes personalities with motivation and an open mind. In such a collaboration, it is important to maintain a balance between high achievers and big personalities. When approaching the task of team building, consider members who have:

- The questioning skills to understand the unfamiliar area and the willingness to learn with an open mind
- The ability to break down complex ideas and communicate them to other team members simply
- The ability to teach and motivate people who do not belong to their team or department
- The capacity to accept mistakes and make improvements

Build Buy-in and Trust

Working on a cross-functional project is a great way to combine talent and make new connections with people working toward a shared goal. The new opportunities are exciting for teams and a great way for leadership to develop trust and promote healthy communication among team members.

During team building, all members of a cross-functional collaboration should have the chance to:

- Introduce each other
- Understand the purpose, goals and timeline of the project
- Learn about the policies and procedures that support the task. (All members of the team should be familiar with the deadlines, availability schedules, meetings and management process.)

- Understand the level of commitment and accountability required to deliver the project
- Recognize the key performance indicators (KPIs) used to manage challenges and measure progress
- Determine how the collaboration will support business objectives and goals or help the organization accomplish a large project.

Provide Collaboration and Communication Tools

Whether your team is working in the same office or across states, they should be equipped with all the tools required to track metrics, share information and monitor performance and progress. The team should also be allowed to address opportunities and problems as they arise, without any hindrance.

The availability of different communication tools can allow members of a group to establish a virtual office where all plans, progress and problems are shared. A software solution helps centralize data and allows employees to access it through mobile or desktop devices. Process automation minimizes time spent on low-value tasks, shifting focus to strategy and planning.

Initiate Effective Project Management

Effective project management prevents a lack of communication and increases employee interest in cross-functional collaboration. All types of cross-functional projects benefit from:

- The establishment of roles, hierarchies and expectations
- Decision-making and process development
- Accountability to minimize downtime
- Regular updates to the C-suite and stakeholders to implement feedback
- The identification of opportunities and challenges
- The establishment of a platform or method through which questions and concerns are addressed

Establishing goals provides teams with a frame of reference. Project management structures tasks and eliminates confusion, mismanagement and miscommunication.

Develop Key Performance Indicators (KPIs)

KPIs are business objectives stated in measurable values. They are an effective way of objectively measuring collaboration and help organizations keep track of performance in cross-cultural collaborations.

Some KPIs help measure financial performance, such as revenue or net profit. Others measure customer satisfaction and response rate.

Transparency About Repercussions and Rewards

Compensation and rewards are effective HR practices that help increase employee motivation and engagement. Similarly, repercussions and negative criticism push employees to perform better.

While rewards and compensations are openly discussed, most organizations overlook repercussions as a means of encouraging employees to perform better. So organizations should ensure that employees understand both the incentives for and the repercussions of their actions to deliver the highest standard of performance.

Develop a Common Identity

One of the key elements of the success of a cross-functional collaboration is the development of a common identity. The sense of unity provided by a shared identity allows different members of different departments to perform with higher motivation. An organization should provide collective training and ensure all employees are equipped with the necessary resources.

Encourage Teams to Communicate for Optimal Performance

In a business environment, building competitive strength and growth requires communication and collaboration between teams. In a cross-functional collaboration, the key to securing optimal performance and achieving goals is to establish a proactive system of communication that caters to all questions, concerns, levels of progress, plans and strategies.

Organizations should provide teams with instructions on how to deal with interpersonal conflict and differences of opinion. This helps employees refer to a set method of resolving problems and challenges.

Chapter 4: Business Best Practices to Mitigate Risks

Risk management is the process of identifying and preventing potential threats in a workplace. The HR department in an organization is responsible for developing risk management plans aligned with company policies.

Risk is inevitable and comes in a variety of forms, each causing different levels of disruption in an organization. Although no business can fully escape threats, organizations have a legal and moral obligation to develop risk management strategies to limit the extent of damage, ensuring the well-being and safety of those who perform for the organization. Risk management is also known as duty of care.

Effective risk mitigation starts with understanding the various types of threats to a business and developing a risk management plan that is strategic and versatile enough to protect the company during a crisis.

Areas of Risk Management

Potential areas of risk vary by organization and operations. There are various methods used to identify risk. A comprehensive analysis of different organizational activities is the key to developing strategies that help identify risk.

Organizations face strategic, external and preventable threats that can be avoided by putting an effective risk management strategy in place, including:

Compensation and Benefits

Different forms of financial abuse—such as fraud, theft and embezzlement—threaten compensation and benefits. Examples of embezzlement include cash skimming and computer or credit card embezzlement.

To mitigate risk against financial abuse, the development of various protocols is required, including multiple signatures on all financial documents, identifying authority for final financial transactions, etc. Stringent accounting procedures should be established to identify fraud or theft.

Recruitment Process

Discrimination in the recruitment process is widely known. Although it is illegal to discriminate during the process, practicing bias based on sex, race, color, religion or disability is common in companies. Hiring managers, recruiters and other parties involved in the recruitment process should follow company policies to avoid discrimination against a candidate.

Hiring Process

Hiring discrimination is widely known and taken very seriously, as it is also illegal. It is described as not hiring a candidate due to a person's race, sex, religion, color, national origin, age or disability. To avoid this, an organization's HR department can educate the company's recruiters, hiring managers and other parties involved in the hiring process.

Similarly, talent acquisition is an integral component of risk management assessment. Performing background checks on candidates is essential to prevent resource-related risks. Improper resource planning—such as unsuitable candidates, overstaffing or understaffing—is damaging and may disrupt functions in the organization.

Occupational Safety and Health

Maintaining a clean and safe work environment is enforceable by law or the US. Department of Labor. Organizations are required to meet the Occupational Safety and Health Administration's (OSHA) guidelines.

It is the HR department's responsibility to maintain operations following OSHA guidelines and provide appropriate training to staff. To protect organizations and employees, regularly maintaining health and safety policies is essential to prevent them from being overlooked during operations.

Location Risks

Location hazards that threaten corporations include storm damage, earthquakes, fires, hurricanes, floods and other natural disasters. It is important to provide employees with training on what to do during a fire, leakages or other emergencies. All employees should be familiar with the emergency exits.

Casualty, property and liability insurance should be in place to prevent financial burden on the organization.

Human Risks

Drug and alcohol abuse is a common human risk in the workplace. Keeping a check on behaviors, developing behavior policies and urging employees to seek treatment are important practices for mitigating human risk. Furthermore, various insurance policies provide coverage for injury and drug abuse.

Health-related delays can cause a loss of productivity and may hamper operations at the workplace. So, training backup personnel is critical to prevent loss of work when employees are absent due to illness.

Strategic Risks

Strategic risks occur when an organization is unable to perform according to market standards. For example, financial institutions, such as credit unions or banks, may be exposed to strategic risk when lending. Strategic risk management identifies risk and its effects to develop necessary plans to mitigate them.

External and internal risks are a threat to business objectives and strategy. The negative effects of strategy risks can be mitigated by developing and maintaining processes that support high-risk projects. For instance, establishing healthy cash flow and adding diversification in projects can control financial damage when a venture fails.

It is important to evaluate the impact of strategic risks to develop an effective strategy. The two key metrics by which strategic risks are assessed are:

- **Economic capital** – The amount needed to bear the impact of unexpected losses. Economic capital is derived from the organization's target debt rating.
- **Risk-adjusted return on capital** – An evaluation of the return on investment (ROI) according to the risk involved. It measures the risk taken against the expected return.

Assessment of Risk Management

Risk assessment is divided into two parts: analysis and prioritization. In the risk assessment process, various actions and events are identified that can pose a risk to the company, projects or employees.

Each risk is assessed based on the level of risk it poses and the probability of its occurrence. The four different risk levels are:

1. Extreme probability
2. Moderate probability
3. Minor probability
4. Minimal probability

Risk Analysis

Risk analysis is a technique that identifies and analyzes potential factors that may cause harm to business initiatives or projects. The following are some effective risk analysis techniques that can help identify potential risks:

- **Cost risk analysis** – It reviews uncertainties and risks that may impact a company's expenditures.
- **Schedule analysis** – It reviews challenges and issues that may arise during a project.
- **Reliability analysis** – It measures a project's reliability and effectiveness with the help of statistics.
- **Decision analysis** – It measures different options in business decisions.

Risk Prioritization

Risk prioritization is the process of prioritizing risks for further analysis or action by assessing and combining their probability of occurrence and impact. It assesses identified risks, their impact assessment and their probability of occurrence to help managers determine which risk they should prioritize or apply their limited resources to.

Risk Management Control

Risk management control allows businesses to detect, mitigate, prevent and prepare for any hazard, danger or other potential disasters before they interfere with business objectives.

It involves risk resolution, risk monitoring and risk management planning.

Risk Planning

Risk planning seeks to eliminate risks, transfer them or reduce the chances of them happening. It includes:

- **Risk avoidance** – The process of eliminating potential hazards that may damage a project or disrupt an operation
- **Risk transfer** – The process of moving the burden of risks, such as insurance that transfers the financial burden to the insurance company in location or human risks
- **Risk reduction** – The process of minimizing risk within an organization

Risk Resolution

Risk resolution allows organizations to evaluate and mitigate risks. The following are the steps required for risk resolution:

- **Research** – The process of studying and assessing threats likely to affect a company or a project
- **Accept** – The process of identifying if the risk is avoidable and foreseeing the events that may lead to risk
- **Reduce** – The process of being proactive and minimizing potential risks to prevent them from recurring
- **Eliminate** – The process of identifying the problem and solving it to prevent the company from being severely impacted by a crisis

Risk Monitoring

The HR department is responsible for tracking and monitoring risk by following up with parties involved to mitigate risks. Risk management plans should align with the company's policies and procedures and meet the present-day standards.

Parties Involved in the Development of Risk Management Plans

Risk management is critical to an organization and involves the cooperation of various parties with different authorities. Based on the size of the corporation, a risk management team is formed to develop strategies and plans. Generally, HR and the company's leadership are responsible for developing risk assessment protocols, but implementation may be carried out by designated teams. All employees in an organization are required to follow the guidelines enforced by the authorities for risk management.

Chapter 5: Significance of Data in Deciding Organizational Strategies

An organization's HR department plays a critical role in utilizing data to develop business strategies and improve decision-making. In fact, an organization adopts HR strategies that integrate the culture, system and employees in a set of actions to achieve business goals.

Two types of data enable the HR department to measure and track operations and performance: HR data and HR metrics. HR metrics measure an organization's HR-related functions. Measuring the number of sick days for staff is an example of HR metrics. Tracking data gives the organization a better understanding of trends and performance, and it is invaluable data that identifies problems and challenges that must be addressed to develop an effective organizational strategy.

One of the most valuable assets of an organization is the people. Globally, evolving machine learning and artificial intelligence technologies are empowering HR departments with data analytics to help organizations inform decisions. Tech-driven data analytics has played an important role in the recruitment process; however, a growing number of organizations are now applying HR metrics to make sophisticated people-related decisions that will drive the experience of employees within an organization.

Employee-related decisions that were previously based on human feedback—including salary, promotions, training and retention—are now increasingly backed with data powered by artificial intelligence as well.

Data to Develop HR Strategy

With the help of data, the HR department can identify and address factors related to an organization's future, such as cost management, outsourcing and succession planning.

In conjunction with data analytics and succession planning, it is the HR department's responsibility to develop improved training protocols and processes. The HR department is responsible for overseeing the organization's various strategic plans, including recording information, identifying best practices to increase employee productivity and developing efficient management tactics that align with business objectives.

The purpose of data is to increase clarity about overall organizational performance. More information and data points increase accuracy in forecasting and modeling plans that improve decisions in different areas, such as:

- **Turnover** – The rate of turnover measures the percentage of employees leaving the organization in relation to the total number of employees. A data-driven HR department can analyze turnover to identify why employees leave, and model scenarios can be created in advance to boost retention and reduce loss.
- **Churn/retention** – Data identifies the high-risk areas of churn. It helps discover resources that will be beneficial for those who are at risk of churn to improve performance and retention.
- **Risk** – HR data helps develop realistic profiles of candidates who are at risk of prematurely leaving the job. It also aids in the development of models of employees who may show a drop in performance.
- **Talent** – HR data helps identify high performers and high achievers and increases their usefulness to the organization.
- **Future casting** – Future forecasting helps model changes with the help of data that an organization may experience from a political, economic and global perspective. It can also identify the impact of different activities, such as hiring new talent and increasing retention and productivity.

How Data Benefits Organizational Strategy

Data helps organizations assess risk and allows them to map out processes and develop organizational strategies that reduce bottlenecks and increase compliance. Though data does not solve all HR challenges, it gives an insight into business functions and helps HR professionals develop strategies that optimize investments; monitor recruiting; and increase engagement, development, productivity and retention initiatives.

Here are some other ways data benefits organizations:

1. Measuring Performance

Data allows organizations to set performance benchmarks and develop training programs for incoming and existing employees to understand and embrace those qualities.

Leading organizations analyze performance data, billing hours and travel data to boost employees' professional performance as well as their energy and willingness to perform better. So, data collected from high achievers and top-performing teams can help establish organizational processes and standards of expected performance.

2. Informing Salary and Promotion Decisions

Promotions of underperforming peers employees are common in organizations. Various factors, including nepotism and human bias, play a part in such decisions.

A data-based approach to salary and promotion decisions can prevent the demotivation of high-performing employees by allowing leaders to drive their decisions based on performance data. For example, a relatively new employee may have done well on a single project, but an older peer may have delivered consistent quality performance. In such cases, various aspects are taken into consideration, such as tenure or impact of performance, etc.

So, collecting different types of data allows managers to make less biased decisions that will be beneficial for the organization in the longer run.

3. Increasing Retention and Understanding Attrition

Performance-based data helps predict which employees are more prone to exiting the organization prematurely, while attrition data helps HR personnel identify reasons for exits, positions worked and types of employees who are more likely to leave. This helps HR focus on the areas of improvement to increase retention.

A popular case study of a US-based company states that money holds less value than the quality of supervisors and managers. The company developed a bonus program to increase retention but experienced little success. By conducting data analytics, it was discovered that teams working under lower-performing managers were more likely to exit. Therefore, leaning toward providing resources is a stronger method of employee retention than pouring money.

Organizations can also use data for their turnover rate to understand organizational trends and prevent sudden spikes by addressing the challenges in a timely manner. For example, a rise in involuntary attrition may indicate the need to look into the training and recruitment process, whereas a surge in voluntary attrition may indicate low-performing managers and departments.

4. Examining Employee Engagement

Employee engagement is important to HR departments across all organizations. Employee engagement data is collected through surveys commonly conducted by third-party sources. Recently, organizations have started to witness the benefits of bringing employee engagement surveys in-house to be conducted by HR departments to collect faster results.

HR departments can replace lengthy surveys with brief surveys to consistently monitor engagement and immediately access data insights. HR can also run reports to measure low engagement based on two key signs: turnover and absenteeism.

Collecting feedback from employees leaving the business can also help organizations make improvements and attend to problem areas. For example, HR managers can standardize an interview during an exit to collect responses to discover areas of improvement in the current process.

So, employee engagement is the key to strategic decision-making in businesses, as understanding the performance and effectiveness of employees drives decision-making in management. And with the help of data, managers and leaders can predict the impacts of their decisions.

5. Measuring Training and Learning Outcomes

In the data-driven business world, the training and development of employees is a key factor of organizational success. Professional and skilled employees have higher productivity and generate more profit for the business than under-skilled workers.

With the help of HR data, organizations can identify and shortlist employees who require training and development. This information can be collected from the performance metrics that reveal how employees perform designated responsibilities and roles as well as the pace at which they work.

Different performance metrics enable HR to evaluate employees' skill levels based on their pace and performance. By training employees, organizations can save costs on hiring new employees.

An effective training program also increases retention and productivity. Organizations can use predictive analytics to develop customized learning and development content to meet individual levels and learning styles. Predictive analytics helps identify weak points during a training program, such as when an employee loses focus, to improve the content and direct changes in the right direction. Therefore, data makes training and development more successful.

6. Developing Safe Working Conditions

Employee safety is one of an employer's key responsibilities. In fact, business owners are legally obligated to provide a safe work environment for the employees.

HR data helps managers identify safety hazards, causes of accidents and injuries to create viable solutions. Data highlights areas with the highest number of accidents and injuries and their impact on business performance.

7. Improve Payroll Management

Payroll is any organization's largest expense and requires careful management and oversight. HR data helps track and report payroll expenses by documenting costs by department, location and position. Data supports the efficient breakdown of total payroll expenses to help the business administration make policy changes to effectively manage costs.

HR data analytics allows you to determine if the compensation and benefits offered to employees are meeting their needs. In-house reports can be generated to determine what kinds of rewards employees like best.

Data analytics also helps HR calculate expenses on total benefits to identify areas where costs can be saved through comprehensive and competitive compensation.

Chapter 6: Federal Laws and Regulations Related to Talent Planning and Acquisition Activities

Title VII of the Civil Rights Act, 1964

This historic piece of legislation is considered a landmark when it comes to prohibiting discrimination in the workforce based on race, color, religion, sex or national origin. This legislation is considered to be most inclusive when it comes to protecting the rights of people in workplaces.

Title VII applies to private employers that have 15 or more employees; federal, state, local governments; employment agencies, labor organizations, education institutions that employ 15 or more individuals; private and public employment agencies; labor organizations and joint labor-management committees controlling apprenticeship and training.

The 1964 Civil Rights Act also established the Equal Employment Opportunity Commission (EEOC), whose mission is "to promote equal opportunity in employment through administrative and judicial enforcement of the federal civil rights laws and education and technical assistance."

Under the act, all discrimination against protected classes is prohibited when it comes to all of the following functions of a workplace:

- Hiring and firing
- Compensation, assignment or classification of employees
- Transfer, promotion, layoff or recall
- Job advertisements
- Recruitment
- Testing
- Use of company facilities
- Training and apprenticeship programs
- Fringe benefits
- Pay, retirement plans and disability leave
- Other terms and conditions of employment

Along with acquisition, Title VII also applies to any possible retaliation against an employee who acts against discrimination and wants to either participate in an investigation or oppose any discriminatory practices.

Uniform Guidelines on Employee Selection Procedures, 1978

These federal guidelines aim to bring uniformity in the employment process to deal with the concept of "disparate impact," which refers to unintentional discrimination against protected groups as a result of procedures. Another purpose is to ensure a reliable and valid selection process in workplaces.

Reliability

Reliability means the consistency of an instrument. When it comes to recruiting talent, the selection process needs to be consistent across all candidates to ensure fairness. For example, in the interview process, a list of job-related questions should be compiled and practiced by interviewers to ensure consistency of selection criteria.

Validity

Validity refers to whether an instrument is measuring what it is intended to measure. And when it comes to talent acquisition, interviews are supposed to measure an applicant's skills. Interviews need to accurately measure the needed skill for a particular position, and all selection procedures need to be valid to ensure performance on the job.

There are various subtypes of validity, including content validity, criterion-related validity and predictive validity. HR professionals need to be aware of these standards to ensure a fair selection process.

Title I of the Americans with Disabilities Act

Title I prohibits discrimination against people with disabilities and applies to all private employers and state and local governments. The ADA provides guidelines on when an employer can require a medical examination for applicants and employees.

Under the ADA, an employer cannot ask any questions related to an applicant's disability or ask for any medical examination until a conditional job offer has been made. After the job offer has been made, any relevant questions can be asked as long as this process/inquiry remains the same for all individuals entering the same job position.

The following points are also highlighted in the ADA:

- An employer cannot use employment tests that screen out an individual with a disability or a class of individuals with disabilities unless the test is shown to be related to the job and consistent with business necessity.
- Employers must select and administer employment tests with results that accurately reflect applicants' skills and aptitudes rather than their impairments.
- Employers must make reasonable accommodations, including in the administration of tests, to the known physical or mental limitations of an otherwise qualified applicant with a disability—unless such accommodation would impose an undue hardship.

The Age Discrimination in Employment Act

The Age Discrimination in Employment Act (ADEA) prohibits age discrimination in the workplace concerning any term, condition or privilege of employment. So, hiring efforts, promotions or reduction activities must not be conducted in a manner that unlawfully discriminates based on age.

For example, if an employer gives a physical agility test only to applicants over age 50 but does not test younger applicants due to the belief that the older applicants would not be capable enough, the employer's actions would fall under disparate treatment and go against ADEA.

ADEA also prohibits employers from using neutral tests or selection procedures that can have an unintentional discriminatory impact on people based on age unless the procedure is a requirement for the position in other factors than age.

Under ADEA, it is also unlawful to put age limitations on apprenticeship programs unless these limitations are validated by some exceptions in ADEA or EEOC. Similarly, no age limitations can be put in job notices and advertisements when planning to recruit new talent. A job notice or advertisement may specify an age limit only in rare circumstances, for example, when age is shown to be a bona fide occupational qualification that is necessary for the normal operation of the business.

Fair Credit Reporting Act, 1970

The Fair Credit Reporting Act (FCRA) intends to ensure fair and accurate consumer reporting. Employers need to adhere to this law when it comes to workforce planning and employment. This is particularly important for employers because they base hiring and promotion decisions, in part, on credit reports.

Employers must tell applicants that they will be using the information in their consumer reports in the decision-making process. This notice must be in writing and in a stand-alone format. Employers need applicants' written permission to use the consumer report on this notice.

To attain an applicant's consumer report, an employer must certify to the company that the applicant has been notified and has granted permission. The FCRA also requires that employers do not use any information in the consumer report to discriminate against any protected classes as categorized by the Civil Rights Act, ADEA and EEOC.

Chapter 7: The Process of Recruiting

Recruiting is an essential process for any organization to keep the business functional. Recruiting refers to the process of attracting qualified candidates for open positions and creating a pool of potential candidates who can successfully take on the responsibility.

Branding

Just like a product or service that the company offers, employers need to market themselves in the labor market as well. This marketing strategy helps promote not only the business itself but the employers that are looking to attract the best suitable candidates for their positions. How employers brand themselves affects how they will be perceived in the labor market.

Relevant Labor Market

To create a pool of external candidates—those who are not part of the organization yet—it is important that the suitable labor market be defined. The size, scope and boundaries of what geographical area needs to be targeted must be determined.

This can vary for various positions and branches of the same company. What skills are needed for a certain job and what personal characteristics would be preferred should be outlined before the active recruitment process starts. Another key thing to note when defining the labor market is how much competition already exists for that specific type of candidate and position.

Selection Criteria

Making the selection criteria for the pool of candidates is a good first step in the broader recruitment process. These criteria could be looked at as a checklist that details the must-haves in the candidates on the KSAs (knowledge, skills, abilities), job specifications and competencies for the job. All potential candidates in your pool will then have to meet this list.

After you have set up the employer branding, defined the suitable labor market and made the selection criteria, you can start actively recruiting potential candidates.

Internal and External Recruiting

When you have a position to fill in the company, you have the option to either recruit internally or externally. Internal candidates are your employees who are already working in your organization. The new position is essentially a promotion for these employees, whereas external recruits are new hires outside the organization and are attracted using different mechanisms.

Recruiting Internal Candidates

There are many advantages when it comes to recruiting internally. The employees get a chance for growth and progress without leaving one organization; employers can save a lot of manpower and money that would otherwise be spent on advertisement, selection, etc. It also creates a strong sense of loyalty within the organization. Employers can recruit internal candidates using a few methods.

Job Posting

This is a straightforward method of announcing an opening for the current employees working within the organization. Eligible employees can choose to apply for the position as they would for any other job. This method is often used before an external recruitment campaign is started to first assess potential within the company.

Job Bidding

Unlike job postings, where the position is announced by the higher-ups once it opens, in job bidding, the employees are welcome to show interest in a desired position at any time. This motivates the employees, who can set a position as a goal for themselves, and saves time for the employer, who is already aware of potential candidates whenever the position opens.

Succession Planning

Proactive planning and assessment for future fill-ins for opening positions is a step taken by many professional organizations. Members of leadership keep their eyes open and identify individuals within their team who can take on bigger roles in the future. These planning and predictive efforts ensure that recruitment efforts are not impacted by the possible departure of a potential candidate.

Employers must keep the process streamlined and fair, as identifying individuals ahead of time and making it known within the company can be detrimental to the morale of other employees and undermine overall recruitment efforts.

Recruiting External Candidates

External candidates can be recruited by advertising the job position using various available mediums. These include:

- Internet job listing websites
- Newspaper advertisements
- Radio advertisements
- Job fairs
- Open houses
- Alumni networks (alumni of colleges/universities, as well as alumni of companies)
- Walks-ins
- Professional organizations
- Referrals from current employees or industry network colleagues
- State unemployment offices
- Organizational websites
- Prior applicants
- Social media

Finding Candidates Using Social Media

There are many platforms now on social media—both professional and casual—where employers can find potential candidates. For example, LinkedIn is a dedicated platform where employers can connect with the labor market and vice versa. Other social media platforms, such as Facebook and Twitter, can also provide unique opportunities and campaigns for external recruitment.

However, employers need to be careful when using social media to inform their hiring decisions, as it is a gray area. What information can or should be used in the selection process? What permissions are required? And does the use of social media in a particular scenario violate any federal laws?

Employment Agencies

Another straightforward method of reaching candidates is using employment agencies. Each state has a state service that gathers the information of all unemployed people looking to get hired. Such public agencies also provide preliminary screening and candidate referral services to employers.

A temp-to-hire model caters to temporary and short-term needs that employers might not have seen coming. These temporary hires are also done through employment agencies. These hires can then be brought on permanently if both the employer and employee find a good match.

There are also private employment agencies that privately hold a pool of potential candidates and offer various recruitment services to employers according to their needs. Various models are followed when conducting business with these agencies.

A contingency employment agency asks to be paid by the employer only when a suitable candidate is successfully found for the position through the agency's efforts. In comparison, the employer pays a retained employment agency upfront for its services in hiring a candidate.

After decisions have been made about what model is to be used for recruitment, the application process starts and a pool of applicants needs to be screened and narrowed down.

The Employment Application

In most cases, after the advertising process, the candidates send in their résumés to employers in hopes of being called for an official interview. In a way, this is a return advertisement on the part of the candidate. Along with the résumés, employment applications are used to collect information from all candidates.

Types of Employment Applications

Organizations can set guidelines on what kind of applications they require from candidates. Employers should be wary of federal and state laws regarding what information they can require and be consistent in their recruitment process. Most organizations want candidates' work history, education and experience at the very least.

- **Short-form employment applications** – These provide the shorter version of an organization's standard application for employment. They can be used as a prescreening tool, the main application for entry-level positions in the company or a preliminary application in a much broader recruitment campaign where candidates later fill out more applications.
- **Long-form employment applications** – These require more detailed information from the candidates. They can include more in-depth and comprehensive information on experience, education and competencies.
- **Job-specific employment applications** – These are used when a large candidate pool is needed to be narrowed down for a particular position. They are tailored to the position that the applicant has applied for.
- **Weighted employment applications** – These allow employers to evaluate the candidates objectively by allotting relative weights to different sections of the applications. In this way, all applications can be weighed following a consistent system, depending on the relevance of each section.

Pre-Employment Testing

Pre-employment testing can let employers assess the knowledge, skills and abilities/behavioral characteristics of candidates. These can then be evaluated to see whether candidates are suitable for certain positions. These tests have to conform to the Uniform Guidelines on Employee Selection Procedures and other laws.

Several tests are performed during pre-employment testing, such as:

Agility Tests

These tests are done to ascertain candidates' physical capabilities and must be related to the job they have applied for. For example, if the job requires a person to lift heavy boxes, these tests must be able to demonstrate this ability.

Aptitude Tests

These tests evaluate the level of knowledge or skill potential candidates hold when it comes to the job they have applied for. These can be written or skill-based tests.

Cognitive Ability Tests

These tests assess candidates' intelligence or other cognitive skills that are relevant to the position they have applied for. For example, for a finance position, a candidate's mathematical skills and problem-solving skills can be tested.

Medical Tests

These tests can be employed only when they are relevant to the job being applied for and must have a reason directly associated with business functioning. These tests can be required only after the employer has made a conditional job offer. Under strict federal laws, these tests cannot be used to refuse a position to candidates but are valuable for accommodating them in case of a medical need.

The Interview Process

A major part of recruitment is the interview process, where the narrowed-down candidate pool is invited to have an interview with the HR team. Having ample knowledge of what the interview process requires is an important skill for any HR professional.

Styles of Selection Interviews

Directive interviews are more structured and have a consistent pattern of interviewing across all candidates. The control lies mostly with the interviewer, and the structure is prioritized over circumstance.

A non-directive interview is relatively unstructured and gives candidates a chance to control the interview process. This provides a more flexible atmosphere but is not consistent across all candidates due to them controlling the flow of information.

Interviews can be carried out in person, over the phone and via the Internet. There are also several types of interviews designed for different kinds of employer needs. For example, a behavior-based interview focuses on candidates' behavioral characteristics along with their skills and knowledge. The interviewer can ask for examples from previous jobs where candidates demonstrated a certain skill or dealt with a relevant situation.

Similarly, stress interviews are designed to put candidates in an orchestrated high-stress situation where the primary aim is to assess their response to a demanding situation. These interviews are usually reserved for high-level positions.

Background Checks

After testing and interviews, background checks are made before any final candidate is selected for the position. Background testing can be difficult because so much time and energy have already been spent on finding the finalists. However, there are huge advantages to carrying out a thorough and open-minded background check for potential finalists before officially hiring them.

Any potential information that can be brought up during this process is only going to save the organization from possible future problems. If all is good, the results can boost confidence in the decision process.

Making the Employment Offer

Once the background checks have been completed, an offer must be made to the best candidate chosen for the position. The offer represents the whole organization and needs to be well-thought-out to seal the deal.

Tips for Employment Offers

It is up to the type of position and the office policies whether HR directly calls candidates to extend an employment offer, sends an email or has an in-person meeting. Care must be taken when making the official offer to maximize the chances of a candidate saying yes.

Here are some tips that might help:

- Try to package the earning details in an easy-to-understand but impressive manner. Generally, it is better to avoid using annual terms.
- Try not to go in-depth with guarantees when it comes to earnings or prolonged employment just yet.
- Keep the language professional. While you should show enthusiasm for a deal, do not give the wrong impression and mix a professional setting with a personal one.

- Try to use the offer letter as the foundation for a legal relationship that is being established with the candidate's permission.
- Stipulate the conditions that have been discussed and are relevant to the employment agreement within the offer letter.
- Give a deadline by which the candidate must accept or reject the offer.

Chapter 8: Orientation of New Employees

Employee orientation or onboarding refers to the process of helping new hires adjust to their new work environment. This involves them being able to adjust socially in their workplace and become attuned to their job performance for the new position.

A successful orientation effort is an important process for organizations after fruitful recruitment and selection. In fact, a productive orientation program helps organizations increase their employees' effectiveness and requires some strategic planning.

The goal of an effective orientation plan is to make the adjustment process for the new employee as smooth as possible. After recruitment, the orientation period is crucial because many employees may decide to leave the organization if they are not able to adjust to the workplace.

According to reports, in the United States, more than 25% of workers go through career transitions every year. Here are some important numbers to keep in mind when thinking about the importance of orientation programs:

- Just in the Fortune 500 companies, 500,000 managers go through role transitions each year or begin new jobs every two to four years.
- Almost half of the new hires for senior positions end up failing within 18 months of taking on new positions.
- About half of all workers working on an hourly basis end up leaving new jobs within the first 120 days.

Hence, it is of utmost importance that HR professionals be focused on the orientation period after a successful recruitment phase to secure their employees' positions in the organization.

Different Approaches

There is a truism in the industry, which is also backed by research, that suggests that new employees have about 90 days to prove themselves suitable for their new jobs. However, all organizations have their own cultures and policies. All workplaces also have their own onboarding processes (how new hires are oriented to their jobs).

In the orientation period, employees are told about the attitudes, knowledge, skills and behaviors needed for the job in a specific workplace. In the world of academia, this period is termed *organizational socialization*. It refers to how quickly employees will be able to adapt to their new responsibilities.

Different organizations have different approaches to the onboarding process, which vary in terms of formality and structure. One of the first steps in coming up with an onboarding strategy is determining what approach would be better suited for the organization: formal onboarding or informal onboarding.

In informal onboarding, a new employee goes through the learning process without any explicit plan from the organization. On the other hand, formal onboarding includes employees getting proper written policies and procedures that are designed to help them adjust to their job and the workplace's social culture.

According to research, a formal onboarding program that includes a step-by-step process of teaching employees their roles, the norms of the workplace and overall expectations in terms of behavior are more effective than an informal approach. Formal onboarding also helps provide structure to the workplace and build organizational role models.

It is also important for HR professionals to keep in mind the sequencing of the new hires, how they are being grouped, what hierarchy is being followed and how the organization as a whole is providing support for them. These are impactful variables for the onboarding process but can be difficult to measure concretely.

The Four C's

When it comes to onboarding in the HR world, the four C's are several agreed-upon elements that must be focused on to have an effective orientation program:

<u>Compliance</u>

Compliance is the lowest level of the onboarding process and refers to giving newly hired employees basic knowledge about the organization. This includes basic legal information and policy-related rules and regulations.

Clarification

Clarification is the level where specific job-related knowledge is given to the new employees. This includes the technical skills that they need as a part of their job responsibility and the related expectations.

Culture

Every workplace differs in terms of its culture. A group of people coming together naturally form their own dynamics. New employees need to be oriented to the culture of the organization and develop a sense of organizational norms.

Connection

Having a strong sense of connection goes a long way when it comes to an employee's performance and loyalty. Helping new hires form genuine interpersonal connections with their colleagues is an important element of the orientation process. So, having people there to guide the new hires and make them feel accepted should be one of the goals of onboarding.

HR professionals need to be mindful of these four elements and use them strategically in their orientation planning to maximize their recruitment efforts.

Levels of Onboarding

The use of the four C's determines the difference in onboarding across various organizations. Depending on how HR plans the programs, organizations usually fall into one of three levels:

Passive Onboarding

At this level, only compliance, possibly with some clarification, is included in the onboarding strategy. There might be some informal efforts put into orienting the employees in terms of culture and connection, but there is no official strategy on behalf of HR to formally maximize the orientation process.

Usually, the organizations that fall under passive onboarding have a robotic checklist of different tasks that need to be marked off. According to research, approximately 30% of all kinds of organizations fall into this category. Passive onboarding addresses the orientation of employees but is not systematic.

High-Potential Onboarding

At the second level, organizations cover the compliance and clarification elements very well and have some culture and connection mechanisms put in place. The difference from the first level is the detail put into the first two C's and at least an effort to formally include the latter two. About 50% of all firms fall into this category.

However, at this level, culture and connection are still not systematically incorporated into the orientation program.

Proactive Onboarding

The third level of onboarding formally addresses all four C's within orientation programs. Only 20% of all organizations fall into this category and include a fully structured, formal approach to the orientation process. Compliance, clarification, culture and connection are all given importance and strategized accordingly.

Onboarding Outcomes

Onboarding as a process has specific goals and purposes. It is about making the employees feel welcomed and helping them settle into their roles as quickly and smoothly as possible.

When coming up with a strategy for onboarding, HR professionals need to understand specific organizational needs and goals that must be kept in mind for the program. There are two kinds of outcomes of onboarding: short term and long term.

Short-Term Outcomes

The main agenda of orientation efforts immediately after hiring is to help employees adjust to their jobs. Research identifies four levels of adjustment for new hires that need to be focused on. These four levels are related to employees' job expectations and social adjustment.

The first is employees' self-efficacy regarding their job performance. The degree of confidence employees have determines their motivation and success. This is important to be kept in mind when designing onboarding strategies because it will help HR personnel integrate specific steps that address the self-efficacy of new hires, as it has shown to be impactful on organizational commitment, satisfaction and turnover.

The second level is role clarity, which refers to employees' understanding of their roles and expectations within the organization. If employees are not clear about their roles and overall expectations, this will eventually be reflected in their performance. Role clarity signifies how well adjusted new employees are and can be used as evaluation tools at regular intervals to intervene when needed. The opposite of role clarity, which is role ambiguity, can lead to a poor attitude and poor performance.

The third level is social integration. This is achieved through having existing employees, the "insiders," involved with the newcomers and helping them learn about the organization. When new employees feel socially comfortable and accepted by their peers and superiors, it reflects directly on their work performance. Research has found acceptance by peers to be a strong indicator of adjustment. Feeling integrated into one's workgroup is also positively related to commitment and turnover.

The HR staff is there to facilitate the process of socialization for new employees, which is eventually better for the organization. This also depends on the individual employees because there needs to be a personal effort in forming interpersonal relationships and being proactive in the process of integration into the culture.

The fourth and final level of short-term outcomes is the knowledge of and fit within an organizational culture. As covered above, workplaces vary when it comes to internal culture and norms. A successful orientation process helps individuals fit into their new place. This includes a deeper understanding of the organization's politics, goals and values and learning the firm's unique language. This level is related to employee loyalty, commitment, satisfaction and turnover.

Long-Term Outcomes

Long-term orientation outcomes go beyond the initial immediate levels that are focused on the employee. These outcomes affect an organization's bottom line. According to a survey of organizations, 52% of the participating pool saw improved retention rates, 60% mentioned improved productivity and 53%

regarded overall customer satisfaction as an effective outcome of onboarding in the long run.

For individual employees, the long-term effects of a successful orientation effort are job satisfaction and organizational commitment. This results in new employees helping the organization be focused on its specific goals.

Without a doubt, performance is an essential long-term outcome of onboarding. One study conducted on an American technology-related company found that employees who underwent an improved onboarding program became more productive two months earlier than employees in a traditional program.

An onboarding process that fails to hit the right mark enhances the risk of the organization losing good employees. This can happen if the new employees feel lost in their new workplace and do not have enough company support to make the needed adjustments for their new responsibilities. A good orientation program can address these possible problems and help save the organization time and money on further recruitment efforts.

Important Key Points of Onboarding

HR professionals must understand the need for good onboarding programs and tailor them to fit an organization's specific needs.

Here are some key points that should be kept in mind when thinking of orienting new employees:

- **Clear communication** – Be it an informal strategy or a formal one, having unambiguous language for all communications is imperative. The new employees are looking for guidance, so having any confusion within the hierarchy or structure in the workplace can have detrimental effects.
- **Put it in writing** – Try to make the communication process as seamless as possible by providing new hires with official documents regarding their adjustment period. These can include copies of the policies, their job requirements, etc.
- **Appropriate attention** – It is essential that new employees feel welcomed and taken care of in their new workplace. The HR department

should try to strategize tasks and meetings in a way that the new employees do not feel left out or completely on their own.

- **Regular check-ins** – Within any kind of orientation strategy, be sure to include regular check-ins with the new employees to gauge how well they are adjusting and getting along in the workplace.

Chapter 9: Staffing Alternatives

Traditional staffing methods come to mind whenever the process of recruitment is mentioned. These usually include hiring full-time employees after an elaborate recruitment campaign. However, HR professionals must make themselves familiar with other forms of staffing that are nontraditional but can be used for the organization's benefit.

Alternative methods are not necessarily only internal or external. Employees within the organization and outsiders can both be targeted by these methods. These methods also encompass outsourcing of processes that the organization currently performs in-house.

Looking at alternative methods of staffing can bring flexibility to the organization. These come in handy when the organization requires a very specific skill set that might be harder to target through traditional means of recruitment. Another application is when the labor market is complicated or too competitive. Alternative staffing methods also provide organizations access to highly qualified candidates who are hard to reach.

Telecommuting

Rapidly advancing technology has paved the way for alternative staffing in the form of telecommuting. Telecommuting makes it possible for people to work from home while being connected to the workplace electronically. This saves employees hours of commute time and makes work accessible for people who might have issues traveling.

However, telecommuting is also beneficial for organizations. An organization can cut back on a lot of overhead costs when fewer employees are required on-site. This also reflects on the organization's overall energy consumption and transportation costs.

Job Sharing

This alternative allows two people to share the duties of one full-time position. Both employees have complementary skills and competencies that allow them to share job responsibilities.

Job sharing allows people to work fewer hours in the workweek and is especially beneficial for people who have home commitments. This flexible work arrangement also works in favor of the organization, as less work requires the company to provide fewer benefits to employees.

Part-Time Employment

This alternative method is cost-effective and can be used by organizations looking for a particular skill set needed for the time being but not regularly.

Part-time employment allows organizations to get projects done related to their business without having to take on more full-time employees. Part-time work also allows individuals to maintain a better work-life balance.

Internship Programs

These programs are mostly targeted toward students or fresh graduates to give them experience in a field. These programs are beneficial not only to trainees and young professionals but also to organizations, as they provide low-cost access to creative minds.

For interns, such programs are valuable for the meaningful learning experiences as well as the opportunity to make connections. Organizations can discover talented young individuals by observing them during the internship period and later extending a full-time employment offer to them.

Temporary Workers

This arrangement is vast and has different models. Usually, a temporary worker (temp) is employed by a single agency that takes on the responsibility of screening and testing candidates before sending them to other organizations for a specific time.

The workload and timing can depend on each project and the type of arrangement being made between the agency and the organization. It can range from one-day assignments to those that span months. Organizations often hire temps for project-specific work.

The difference between part-time workers and temporary work is the regulation of the employees through an agency dedicated to having a pool of competent candidates. This allows organizations to use fewer resources in recruitment efforts and candidates to spend less time finding each job.

If an organization likes a temp, it can extend a full-time employment offer. This is usually done by using a temp-to-perm arrangement.

Contract Work

Contract workers are independent workers who work with organizations on a project or fee basis. These workers provide organizations with another type of staffing alternative, especially during a time of crisis when immediate work is required.

There are strict guidelines on the federal as well as state level differentiating between contract workers and employees. Misclassifying an employee as an independent worker to cut back on benefits cost is a common practice that carries substantial penalties.

There are dedicated employment agencies and brokers that assist contract workers by providing the workers' payrolls, marketing their skills and negotiating the contract with clients on behalf of independent workers.

Professional Employer Organization

A professional employer organization (PEO) is a company that works as the HR department for another organization. When employed, a PEO employs candidates and "leases" them to the organization.

PEOs can provide all the services of a full HR department, including payroll and benefits services. They are suitable for smaller companies that need to offer better benefits to their employees in a cost-effective manner.

Outsourcing

When an organization needs to complete a project that is proving to be difficult or needs a side project done in relatively less time, outsourcing provides a great alternative.

The trend of outsourcing is becoming increasingly popular because it allows organizations to not take on too many functions that can be completed by specialists in a cost-effective arrangement.

These functions can be time consuming, too costly or require a specific skill set that would be too intricate to cover in a broad recruitment campaign starting from scratch.

Interestingly, HR departments are famous for outsourcing their various functions. These can include:

- 401(k) or 403(b) programs
- Pensions/benefits
- Stock option administration
- Learning and development
- Payroll
- Safety and security

Reasons for Rapidly Growing Alternative Staffing

There are many reasons that we are seeing these alternative staffing methods become more popular and almost a standard of their own in the face of traditional recruitment.

The rapidly changing world and technology play a major role in this industry shift. Due to the flexibility provided by the Internet, physical presence in many jobs is seen as unnecessary. Why waste resources and time on getting people in the same building when a business can be conducted online more efficiently?

This change also allows employees to pursue different passions and be involved in more projects that can boost their productivity. The opportunities for part-time workers and freelancers are increasing with this fast-paced shift.

Benefits of Alternative Staffing for Employers

Just like there are many models and arrangements available within the world of alternative staffing, the benefits vary as well. First, these options allow organizations to be more adaptable to the uncertain market.

In the rapidly shifting world, alternative staffing allows employers to think on their feet and not be held back because of the daunting structure of traditional recruitment measures. Any sudden changes in the market or even the internal workings of a company can be swiftly dealt with within a reasonable time by making use of alternative staffing methods.

Second, cost-effectiveness is a big plus when it comes to alternative staffing. Most of the methods included in alternative staffing cost the employers less time and money than would any traditional means of handling the same situation. Alternative staff also does not require the usual benefits packages or payroll taxes.

With the booming gig platforms and freelancing markets, organizations can benefit from reaching independent contractors for specific projects. These methods almost guarantee time-effective strategies for tackling unexpected situations and less capital than would any traditional means of acquiring the needed skills.

Alternative Staffing and HR

No one can deny or challenge the benefits provided by alternative staffing to both employers and employees. HR professionals need to keep up with the rapidly changing environment and familiarize themselves with the newest alternatives to traditional recruitment. These methods can prove to be not only cost-effective but time effective as well for organizations of all shapes and sizes.

HR professionals also need to understand the benefits that alternative staffing offers to employees. From flexible hours and increased productivity to a more creative outlook and a better work-life balance, alternative staffing provides many benefits. These are important points of negotiation and persuasion.

These alternatives provide useful solutions to people who are at a disadvantage in traditional recruitment efforts, such as people who need to stay at home or have other commitments that do not allow them to work full time. HR departments can maximize the gain to their organization by tapping into this pool of potential workers while also doing something valuable for the community.

Chapter 10: Transition Techniques for Corporate Restructuring and Measuring Staffing Effectiveness

Corporate restructuring refers to the changes made in the individual units of an organization to reduce or eliminate redundancy. It also encompasses any bureaucratic process applied to reduce organizational costs while increasing production.

With the rapidly evolving business environment, shifts in organizations are becoming more commonplace. Organizations need to be quick in replying to market change and demand. For example, more businesses now seem to be decentralizing different functions of their operations to keep up with the market.

Corporate restructuring also occurs when there is a change in the company's vision or strategy. Depending on an organization's size and framework, any restructuring can have a huge impact on both the overall workplace environment and individual employees.

This is where HR needs to play a crucial role and be the glue that keeps the organization together while it is transitioning between different structures. The HR department delivers on the changes that the company needs in order to change its structure, focus on the new strategy and carry out change management.

The HR department needs to be aware of the impact any restructuring will have on employees and try to understand which approach will work best to stabilize the workplace atmosphere during an uncertain period.

HR and Change Management

When it comes to corporate restructuring, layoffs are inevitable. It might be a difficult process both for the organization and employees but is inherent to the nature of corporate restructuring.

It is HR professionals' responsibility not just to work for the benefit of the organization and its brand but also to be thoughtful in their approach to individual employees who have been loyal to their jobs. The HR department needs to make sure that these employees are treated well and leave the company on good terms.

HR professionals need to be cautious because of the intricacies involved in change management, which is why it can become a challenge. This is especially true when corporate restructuring involves significant cuts in the workforce or moves to other markets to serve a strategic need.

In this unstable environment, the HR department also needs to be cognizant of possible legal disputes. There is a lot of sensitive material that needs to be handled carefully, and if one party is displeased, the organization can be at risk of a legal battle.

Successful Change Management

The HR department needs to be involved in the organization's strategic choices when it comes to restructuring. It needs to keep in mind the organization's competitive position in the market and the profiles of employees when it comes to their strengths and weaknesses.

Once a strategy is chosen and a plan is finalized, the HR department needs to actively work with employees to make the change process as smooth as possible. There are some key points in this phase that must be focused on, including:

Effective Communication

Research has found that employees are more uncomfortable with feelings of uncertainty during times of restructuring. They prefer to hear the bad news upfront rather than work for a significant time while hearing nothing but rumors.

During any kind of restructuring process, HR needs to have clear communication with the employees. It is not just better for the overall transition of the organization, but it also dignifies the individual employees by not leaving them hanging. Having transparency and honesty in the workplace will keep the expectations in check while also minimizing the risk of chaos and confusion.

Administrative Tasks

Corporate restructuring is an intricate process that involves a lot of paperwork. So, HR professionals need to make sure that they are doing their due diligence when it comes to tying up any loose ends. These tasks include the employee payroll and possible additional packages that need to be given to employees who are being laid off.

All the legal regulations also need to be followed when it comes to documentation. These are not just important while restructuring is happening but also for future audits and any possible disputes.

Supporting Employees

Supporting employees is an essential function of the HR department in any organization. The only way an organization can uphold good standards of HR and employee care is by caring about employees. When it comes to restructuring, the overall morale of the workforce is naturally down. Employees are either aware they are being laid off or are in fear of it. HR professionals should dedicate themselves to helping employees consider professional outplacement services and may even provide contacts for them.

Outplacement services help rehabilitate laid-off employees back into the workforce. They offer both practical and mental support for employees and help them transition into their new jobs.

Plan Ahead

It is imperative that the HR department first takes its time to go over all the essential parts of the new strategy and be ready for any kind of development in the restructuring process. These can include any legal setbacks or hurdles in the allocation of resources according to the new strategy.

It is also important for HR to make sure that different departments are on the same page when planning what needs to be changed. If all involved units within the organization are not kept in the loop, the change process can suffer when it comes to implementing the plan.

Measuring Staffing Effectiveness

Planning and employment are more measurement friendly than some other functions of HR.

Business Impact Measures

First, the most obvious measure of effectiveness comes in the form of productivity metrics. Employee productivity informs the department of the implemented strategy that has been used for staffing.

These metrics are calculated by dividing total output (either the revenue generated or product inventory) by the number of employees. This metric can be applied to the whole organization or individual work units, depending on what information is needed.

Tactical Accountability Measures

When it comes to HR's performance in terms of staffing, various accountability measures can be used. The following are the most common methods:

- **Accession rate** – This metric measures the number of new employees against the total number of employees. It is used to determine the different HR programs needed to manage and support the workforce that is already accumulated. Accession rate is calculated by dividing the total number of new employees by the number of employees at the end of the previous measurement period. This rate can then be used in conjunction with other performance metrics to get an idea of how effective the new staffing strategy has been.

- **Quality of hire** – In this measurement, HR first develops some criteria of the quality to be measured. For example, HR needs to determine what qualifies as a "quality hire." These criteria usually include information from job descriptions and job expectations. HR also needs to verify if these expectations have been communicated to the employees. After this, performance ratings gathered from managers can be compared to evaluate new employees, which ultimately reflects on the quality of staffing.

- **Cost per hire** – There are several costs associated with the hiring of an employee, such as advertising, in-house recruiter fees, candidate screening fees, HR staff salary, salaries for hiring managers and other members of the interview team, assessment tests, pre-employment inquiries, administrative costs and any other costs associated with the hiring process. This metric is calculated by dividing the total costs by the number of hires for the measurement period.

- **Time to hire** – The time-to-hire metric is calculated from the date a job is posted to the date a new employee accepts a job. This lets HR know whether the strategies are time effective and what kind of response they are getting from the market. This informs future decisions that need to be made, keeping in mind the urgency of some hires for the organization.

- **Replacement cost** – HR needs to be aware of what value they are putting in and getting out of employees. A good staffing strategy keeps in mind the cost that a possible replacement would entail. These measurements can be an eye-opener for managers and executives. In addition to the costs calculated for the cost per hire metric, this measurement includes costs for training, lost productivity, temporary replacements, overtime for employees who fill in while a position is vacant and other costs.
- **Turnover analysis** – This analysis is calculated by dividing the average number of total employees in the measurement period by the number of employees who have exited the organization. This turnover analysis can vary depending on what information the organization needs. Some variations include calculating on a monthly or annual basis. This analysis can be run separately for voluntary exits and layoffs to accrue more meaningful data.

Chapter 11: Organizational Development

Organizational development in HR is the strategy of improving an organization's structure and processes through the implementation of policies, leadership, learning, training or job redesign.

The purpose of an organizational development strategy is to improve effectiveness and efficiency within an organization. Organizational development advances and unites different business objectives.

The focal areas of effective organizational strategies are:

- Organizational effectiveness
- Organizational structure
- Organizational learning
- Performance and productivity

The Purpose of Organizational Development

The purpose of organizational development is to improve an organization's competitive advantage in the marketplace. It is achieved by increasing cultural values, employee productivity, market share, margins, morale and other factors that boost organizational strength.

Present and Future-Oriented Talent Acquisition

Talent management is the process of identifying an organization's present and future employment needs in relation to its potential and competencies. The stronger the correlation between employee-organization interests, the greater the results of talent acquisition initiatives will be.

Career management focuses on an organization's talent needs, whereas career development reflects employees' desires and interests. Talent management is the bridge between these two interests, identifying the sweet spot that represents the shared objectives of the organization and its employees and aligning the interest of two leads to increase joint satisfaction and organizational strength.

Activities that help achieve talent management objectives include:

- Mapping tasks to competencies and establishing assessment metrics and standards of performance
- Comparing employees' formal and informal skill sets to selected competencies
- Studying deficiencies that lead to incompetence

The HR department can provide development opportunities to current employees by:

- Identifying existing talent for training and development
- Evaluating career development opportunities, including the interests of employees in advancement and nontraditional careers
- Planning resources to provide development interventions to the internal audience

The HR department can establish long-term strategies to develop talent strength in the organization by:

- Starting a performance management program to identify performance expectations, institute stretch goals, provide regular feedback and objectively measure performance
- Establishing training programs to promote the concept of knowledge sharing between experienced and junior staff members

A future-focused system of talent management will help the organization achieve its business objectives and ensure that it is equipped with skilled employees in case of changes that affect the strategic direction in the future.

Organizational Effectiveness

Organizational effectiveness helps leaders ensure different departments in the organization are performing at peak efficiency with the help of improvement programs. Organizational effectiveness also maintains leader-member relationships. The approach to achieve this is to practice active vigilance, as it limits damage and offers a challenge. Accurate identification of sources of the problem helps develop effective practices to eliminate functional barriers in an organization.

Unfortunately, most organizational development interventions are implemented incorrectly by assuming dysfunction instead of following a procedure of assessment and analysis to reveal problems. To prevent this, it is important to develop a data collection process to extract information. The most useful information comprises qualitative and quantitative data collected from various sources.

There are various methods of intervention and assessment used based on indicators being observed. The majority of productivity and performance dysfunctions are found in the following categories:

- **Behavioral** – Problems with employee behavior can cause communication gaps, reduce the quality of performance, deliver inadequate performance and disrupt the environment of the workplace.
- **Technological** – Problems with materials, information and technology used to complete tasks or conduct work can lead to performance inefficiencies.
- **Skill and knowledge** – Deficiencies in employees' skills and knowledge can be corrected with targeted learning and development opportunities.
- **Process-related** – Inefficiencies in the system can cause problems with how tasks are performed. Impractical procedures, outdated policies and inefficient systems or reporting structures are common process-related problems.
- **Cultural** – Workplace difficulties and an unhealthy work environment are challenging problems that are difficult to remedy.

Different problems require different solutions. For example, learning and development programs can correct skill, knowledge and behavior problems but cannot improve a flawed process or technological barriers.

Organizational Structure

Organizational structure is the framework around which an organization operates, designs its goal and performs a function. Organizational structure aligns different parts of a business and allows it to reach maximum performance. How an organizational structure is developed impacts the success of business objectives and strategies. It is important for the leadership to understand the benefits, characteristics and limitations of different organizational structures to accomplish strategic alignment.

The following are the four types of standard organizational structures:

Functional Structure

The functional structure aligns employees and works according to specialization. It positions each department in a hierarchical order, so employees can directly report to their supervisors within their functional area. The functional structure works most effectively in organizations where decision-making and operations remain centralized, as centralized decision-making allows businesses to benefit from economies of scale, which is otherwise not possible when all functional areas make independent decisions.

Functional structure works in a traditional organizational setting with standard departments, such as sales, production, development, accounting, marketing and HR. All departments specialize in different functions. For instance, in an HR department, all employees work within the same functional area and report to the senior HR manager or head.

Divisional Structure

Divisional structure arranges an organization by its region, market and product. For example, a clothing business that sells clothing items for men, women and children in the south, east and north can have three types of divisional structure:

- **Market** – E-commerce, retail and catalog
- **Region** – South, east and north
- **Product** – Men's, women's and children's clothing

These structures work because all divisions must collaborate because they have shared needs. Collaboration takes place with shared products, distribution processes, vendors and products.

Divisional structure works effectively because the authority to make decisions goes through different levels of the organization, making the process faster and more independent. Furthermore, there are two reporting direction options available to employees in this structure: dotted-line reporting and straight-line reporting.

In a straight-line reporting system, employees report to their division heads, whereas in a dotted-line reporting system, the employees report to their functional managers. These systems align tasks for each divisional and functional objective and operation.

Matrix Structure

Matrix structure is the most complicated organizational structure because it requires employees to report to multiple leaders.

Direct reporting to a functional and divisional manager is a unit arrangement similar to the divisional structure; however, the multiple-personnel chain of command requires understanding, cooperation and efficiency of supervisors to determine employee assignments, work priorities and performance standards.

In a matrix organization, along with the two reporting structures mentioned above, team members also report to department managers. Reporting to the primary manager of their department is similar to a traditional organizational structure. For example, teams working in the IT department report to the head of the department. The head reports to the divisional head and eventually, all reports are carried to the CEO.

Organizational Learning

Positive behavior and cognitive skills are the keys to organizational strength. The responsibility for developing employees' cognitive and behavioral skills is shared by departments and remains a consistent business objective.

There are various ways to improve organizational learning. It can be done by:

- Developing a culture of learning and providing developmental opportunities within the organization
- Establishing personal development as a key business objective and performance requirement for all teams
- Creating learning opportunities with effective evaluation after each project

- Encouraging cross-disciplinary skill development and learning opportunities
- Matching the required competencies to accomplish organizational goals against the inventory of skills
- Establishing advancement and development of subordinates as a key metric for leadership assessment
- Creating and monitoring different appraisal tools to discover trends in employees' development needs
- Determining the value of learning programs to identify, retrieve, harvest and transfer skills and knowledge

The efficiency and credibility of an organization's learning program are measured by the ROI. This is a simple calculation that reveals that the return is more than the investment.

- **Sample returns** – A sample return includes the value to improved service and production units and proficiency, quality of units, minimized errors, reduced waste, downtime, accidents, damage and absenteeism, as well as improved employee/customer and public relationships.
- **Sample investments** – A sample investment includes the cost of lost time, opportunities and delivery and its impact on relationships and reputation.

In addition to investing in different learning opportunities, it is also important to identify the need for necessary skills that are presently missing within an organization.

Chapter 12: Instructional Design Principles and Processes

HR development integrates career development, organizational development and training to improve organizational and individual performance. The purpose of instructional HR development is to increase employee productivity/performance that directly impacts profitability and the success of organizational operations.

HR professionals have the responsibility to develop programs and encourage the participation of the workforce in performance management. The success of this process is based on business objectives, identified competencies and expected project outcomes. Developing performance standards and problem-solving procedures is key to enhanced organizational performance.

To successfully implement HR development, the HR department is divided into distinct roles and responsibilities. These roles can be categorized as learning agents, managers, performance engineers and instructional designers.

What Is Instructional Design?

Instructional design is a systematic approach to identifying performance gaps; assessing problems with performance; developing interventions that address gaps in performance; and successfully implementing solutions, such as employee training programs, support tools, reward programs and organizational restructuring.

The first step in instructional design is developing a performance objective that asserts the learning outcomes of the instructional experience. There are four key components of performance objectives:

- Audience
- Behavior
- Degree
- Condition

The performance component states the tasks to be performed when demonstrating optimum performance. The ABCD formula allows clear goals and objectives to be established:

- **Audience** – Determine who will receive the learning to achieve the objective
- **Behavior** – Describe the ideal behavior that demonstrates command of the objective
- **Degree** – Establish the degree of command required, meaning the acceptable accuracy, speed, quality and performance
- **Condition** – Determine the condition under which the learning will be performed

Adult Learning Theory

Adult learning theory was developed by Malcolm Knowles in 1968. It underlines five assumptions in providing an effective knowledge and learning experience to adults. These assumptions can help organizations create meaningful learning and development experiences for employees. They include:

Self-Concept

Adults are more independent and prefer self-directed methods of learning compared to instructor-led learning techniques. To engage with the learning experience, adults prefer to be involved in the evaluation and planning of the learning process.

Experience

Compared to children, adults have more exposure to different experiences and learning opportunities. Being able to relate to previous knowledge and experiences keeps them engaged and motivates learning of new concepts.

Orientation and Readiness to Learn

Adult learners are more engaged in a learning experience that can be practically implemented. The knowledge that is implemented in the form of a task is more readily accepted than conceptual information that is not immediately required.

Motivation to Learn

Adults learn better when they are motivated to learn. It is important to provide adults with a reason to learn and explain how it will benefit them to engage their attention.

Instructional Systems Design (ISD) Process

The ISD process model helps HR professionals effectively develop an instructional design. It is a methodical approach to training that takes into account various factors, including the environment in which learning is taking place, the personalities of the learners and the characteristics of the system in which the learner will perform the task.

The ISD model comprises various steps that identify the purpose of instruction and its method of delivery. To ensure the effectiveness of the instructional process, thorough evaluation and careful implementation are applied. The ID process also ensures that the learning will solve organizational problems and challenges and help achieve organizational goals.

Responsibilities of an Instructional Designer

The primary responsibilities of an HR professional dedicated to the role of instructional design are identifying objectives, defining content and preparing learning activities. Instructional designers have the responsibility to design and develop different interventions that promote behavioral change and the effectiveness of the organizational process.

The five sub-roles of an instructional designer can be categorized as program designer, task analyst, instructional writer, media specialist and theoretician. All responsibilities attached to these roles are carried out at the same time:

Program Designer

As a program designer, the HR professional is responsible for identifying performance objectives; developing and ranking learning activities required to accomplish these objectives; and selecting relevant materials, media and training aids required for intervention.

Task Analyst

As a task analyst, the HR professional is required to develop the necessary steps required to perform a task. The listed steps are the key to developing performance-based learning objectives, content and evaluation processes. Task analysis gives a detailed sketch of the task needed to be learned and establishes different levels of learning and training prerequisites.

Writer

The writing role requires the development of course materials, such as training manuals, used during development training.

Media Specialist

As a media specialist, the HR professional studies and selects appropriate technical training and audiovisual tools to engage learners. The selection of media depends on various factors, including time available, group size, learning styles and training content.

Theoretician

The theoretician is responsible for developing theories and models related to the development process to drive changes in performance and organization.

Key Practices

The key practices of an instructional designer are to:

- Identify the audience of learners
- Adhere to adult learning theories, curriculum, design and education
- Conduct an analysis of needs to identify gaps and determine outcomes and potential interventions
- Develop learning objectives in relation to the desired outcome
- Identify the indicators of success, such as behavioral changes, evidence of learning, rating percentage and impact of change on the organization
- Develop and rank instructional strategies and content
- Design interactive and innovative content that reflects the diversity of learners with the help of current and new technological tools, such as social media, e-learning and virtual training

- Oversee the implementation of programs and products
- Develop benchmarks and best practices in learning models to enhance the quality of the programs
- Assess and evaluate the impact of instruction according to the success indicators and make revisions and updates to the programs if required

Competencies of an Instructional Designer

The competencies required by an instructional HR designer include understanding of areas of business and technical, intellectual and interpersonal skills as categorized by the American Society for Training and Development. Understanding adult learning, developing objectives, identifying skills, understanding business and its operations, understanding organizational behavior and performance, questioning skills, presentation skills and research skills are the core competencies of an instructional designer.

HR professionals must have good communication, interpersonal and facilitation skills. They must be able to create and manage different learning environments effectively using media, motivation and feedback techniques. Instructional designers should be able to innovate and be creative when developing learning opportunities for employees. A competent ID professional must have an in-depth understanding of learning patterns and different environments in which learning takes place.

There are three key learning styles identified by experts: visual, auditory and tactical. Visual learners tend to prefer written instruction. Auditory learners prefer listening to instructions, and tactical learners prefer learning experiences that involve the sense of touch.

It is an HR professional's responsibility to understand the weaknesses and strengths of different learning theories to develop an effective instructional design strategy. The ID professional must have an awareness of learners' cultural and environmental differences to understand their psychological and social composition. Without an understanding of learners' unique needs, an HR professional cannot motivate, encourage and support people to lean toward change.

Importance of Instructional Design

ID is one of the most important components of an organization's structure. It is the development of different learning materials to ensure the quality of delivery, design and effective transfer of knowledge. Instructional designers improve employee performance and productivity and increase customer satisfaction. By analyzing human performance, instructional designers identify problem areas, develop different solutions and implement them effectively.

Rapid changes in the work environment, economies, technology and globalization are driving the need for effective instructional design. The need for new skills is pushing organizations to develop training programs to help employees develop and implement new skills. All organizations may not be able to procure instructors for implementing learning programs but may be able to provide tools and learning materials that boost productivity and creativity.

Chapter 13: Consultation on Professional Growth and Development Opportunities

Great organizations have a structure in place that identifies how employees progress and grow during their tenure with the organization. All departments have a career development model in place that develops steps to education, learning, experience and professional development. It identifies the essential *what* and *when* in employee career timelines.

The workforce of an organization needs to understand the performance benchmarks to advance and grow. For employees who do not intend to advance to supervisory roles or take increased responsibility, activities should be planned to enrich and maintain engagement in their current roles.

An HR professional can develop a career development map that facilitates switching career paths or jobs by identifying roles that require similar skills. This can help employees create a career development plan that incorporates the company's needs and their personal goals.

Aligning the company's requirements with an employee's aspirations and career goals is a challenging task. Leadership plays a critical role in making this happen by coaching, motivating and providing benefits to employees to maximize their productivity and contributions to the company. Some high-performing leaders and supervisors also identify skill gaps and minimize them by developing training programs.

The functional area of HR development demands responsibilities from the HR professional that are critical to the organization's success; however, small-scale organizations often outsource development tasks. Other functional area tasks—such as payroll, recordkeeping and compliance—have an immediate impact and are therefore given more priority than development tasks.

Unfortunately, because of the overwhelming short-term needs of employees and organizations, development responsibilities are viewed as a bonus and not requirements of an organization. It is important for HR to strongly advocate for the professional growth and development of the organization's talent.

Provide Consultation

It is HR professionals' responsibility to provide consultations to employees and managers on internal and external professional growth and development opportunities to maximize the company's human potential.

HR professionals are required to coordinate with managers and supervisors throughout the development and learning process. Sometimes managers are highly knowledgeable and skilled but cannot tap into the potential of their teams. In such cases, HR personnel must apply their interpersonal skills to help managers encourage employees to consistently and constantly achieve the performance benchmarks set to meet business objectives.

HR professionals act as advisors to managers, encouraging them to coach employees about development plans. Managers should have regular discussions with their team members about their career goals, desire for growth and future development plans. Managers and HR work together to develop training programs that support the learning of new skills. The HR department is also responsible for identifying internal biases and preventing discrimination in terms of growth opportunities.

Employee and Organizational Development

To help the organization grow, HR professionals must meet the changing needs of the organization's stakeholders, customers and employees. There should be a systematic process in place that ensures no employee, department or team is left behind during transformation and change. HR professionals need to understand the impact of change and be able to mitigate the negative consequences following the change.

These are some of the other responsibilities of HR professionals:

Develop and Implement Training and Career Development Programs

HR professionals develop, implement and evaluate training and development programs by collecting data and insights. Data includes statistics about employee performance, trained number of employees, employees eligible for retirement, replacement candidates and high-potential employees.

Talent Management

HR professionals are required to manage and grow organizational talent to benefit the company. Different development models should be designed to identify high performers to ensure they are given increased responsibility to maximize their potential and utility to the organization.

Career Mapping

Mapping career progression is an essential responsibility of HR professionals. Career ladders and paths are two methods of encouraging the development and growth of employees. The career ladder is defined as progression in particular fields within an organization classified from high to low according to the level of pay and responsibility. Career paths refer to different forms of progression, including vertical, horizontal, dual-career ladders and progression outside the organization.

HR professionals must have an understanding of how to map career progression for different positions to develop internal talent and stabilize the workforce. Career mapping requires an understanding of skills, abilities and knowledge required in different fields and how employees progress to more senior positions. These models also include HR planners who enable transfers across departments and provide cross-training.

Ideal career development models demonstrate the career progression of a new employee. They also explain how employees can advance and develop their skills in the organization. The career development chart reveals a combination of education, experience and professional development required to progress. However, note that a career development model may show what is required to progress but may not evaluate the performance or potential of an employee.

Management of High-Potential Employees

High-potential employees can perform complex tasks with a wide potential for progression into supervisory and management responsibilities. HR professionals have to help supervisors identify high performers within an organization to train and promote them to higher roles.

Various tools and techniques are used to evaluate the potential of employees and support managers to cultivate skills and maximize their potential. HR professionals may have to develop an individual development plan to encourage talented groups of individuals to increase their learning and development and groom their leadership skills.

Develop Job Enrichment Opportunities

There are cases where employees have reached their capacity for growth but still competently perform their roles. Keeping these employees engaged during their tenure is important to prevent a decline in performance. HR professionals are responsible for finding creative job enrichment opportunities for these employees.

In certain cases, developing a training program for learning new processes or technologies can help these employees perform better. For example, competent employees may not be eligible for supervisory positions but can be given the role of team leads. Instead of leading departments, they may train new employees and perform quality checks on the team's performance.

Training for Evaluators

Training managers and supervisors about the evaluation process is also the responsibility of the HR personnel. Providing training about how evaluations are performed and submitted, including the appropriate time frame, is an example of training.

Another advanced form of training requires helping managers and supervisors to identify and establish performance criteria. The evaluation process cannot be haphazard, but it is difficult to evaluate tasks from a quality perspective.

HR professionals should train supervisors to measure behavioral and technical competencies to evaluate employees' performance. Technical competencies can be evaluated according to the completion of tasks. Behavioral competencies reveal an employee's performance level.

It is common for supervisors to overlook one aspect of performance for the other. Difficult situations, such as an employee performing well on tasks but having behavior problems or having a positive attitude while struggling to perform well, can be challenging for supervisors. HR professionals can help managers and supervisors navigate difficult situations.

Support Succession Planning

Succession planning takes place at a higher level of HR; however, all HR professionals have the responsibility to support succession planning. Senior HR generalists or managers have a higher understanding of employees and their capacity to perform. The information available to them has more value than information systems.

HR professionals are responsible for evaluating skills, knowledge and abilities for the job in question and then identifying gaps that can be filled with training and development programs. HR professionals also determine the cost and time required to close the skill gap and identify where the resources should be applied in the process.

Succession planning is not limited to identifying individuals who may have the potential to progress to senior-level positions. Doing so is considered a failure and discrimination in providing equal opportunities. HR has to determine the skills required and identify high performers and different potential replacements with the capacity to learn. Succession planning may require recruiting talent from outside the company if no employees match the required skill set.

Chapter 14: Training Program Facilitation, Techniques and Delivery

Employee Training Programs

Training is the process of improving and expanding employees' skills, capabilities and knowledge for doing a particular job. It is an effective tool used by many organizations to enhance productivity and improve efficiency.

Training takes place at three levels: organizational, task and individual.

The Organizational Level

In organizational-level training, the entire organization or just one particular department focuses on preparing employees for expected future needs and/or goals. Factors such as a downward trend in metrics representing employee satisfaction and productivity, a change in the company's strategic plans or direction, a new product being launched and an increase in the number of casualties all indicate training is needed at this level.

The Task Level

Training that occurs at a single job process or category is known as task-level training. Low performance in a specific task/process would indicate training is needed at the task level.

The Individual Level

Individual-level training, as the name implies, occurs at a personal level. The need for this training is indicated by poor performance by a particular employee.

Training programs at any of these levels are designed using the ADDIE model, which stands for analyze, design, develop, implement and evaluate.

Analysis

This step begins by identifying the desired outcome or goal, gathering data relevant to that particular case—which can be done through surveys distributing questionnaires and conducting job analyses—and using this data to highlight the performance gap, identify the instructional goals, draft possible solutions and choose the best solution after careful evaluation of each.

Summary of the Analysis Process

Here is a summary of the analysis process:

1. Identify the goal(s)
2. Gather data
3. Find performance gap
4. Identify institutional goals
5. Draft solutions
6. Evaluate

Design

The design step begins by compiling all the tasks in the job to create the task inventory list. An action verb, a function and an object should be included in the task description. An example could be *Informing employees of the upcoming meeting by sending emails using a computer.*

The second sub-step is identifying the target audience (the people who will be attending the training session). As noted earlier, there are three types of learning styles that should be kept in mind when attempting to engage the audience: visual, audio and kinesthetic.

Once the audience has been identified, the training objectives are formulated. These describe the desired outcomes in quantified/measurable terms and highlight what exactly is to be achieved.

Then, keeping the training objectives in mind, the course content is developed. Only material that can be utilized immediately after the training is included.

Finally, the evaluation criteria are selected. This will test whether the employees, after training, can meet the goal that was initially set.

Development

In the development phase, the design component covered earlier is translated into a presentable format. This is done using different training materials, such as manuals and handouts and different instructional methods.

Instructional Methods

The manager can choose from a pool of different instructional methods, depending on the situation.

1. **Passive training methods**

In passive training methods, the learner only listens to the lecturer without any active participation. The training can be delivered using lectures, presentations and conferences.

To inform and answer any queries, lectures are used in combination with other tools, such as demonstrations. Information is delivered to a gathering of individuals using a presentation. A conference is usually a lecture or presentation combined with a question-and-answer session with the audience.

2. **Active training methods**

Active training methods place the focus on the learner, who is asked to participate in the training exercises frequently. They include:

- **Facilitation**

This technique involves a facilitator—a subject specialist—leading a group of employees to brainstorm and share ideas that are used to solve problems.

- **Case study**

Case studies replicate real-life scenarios and help learners identify strategies they could use to deal with similar situations.

- **Simulation**

Simulation training helps inexperienced employees learn new skills in a scenario that is not dangerous for them or the public. Simulation training that acquaints novice employees with hazardous equipment or job operations that demand speed, such as a checkout scanner, is a type of vestibule training.

- **Socratic seminar**

A Socratic seminar helps employees understand a certain topic through a question-and-answer format. For example, the leader may ask the group a question at the beginning of the seminar, which will then be answered through a discussion.

3. **Experiential training methods**

Experiential training methods, also known as "learning through experience," allow employees to gain knowledge and experience by going through real-life situations.

In this type of training, trainees may have to undergo demonstrations, one-on-one training sessions (a situation where the trainee is paired with an experienced expert) and performance-based methods in which the employee is trained to gain expertise in the particular skills needed to finish the job efficiently.

Implementation

In the implementation phase, a place that will help implement the desired training is selected.

Some of the selected styles include:

- **Theater-style seating** – Theater-style seating is best suited for lectures, films or video presentations.
- **Classroom-style seating** – Classroom-style seating is best suited for situations where employees will be seeing manuals and taking notes.
- **Banquet-style seating** – Banquet-style seating is best suited for small-group discussions.
- **Chevron-style seating** – Chevron-style seating is best for when the audience is expected to interact with both the speaker and each other.
- **Conference-style seating** – Conference-style seating is best suited for scenarios where the debate is led by a facilitator rather than a professor.

- **U-shaped seating** – U-shaped seating is best suited for situations in which collaboration plays a key role, and the central area may be used for role-playing, etc.

Evaluation

The final phase in the ADDIE model is evaluation. Evaluation occurs after the training has been completed and uses the initially set criteria as the basis.

There are four main types of evaluation techniques:

Reaction Evaluation Method

The reaction evaluation method collects information about the initial reaction from participants through a survey. It does not measure the organizational impact of the training but does help trainers gauge how efficiently they presented the description.

Learning Evaluation Method

A test is used in the learning evaluation approach to see how effectively employees have recalled the material. The approach employs a pretest/post-test comparative experimental design. In this technique, the test results of two groups—only one of which received the training—are compared to gauge the effectiveness.

The selection of groups must meet three criteria: the creation of more than one group, the random allocation of group members and a measurable outcome that both groups share.

Behavioral Evaluation Method

The behavioral evaluation method evaluates job performance around six weeks after training.

Results Evaluation Method

The results evaluation method is most relevant when determining the impact of training on business productivity by comparing objective statements, such as, "Following this training program, the number of accidents will be reduced by

25% in one month," to the actual decrease in the number of accidents in a month (the results).

Training Techniques and Delivery Methods

Now that we have covered how training programs are formulated, let's move on to the different training techniques used to train employees once they enter the workforce. This occurs in four steps:

1. **Employee orientation** – The objective of employee orientation is to welcome new employees and help reduce startup costs and turnover. It helps save supervisors' time and reduces newcomers' anxiety by familiarizing them with the job expectations.
2. **In-house training program** – This is the second step and includes any program that is delivered by an employee of the organization.
3. **Mentoring** – This third step, which should involve a formalized program, teams up recruits with experienced employees to assist them in learning specific skills.
4. **Exterior training** – Any type of training that does not occur in-house is included in the final step. For example, employees attend conferences and seminars that improve their leadership skills.

Types of Training

- **Technical training** – Technical training deals with the different types of software and other technical tools that employees must use to carry out their jobs efficiently.
- **Quality training** – Employees become familiarized with the tools needed to generate a high-quality product through this form of training.
- **Soft skills training** – Soft skills training helps teach employees soft skills—like good communication, critical thinking and public speaking—to ensure things like superior customer service.
- **Professional training** – Professional training occurs externally and involves acquiring the necessary certification or information needed to perform a certain job.

- **Team training** – Team training helps employees learn how to work efficiently in teams and allows teams to improve their decision-making and problem-solving skills to enhance communication among employees and boost productivity.
- **Managerial training** – Managerial training provides employees with the necessary abilities to take on a management position.
- **Safety training** – Safety training helps make sure a company is meeting OSHA standards to minimize safety hazards and ensure smooth operations.

Training Delivery Methods

There are different types of training delivery methods. Managers should select the most appropriate, depending on the type of training that will be performed. In most organizations, a combination of different delivery methods is used.

Delivery of On-the-Job Coaching

Delivery of on-the-job coaching involves an amateur employee paired up with a more experienced employee to specialize in certain skills. It is comparable to the mentor-training delivery approach; however, mentor-training delivery focuses more on overall development rather than polishing specific abilities.

Brown Bag Lunch Training Delivery

This training delivery method, as the name implies, is informal and used mostly when employees gather to have lunch. As it occurs in a relaxed environment, it can help hone either personal development or specific job-relevant skills.

Web-Based Training Delivery

Technology is used for web-based training, also known as e-learning or computer/technology/Internet-based learning. There are two types of web-based training delivery: synchronous and asynchronous learning.

Learning led by an instructor is synchronous. Learning that is self-directed and does not require an instructor is asynchronous. This type of training is low cost, requires no travel and is easy to access, but it can also have no personal touch, which may impact learning.

Job Shadowing Training Delivery

Job shadowing, as the name implies, places a fresh recruit in the shadow of someone more experienced and involves on-the-job training.

Job Swapping Training Delivery

In this training delivery method, two employees swap their jobs to learn new skills and gain expertise in different categories. This type of training delivery is useful for organizations, as it enables employees to be cross-trained in different categories. It is also beneficial for employees, as it can be a source of motivation by creating a change of scenery.

Vestibule Training Delivery

Vestibule training happens in a conference room, classroom or lecture room and is useful for skill-based training and delivering orientations. It is utilized by many firms for professional development, technical training, quality assurance and safety training.

For example, company X may use vestibule training to teach its new recruits skills needed to operate the cash register and/or how to deal with customers in a manner that improves customer service.

International Assignment Training

International assignment training focuses on preparing employees for working in foreign countries and new environments. This type of training delivery is becoming increasingly relevant in the modern era because of global shrinkage, which allows companies to operate in different countries.

There are certain key elements that employees should be aware of for this type of training to be successful. This includes awareness of cultural similarities and differences, fluency in linguistics, socially accepted norms and an insight into a country's daily lifestyle.

Chapter 15: Coaching, Mentoring and Employee Retention

Mentoring

Mentoring is defined as an employee training system under which an expert or highly experienced person is assigned as an advisor or guide to less experienced employees to guide them and nurture their development. A mentor can be a supervisor or a colleague who has more experience than the trainees.

Mentoring can occur informally, but a formal mentorship program helps create a pathway that allows employees to navigate on-the-job challenges and hassles.

Mentoring must be integrated into the company's culture for it to be effective, which means mentors should get in-house training and be chosen on the basis of personality, willingness and experience.

For example, mentors are listed according to their attributes in IBM's integrated supply chain division mentorship program, and employees can choose their mentor—a person who possesses attributes most suited to their needs. Some companies, like Starbucks, use short-term mentorship programs to increase productivity.

Coaching

The focus of coaching is to meet specific objectives or skills within a given period of time. A coach is a specialist who works with trainees to ensure certain goals are met.

A coaching session usually follows an already established plan—with listed outcomes—in contrast to mentoring, which is usually much more relaxed.

Similarities Between Coaching and Mentoring

Although certain differences exist between mentoring and coaching, these two training systems are quite similar in what they aim to achieve. A mentor or a coach can be considered an accountability partner who strives for their protégés' best interests.

These systems are not about just telling trainees what to do but rather allowing them to become more self-aware and better critical thinkers by asking the right questions. Mentors and coaches can attempt to teach trainees not just to solve problems but to find the best solutions.

The goals of mentoring and coaching are flexible and can change over time as protégés meet certain goals or learn new behaviors.

Mentoring or coaching is applicable to the following situations:

- Traditional courses that do not benefit senior managers
- Fresh recruits starting a new career
- Employees who have changed career direction
- Employees who are going through challenges or difficulties related to job tasks/processes
- Employees wanting to polish and/or expand their skills/expertise
- Mentors and coaches themselves

Mentoring can help/improve:

- Employees in their professional development
- Individual and team commitment to the organization
- Employees' insight into the processes of an organization
- Communication within the organization
- The work culture within the organization
- Networking of employees by exposing them to new individuals

Mentoring cannot:

- Be used as a substitute for traditional training
- Succeed without an agreed-upon plan
- Succeed without clear objectives that have been discussed well in advance

Coaching can:

- Aid individuals in gaining specific new skills

- Help individuals according to their specific needs
- Create flexibility in the learning process
- Give individuals the freedom to learn what they want and how to go about it

Coaching cannot:

- Implement change unless clear and measurable goals have been set beforehand
- Help protégés without support from senior management
- Be successful without full commitment from both coaches and protégés

An effective mentor/coach is:

- Willing to listen
- Open to new ideas
- Eager to challenge traditional ways of thinking by encouraging out-of-the-box thinking
- Passionate and enthusiastic

How to Start a Mentorship or Coaching Program

The following factors must be considered when devising a coaching or mentorship program:

1. How the mentorship/coaching links to the overall goals of the organization
2. How well-suited mentors or coaches are to protégés to avoid clashes
3. The objectives of tutoring and what it desires to accomplish
4. A support structure to take up protégés' workload while they are being mentored or coached
5. The establishment of mechanisms for assessment and criticism

The Coaching and Mentoring Briefing

The guide/mentor and protégés should get to know the accompanying basic issues when the tutor/mentor and protégé have agreed on a basic level to start a tutoring or training program:

1. A chosen topic for mentoring or coaching
2. Overall objectives agreement
3. Creation of a plan to accomplish the target goal by identifying feasible outcomes
4. Creation of an appropriate mentoring and coaching program
5. Reasonable timeline agreement

The GROW Model

A framework for coaching conversations with more experienced employees is provided by the GROW (goals, realities, choices and wrap-up) paradigm. The process might be time consuming and confusing for less experienced employees. In this style, employees are responsible for their progress, and coaches are less directive.

The GROW model is divided into four distinct stages:

1) Determine objectives
2) Investigate reality
3) Generate options
4) Agree on a course of action and tie things up

Performance Evaluation and Feedback

The program's success or failure is objectively assessed by the mentor or coach. Obtaining informal feedback at various stages of the program is important in addressing any adjustments or challenges. Any mentoring or coaching program should start through a feedback mechanism.

Employee Retention Strategies

Employee retention strategies aim to minimize employee turnover, prevent attrition, maximize employee loyalty and enhance employee engagement. They are critical for the productivity and success of any organization.

Retention strategies are designed using retention plans. A retention plan consists of steps like surveys to assess employee satisfaction, the strengths and weaknesses of current plans, the goal of the retention plan being formulated, and last, the specific strategies that will be implemented.

Most organizations devise many strategies in order to ensure employee retention. Some of these are:

Salaries and Benefits

When it comes to salaries and benefits, companies that provide their employees with health benefits and paid time off (PTO) in addition to salary are better able to retain employees compared to organizations that offer only monthly salary packages.

Companies must also ensure there is transparency and fairness in salaries using standard procedures like the pay banding system. Additionally, there should be open communication with employees regarding pay rates and packages.

Training and Development

Training programs that help improve employees' technical and soft skills allow employees to stay longer because they lead to personal growth and fulfillment of psychological needs. Employees who experience professional growth are likely to feel attached to the organization and will be less likely to leave.

Performance Appraisals

Performance appraisal is a formalized process that helps employees gain constructive feedback about their performance by communicating with their managers. This process improves employee retention, as employees who receive helpful feedback are bound to perform better in their jobs because a sense of accomplishment motivates them and helps them fulfill their self-actualization needs.

Succession Planning

Succession planning helps retain employees by allowing career growth. It occurs in three steps. The first is to identify talented employees capable of fulfilling higher-level positions. Following this, these employees are nurtured to ensure they are ready to take on higher-level positions once those positions become vacant. Last, organizations devise a formal succession planning process to diversify the talent bench.

Flextime, Telecommuting and Sabbaticals

Flextime, telecommuting and sabbaticals help retain employees by offering leisure time and giving them the option to work from home to improve flexibility in the workplace. Paid leaves allow a change of environment and can help employees return to work refreshed and motivated. All these steps help improve work-life balance and ensure a more satisfied workforce that is less likely to quit their jobs.

Management Training

Managers who bully their employees, do not provide proper feedback and do not engage in clear communication are likely to increase employee turnover. Hence, management training is necessary to help create effective managers who are empathetic, take care of their employees' needs, improve their skills and cement employee loyalty.

Conflict Management and Fairness

Managers must ensure fairness and transparency in procedures as well as outcomes of the organization when dealing with any possible conflicts that may arise.

Employees use six main areas to determine whether a process is fair or not. These include:

- **Consistency** – Employees identify whether the distribution of outcomes is consistently fair over a time period or not.

- **Bias suppression** – Employees perceive whether the person responsible for distributing the outcome has any vested interest that prevents equitable and fair distribution of resources.
- **Information accuracy** – Employees discern whether decisions made are based on correct information or not.
- **Correctability** – Employees assess if a mistake made in a decision can be corrected or not. If the employees form the impression that a decision cannot be repealed despite being unfair, they may be tempted to leave the organization.
- **Representativeness** – Employees consider whether the interest and concerns of all stakeholders have been accounted for or not.
- **Ethics** – Employees consider whether the decision-making process is in line with morally accepted societal standards or not. This could be with regard to certain practices, like racism, sexual harassment policies and whether minorities in the organization are protected or not.

Job Design, Job Enlargement and Empowerment

Monetary dissatisfaction is just one of the many reasons that lead to employee turnover. Other major reasons include employees being unsatisfied with the job itself because of a skill mismatch or the job being stagnant. Hence, managers should adopt job enrichment, enlargement and empowerment as strategies to boost employee retention.

Job enrichment means expanding/enhancing a certain job by adding additional meaningful tasks to it. This can be achieved by improving certain factors that have been linked to job satisfaction, such as:

- **Skill variety** – The types of skills needed to perform the job
- **Task identity** – The ability to finish a task once it has been started
- **Task significance** – The extent/degree by which the job impacts others inside or outside the organization
- **Autonomy** – The freedom to make relevant decisions on the job

- **Feedback** – Clear information that indicates how a certain employee has performed

Job Enlargement

Job enlargement is defined as the addition of new challenges to job responsibilities through the modification of a current job. This process can create job satisfaction by tackling the mundaneness that may develop when employees carry out repetitive tasks.

Employee Empowerment

Employee empowerment means giving workers the autonomy to make necessary decisions in their jobs. This leads to an increase in job satisfaction, as employees learn more, and a decrease in the kind of micromanagement that can result in possible clashes and conflicts with managers.

Employee empowerment can be achieved by encouraging employees to bring innovation to their jobs using out-of-the-box thinking, using less authoritative management styles that allow space for interaction and feedback, and making sure employees have all the information they need to complete their tasks.

Performance Strategies Pay

Employees are rewarded for meeting certain objectives and accomplishing their assigned goals. Some organizations also offer bonuses for participating in group activities or completing challenging tasks designed to improve job satisfaction and incentivize workers to perform better.

However, managers should make sure performance strategies are standardized and fair for employees in order to avoid conflicts and increase employee retention. Other retention strategies include:

- Providing a good work-life balance
- Offering free gym memberships and day care facilities
- Providing access to support groups and life coaches
- Conducting recognition programs

Chapter 16: Compensation and Rewards

A systematic methodology of providing employees with financial and/or non-financial rewards in return for services performed is called a compensation package. The components of a compensation package include salaries, bonuses, insurance and health care plans, as well as many other types of rewards. A significant portion of a company's budget is dedicated to employee compensation, as it is vital for recruiting, retaining and motivating/satisfying employees.

Compensation

Compensation is broadly divided into two main categories: monetary and nonmonetary compensation.

Monetary Compensation

The costs incurred by an organization for the benefit of its employees are referred to as monetary compensation. For example, all types of cash compensation, insurance, medical care premiums, retirement plans, 401(k) matching and paid vacations are a form of monetary compensation.

Nonmonetary Compensation

In the present era, nonmonetary compensation is also critical for motivating employees and improving job performance. Types of nonmonetary compensation include flextime, time off, mentorship programs, gym membership, day care facilities, tuition assistance, free parking and short Fridays.

Rewards

Besides their monetary nature, rewards can also be divided based on their intrinsic and extrinsic nature.

Extrinsic Rewards

An extrinsic reward represents something tangible awarded to an employee for meeting certain goals or accomplishments, such as salaries, bonuses, medals, certificates, etc.

Intrinsic Rewards

Intrinsic rewards refer to something intangible, such as a sense of accomplishment or achievement, general satisfaction and the positive feeling associated with being recognized or acknowledged. As these feelings originate from within a person, they are referred to as intrinsic rewards.

Types of Compensation

Compensation may be classified as direct or indirect.

Direct Compensation

Payments that are related to employees' wages and salaries are referred to as direct compensation. Base pay, flexible payments (such as sales commissions) and compensation for performance are all examples of direct compensation.

Indirect Compensation

A payment that is not associated with employee wages and salaries is called indirect compensation. Some examples include benefits like 401(k) or other retirement plans, vacations, sick leaves, leave of absence, paid holidays, government-mandated benefits like FMLA, Social Security and additional advantages.

Now that we have covered the types of compensation and rewards, let's move to how an organization designs an optimal compensation package for its employees.

Developing a Compensation Package

The first step in developing a payment system is asking some general questions. These include:

- What's considered a fair wage by the employees?
- Is the compensation sufficient for retaining employees?
- Are the wages high enough to hinder the organization from achieving its financial objectives?
- Does the pay scale reflect the importance of various jobs in the organization?
- Is the compensation package satisfying state and federal laws?

- Does the compensation philosophy follow the labor market, industry and organizational changes?

Once the answers to these questions have been noted, the organization devises a total rewards philosophy based on internal and external factors.

Total Rewards Philosophy

A mission statement that helps in the development and implementation of compensation packages that attract, motivate, retain and reward its employees is a total rewards philosophy. Several internal and external factors affect this philosophy.

The Internal Factors

Some of the internal factors that impact an organization's ability to draft its compensation packages include:

Financial Constraints

If an organization is struggling to be profitable, its poor revenue and cash flows will ultimately be translated into lower salary packages that are not market competitive. The cost-sensitive nature of the industry and high levels of competitiveness are some factors that may impact an organization's ability to remain profitable.

Pecking Order

Organizations consciously or unconsciously determine the jobs that are most valuable to them for the fulfillment of their long-term goals and objectives. Hence, they include only these jobs in the incentive programs.

Organizational Structure

If the organization has a parent organization that it answers to, then that organization can act as an additional constraint because the total rewards philosophy has to be approved by that organization before implementation.

Organizational Culture

The values and beliefs dominant in an organization's culture have a significant impact on designing a compensation package. Depending on what aligns with the company's culture, an organization can adopt the following payment philosophies:

- **Performance-based philosophy** – In this approach, organizations use what is known as line of sight. Line of sight happens when employees are aware that their performance impacts their monetary and nonmonetary payments. As a result, good performance is correlated with better rewards, and a merit/high-performance culture is created in which employees are motivated to perform their best.
- **Entitlement philosophy** – In entitlement philosophy, the organization values and rewards seniority or employee longevity. In this approach, the time an employee has spent in an organization is prioritized over performance. Organizations with this culture invest in retirement plans and benefits, such as stock options and company-paid vacations.
- **Market compensation philosophy** – In this philosophy, organizations pay the same as the market rate for a job.
- **Philosophy of market plus** – In this approach, payment is higher than the average market rate.
- **Philosophy of market minus** – Organizations pay less than the market rate by compensating with, for example, more benefits than other companies.

External Factors

Economic Conditions

While designing reward packages, organizations are constrained by adverse economic conditions, like inflation and recession. These conditions can affect organizational profitability and productivity.

Building a Pay System

An organization creates its pay system by keeping internal and external factors in mind. The first step is job evaluation, which is used to determine the relative importance one job holds over another. After this, a suitable pay system is implemented.

Types of Pay Systems

- **Pay-grade system** – Specific pay levels are set for particular jobs.
- **Going rate system** – Pay is determined according to the industry compensation standards or the going rate.
- **Management fit system** – Managers have the authority to determine the appropriate pay for an employee or a job.
- **Skill-based pay system** – An employee's skills determine salary.
- **Pay based on competency** – Salary levels are based on employees' traits and characteristics instead of skills.
- **Broad banding** – A pay category is assigned to all jobs in a particular department.
- **Variable pay system** – A surplus is awarded to employees above the base pay for the attainment of certain goals.

Pay Theories

To understand which types of remuneration employees favor, we need to understand the framework of employee remuneration. There are three pay theories: equity, expectancy and reinforcement. These theories are used by HR professionals when they are creating compensation management plans.

Equity Theory

According to the equity theory, people associate their level of satisfaction with their payment by comparing it with that of others. For example, if Katherine and Simone work the same shift and number of hours and have a similar level of education and experience, then they will both expect to receive the same salary. If

Katherine discovers that Simone is being paid much more, Katherine may become less productive and prone to absenteeism.

Expectancy Theory

According to this theory, the amount of effort expended by an individual depends on the payment/reward expected. For example, if employees think they will not be paid or rewarded for doing a task, then they may not put forth their best effort.

Reinforcement Theory

According to this theory, if high performance is rewarded, individuals are expected to repeat similar behavior in the future. For example, if Rowena is rewarded for working simultaneously on five projects, she will expect to receive the same reward in the future.

Chapter 17: Job Analysis and Evaluation Concepts and Methods

Job evaluation is defined as a process that can be used to determine the relative importance or worth of every job in the organization. The basic gist of job evaluation is weighing the efforts required for completing a certain job. Job evaluation is vital in every organization, as it is necessary for setting up orderly and systematic pay scales for each job. It achieves this purpose by ranking each job, also known as job grading. In turn, job grading helps determine the appropriate pay scale for the respective jobs.

Job evaluation is mainly carried out using either the analytical approach or the nonanalytical job evaluation. In the analytical approach, the worth or value of each job is determined by the presence of certain defined factors. In the case of nonanalytical job evaluation, a job's worth is determined by measuring and then comparing it with other jobs in the organization (these methods will be covered in greater detail later).

Characteristics of a Job Evaluation System

- Job evaluation is concerned only with determining the internal worth of the job within the organization, as compared to the external worth or the impact it has on the labor market.
- Job evaluation is independent of the skills and traits possessed by the employee performing the job.
- The relative worth of a job is generally determined by three main factors: duty, responsibility and job accountability.
- As a result of job evaluation, each job is assigned a certain grade or level.
- The main motivation or purpose behind a job evaluation is to determine fair and equitable pay.

Objectives of a Job Evaluation

The objectives of a job evaluation are to:

- Rank jobs within the organization

- Develop an efficient and consistent/uniform system for assigning pay grades to each job
- Ensure there are no biases and prejudices in determining the pay grade system
- Make sure the organization rewards and retains the most talented employees who are performing important jobs

The Job Evaluation Process

To ensure that the job evaluation system is consistent, organizations usually follow a methodical approach. The steps in a job evaluation system are as follows:

Identification of Jobs to Be Evaluated

This is the first step. It helps identify the jobs that will be evaluated. Usually, it is costly and time consuming for most organizations to evaluate every job; hence, in this step, a few key jobs are selected to represent similar jobs.

After this, the organization determines the factors that will be evaluated in the selected job. These include things like mental and physical effort, time consumption, pressure, communication and concentration, leadership skills, educational qualifications, experience and job complexity.

Gathering Relevant Information About the Jobs

In this step, the job evaluators gather the relevant and necessary information for the job being evaluated. The evaluators can do this by utilizing data collection techniques like surveys, interviews, job description statements, observation and job description statements, etc. This step assures evaluators that sufficient information is available about the job being evaluated. Once sufficient data has been collected, it is carefully analyzed.

Determination of Job Ranking

Once the evaluators are finished analyzing all the available information, they rank each job based on the extent to which the factors chosen initially are present in each job. As the weight of similar factors is being evaluated in each job, the ranking assigned reflects the relative importance or worth of each job.

Selection of Benchmark Jobs

As it is not feasible for an organization to evaluate each job in every department, evaluators usually select a few key jobs that are present in all organizations and then determine their pay by comparing it to what other organizations in the industry are offering. These selected jobs are called benchmark jobs, and they serve as yardsticks for determining the pay of other jobs in the organization.

Wage and Salary Surveys

In this step, an organization uses surveys to collect information about the salary of the benchmark jobs in other organizations. These surveys may be formal or informal. Furthermore, an organization may also use a direct survey or gather information from the published professional agencies' reports and magazines.

Most organizations use informal methods like the Internet, telephone or newspapers to determine the monetary value of each job.

Periodic Review and Feedback

As the external environment of all organizations is constantly changing, those external changes also cause changes in an organization's internal environment and affect pay grades. For example, technological changes can significantly alter the requirements of a certain job. Hence, it is important for an organization to periodically determine the worth of a job and update the wages if required.

It is also important to get feedback from important key players like supervisors, managers and jobholders during this process.

Methods of Job Evaluation

Analytical Methods

Analytical methods include point ranking and factor comparison.

- **Point ranking** – In this approach, the value of each job is determined by the presence of certain factors, like time consumption, pressure, education, experience and complexity. Each of these factors is assigned certain points. High-scoring jobs are ranked higher.

- **Factor comparison** – In this method, the rank of each job is determined by comparing it with other jobs using five universal factors common to all jobs. These factors are physical requirements, mental requirements, skills, responsibilities and working conditions. The factor comparison method is considered an improvement over the analytical method and is widely used for job evaluation.

Nonanalytical Methods

These methods include ranking, paired comparison, job grading and market pricing.

- **Ranking** – In this method, a job is ranked vertically after it has been compared with other jobs based on the decisive factors required to be successful in that industry, such as persuasion skills in marketing. This method has the advantage of being simple and less costly, but it is not very accurate due to its subjective nature.
- **Paired comparison** – In this approach, each job is compared with every other job and assigned reward points if found to be more valuable.
- **Job grading** – In this method, jobs with similar characteristics are grouped in a category and assigned the same pay grade.
- **Market pricing** – In this approach, in addition to ensuring internal equity in pay grade fixation, organizations also carry out surveys to make sure their pay grades are on par with those of other organizations in the market.

Chapter 18: Non-Monetary Compensation

A monetary exchange from a business for the services given by its employees on a wide scale is defined as total rewards (TR). A serious TR program, also known as total compensation or the pay package, is vital for selecting, holding and persuading candidates in the present worldwide economy. TR costs are often the single biggest operational expense in many businesses, making them an important part of the HR strategy. All sorts of incentives are included in a TR package, which is classified into two categories: monetary and nonmonetary remuneration.

Non-cash compensation is also closely linked to the concept of intrinsic rewards. Employees' self-esteem is raised by intrinsic rewards, such as satisfaction from demanding and interesting jobs. But extrinsic benefits, like satisfaction from working with peers, are obtained through the demonstrations of others.

Nonmonetary benefits include the employees' relationship with their bosses, acknowledgment of successes, growth and career prospects and collaboration. Nonmonetary rewards like telecommuting, on-site childcare and flex time are examples of nontraditional work-life benefits. These nonmonetary incentives can be employed effectively in the workplace.

Theories like Maslow's Hierarchy of Needs and McClelland's Acquired Needs Theory explain how these reward systems affect an individual's desire for nonmonetary rewards like belonging, esteem and self-actualization.

The term *compensation* is usually perceived as the monetary benefits associated with a particular job or task. It must be clarified here that in the scope of HR, the concept is much more than that. Specifically, it includes pay, health care benefits and other compensation benefits.

Compensation plans usually satisfy an employee's needs. These needs can be classified as nonmonetary and monetary. Nonmonetary needs are satisfied through nonmonetary rewards, while monetary needs are satisfied through indirect and direct cash compensation.

Nonmonetary Benefits

Nonmonetary benefits usually include benefits that do not entail any monetary exchange offered by organizations to their employees. These rewards ensure better cooperation and commitment from the employees. They include job rotation and sharing, promotions or transfers without any monetary offers, flexible hours and telecommuting, free parking and reduced supervision. These advantages usually provide a platform for employees to maintain their motivation and morale and gain intrinsic satisfaction.

Any perks that do not immediately deposit money into an employee's bank account are considered nonmonetary benefits. Where this varies from the conventional definition is that we consider nonmonetary benefits to include those having a monetary value, such as a benefit that gives employees $500 for health exams.

Nonmonetary advantages may be further divided into three categories:

1. **Psychological advantages** – Benefits that enhance an employee's emotional and psychological wellness
2. **Medical advantages** – Advantages that promote an employee's physical well-being
3. **Lifestyle advantages** – Perks that promote an employee's way of life

Non-cash compensation could also include but is not limited to merchandise, gifts, tickets to paid events, prizes, travel costs, meals, lodging and leaves.

All of these incentives demonstrate that employees' efforts are valued and promote a good work-life balance.

Benefits

The most common type of nonmonetary compensation is benefits. Some examples of employee benefits include overtime pay, insurance and retirement funds. Employee benefits are designed to build a sense of community and support among employees, allowing them to focus on their work rather than their personal lives.

A non-cash benefit designed to address a specific need is defined as a benefits plan. Minimal benefits, including paid time off, corporate pension payments and sick pay, are required in many countries. Benefits in the United States may include a company-funded health plan that includes vision and dental coverage in addition to basic health coverage.

Some governments mandate benefits, like matching retirement funds, but employers can supplement their retirement benefits by creating a matching system. Numerous proficient individuals will reject working for an organization that does not give essential fundamental benefits. In American culture, it is not unusual to give full-time, long-lasting employees an essential degree of non-money-related motivators. Part-time and contract employees are rarely given these benefits due to the high cost to employers.

Extra opportunities for professional and personal development also fall under non-cash compensation. According to Randstad's Company Brand Research in 2020, 49% of job seekers consider professional advancement prospects when choosing an employer. One method of providing these chances for employees is to assist them with upskilling or reskilling. Consider the possibility of establishing a peer mentorship and/or peer coaching program. Both may be excellent opportunities for employees to learn from one another, increase their skill sets and strengthen their bonds.

Fringe Benefits

Fringe benefits are another type of nonmonetary incentive. They are extra benefits that organizations provide to their employees, such as fitness programs, free lunches at work or restaurant vouchers, commuter incentives, movie tickets, etc.

Employees can also make use of the benefits of a non-cash prize without having to pay taxes on the award's value, thanks to tax gross-ups. Employees in 37% of firms are given an additional cash payment to cover the tax liabilities of their nonmonetary rewards.

Time Off

Time off varies significantly across different regions of the world. In France, for instance, managers are required by law to give workers five weeks of paid leave. The number of days off available in the United States is an essential financial consideration.

Here are the various types of leave:

- **Paid holidays** – New Year's Day, Memorial Day, Christmas, Independence Day and Thanksgiving are a defined set of holidays offered by many employers.
- **Sick leave** – Employers might have a wide range of sick leave policies. Employees in the United States are given an average of 8.4 paid sick days each year.
- **Paid vacation** – Many organizations give paid leave to full-time employees. As indicated by a Salary.com survey, the average number of paid leave days for one business year is nine, 14 for a longer administration period and 17 for a considerable-length administration period in the United States.

  Vacation time is earned in a variety of ways, depending on the company. Some employers pay their employees per hour, while others require their employees to wait a certain length of time before receiving PTO. Furthermore, some companies permit workers to carry unused vacation time from one year to another, while others urge them to use this time quickly or risk losing it.
- **Paid time off** – One choice is to provide employees with a specific number of days off, which they can use for vacations or sick days. To encourage employees to stay longer, several organizations offer paid sabbaticals (or, in certain cases, 60% of their salary). An employee may, for example, take a one-month paid sabbatical after five years of service.

Incentive Schemes

Once the goals of an incentive scheme have been determined, it is the responsibility of HR professionals to finalize the sort of incentives to be used and how they will be paid. The compensation due to employees for meeting specified performance targets should be determined first. It can be based on an individual or group reward system. Furthermore, HR personnel must decide whether the incentives will be monetary or nonmonetary.

The HR department should also analyze the benefits and drawbacks of various incentive systems before deciding on the best method for achieving their goals.

Non-Cash Compensation Objectives

The objectives of remuneration are to draw in employees to work in a firm and to retain the individuals already working there. Compensation can also be used to motivate staff to perform at their best and increase morale. Non-cash incentives can be delivered in the form of memorable experiences that are added to the employees' overall compensation.

An additional day off, employee incentives and wellness programs are all examples of fringe benefits that help employers recruit and retain Generation Z and millennial employees.

Non-cash awards are more memorable and emotional in nature. The employees at an organization may be eager to discuss the rewards or incentives they receive for their hard work and achievement.

Other Types of Non-Cash Compensation

Childcare

In the current era, facilities like on-site childcare are crucial for motivating and retaining employees. As society is progressively taking an egalitarian shift, stark improvements have been made for female representation in the workforce.

As a consequence of these improvements, there has been an influx of working mothers and fathers into the workforce. As a result, the demand for day care facilities has shot up, as it ensures employees can effectively perform their jobs without becoming worried about their children's needs. Many organizations, like Microsoft and Intel, provide childcare assistance for their employees.

Gym Membership

In addition to other benefits, many organizations now provide their employees with either gym memberships to external gyms or provide on-site gyms. It has been shown through extensive research that exercise aids in stress release and the release of good hormones that fuel motivation. Hence, gym memberships have been linked with greater employee satisfaction and job performance.

With increasing competitiveness among organizations, all the aforementioned types of nonmonetary compensation are no longer optional but mandatory for organizations to provide to their employees if they plan to attract and retain the best workers from the current workforce.

Chapter 19: Functional Effectiveness of the Employee Life Cycle

According to the employee life cycle model, engagement as a planned experience is something that has been woven into the trajectory/path of all the employees in the organization. The HR office plays the part of empowering the entire process and guaranteeing that the change to each stage is obvious and organized. In today's fast-paced corporate environment and economy, each phase of the employee life cycle is becoming increasingly important.

Stages in the Employee Life Cycle

The stages of the employee life cycle model are as follows:

1. Hiring
2. Onboarding
3. Development
4. Retention
5. Exit process
6. Alumni program

1) Hiring

The hiring and selection process is the first step of the employee life cycle model. Hiring happens when a current position has opened or another position has been created in the organization.

The best hiring strategies ensure a positive candidate experience, encourage cooperative recruiting based on standards and processes that have already been defined, and provide significant data that can be used to improve/upgrade recruiting results.

The common elements present in these strategies include employer branding, assessments, the selection process and talent acquisition.

HR professionals should:

- Examine the benefits provided to employees
- Outline the employer's expectations

- Make a timeline for the hiring procedure (i.e., the number of interviews, the status of interviewers and a timeline/schedule)
- Indicate any tests that will be conducted as the process continues
- Create a job description that highlights/outlines all duties and responsibilities, as well as the skills needed for carrying them out effectively

The following are a few crucial recommendations that should be included in the recruitment stage to succeed in attracting the ideal talent:

Request References from the Current Team

Using referrals from experts/professionals in the field is one of the best methods for hiring/recruiting employees. However, the manager should try to avoid hiring friends. This could lead to complications like biases, etc.

Use Various Recruitment Platforms

To attract a wider range of candidates, advertise the post on numerous platforms. There are fewer chances of finding extraordinary competitors when you use only a few social sites. Going broad is fantastic, but HR should not overlook the worth of the organization's internal talent pool, which may contain employees looking for a promotion, a career change or an employee referral.

Be Specific in the Talent Acquisition Process

To hire the right individual with the relevant skills and traits, an organization needs to be specific in its ads and posts. Being broad in the search process may help reach a wider pool of candidates, but it can lead to the hiring of employees who may not be a good fit for the organization's needs.

Prioritize Diversity

There are numerous advantages to developing a diverse workforce. Various businesses associate improved bottom lines, staff performance and even cash flow per employee to a diverse workforce.

Recruiting diverse people is the first step in creating a diverse workforce. HR should take steps to minimize bias during the interview process to prioritize diversity and inclusion when hiring. It should also create varied sets of interviewers and instruct them on how to overcome unconscious prejudice and provide subjects to avoid during interviews.

2) Onboarding

Employee onboarding refers to the process of bringing new staff up to speed. This is the journey from the time employees join the company until they reach peak production. The process helps new employees assimilate into the company's culture.

After the assimilation, individuals are completely onboarded and fully productive. Depending on the job's intricacy, this might take anywhere from three to nine months.

Two of the methods that companies can adopt to make sure the onboarding process goes smoothly are as follows:

Sharing the Values, Vision and Mission of the Company

Customer empathy, ownership, transparency, team spirit and social responsibility are examples of values. A crucial part of any onboarding process is laying out the corporate strategy, explaining what it means to new hires and clearing up any confusion.

Job Description

There is no need for lengthy job requirements in a job description. Optimally, companies should attempt to draft a one-page outline that covers the role's most crucial responsibilities, as well as any relevant experience and skills.

3) Development

Employee development is the focal point of this phase of the employee life cycle. It includes fortifying the employees' present abilities, informing them of the abilities they need to qualify for advancement, or providing them with general upskilling opportunities as times change and new skills are required.

Onboarding digital technologies that make it easier for new hires to fit in are essential for increasing employee productivity.

The development stage of the employee life cycle model can be refined using the following suggestions:

Encourage People to Learn More at All Phases of Their Lives

Conferences, seminars and lunch-and-learns are all good options for internal or external learning. They keep staff informed about current trends while also allowing them to deepen their skills. It is a win-win situation for everyone if they can share what they have learned with the rest of the team and make adjustments based on new information.

Use a Learning Management System

A learning management system (LMS) serves as a platform for managing and delivering online training content in various formats. It enables access from any location and allows employees to develop whenever and wherever is convenient.

Following this, the organization can monitor the progress and decide whether the required development goals are being met or not. An LMS helps create a personalized learning experience, allowing the creation of new courses, and can even create learning paths that help employees learn in the way that best suits them.

Encourage Knowledge Sharing

Encourage knowledge sharing among staff through coaching and regular sessions where they can share their hard-won experiences. Employees will be driven to learn if they are rewarded for meeting their growth goals.

4) Retention

The retention stage is critical in the employee life cycle. That is because once employees have been with a company for a time, there is a real danger that their bosses may take them for granted.

The struggle to keep employees starts the moment they are employed. This is particularly true for organizations with a high staff turnover rate. It is the organization's responsibility to earn the trust of its employees and demonstrate that it is deserving of their continuous loyalty on a daily basis. Improving the retention stage is a wonderful way to reduce the risk of losing employees while also improving employee happiness.

The following are some ways HR can increase employee retention and reduce turnover:

Hire the Correct Personnel

If organizations are careful in their recruiting process and techniques, they will have a greater shot of retaining talented workers.

Have a Positive Work Relationships With Coworkers

It is crucial for HR and managers to have open, fair and conscious relationships with employees if they want them to stay with the organization. Positive work relationships have been shown to affect employee satisfaction and retention rates.

5) Exit Process

The exit process can take one of two forms: employees choose to leave on their own (resignations and retirements) or employees are asked to depart in some fashion (termination, downsizing or layoff).

Exiting an organization can be a stressful experience. Even when an employee chooses to leave and leaves on good terms, the business faces challenges in replacing the person or delegating responsibilities to remaining coworkers.

Coworkers may also be affected by the move, so planning an exit strategy that reduces stress and creates a smooth transition will pay off in a variety of ways.

Processes for Voluntary Exit

Employees willingly leave the organization by resigning or retiring. When employees decide to leave the company and explore other options, they resign. Resignations provide little legal concerns for HR, but they do create the need to make decisions about replacements or work reassignments, which may result in promotions or transfers of other employees, all of which have an impact on the workforce planning process.

The HR department should perform an exit interview before an employee quits the organization. An exit interview allows employees to share with the company why they decided to leave, any specific issues that need to be addressed and any adjustments the company may make to improve the employee experience.

If the employee has made a major contribution and the company is considering rehiring the person in the future, an exit interview is a moment to leave the door open for that possibility.

Exit interviews should ideally be conducted by a third party so that employees are free to share their thoughts. A variety of organizations offer this service, which is usually delivered via phone or online interview. Collecting and analyzing this data over time will help identify potential problem areas that, if addressed, will decrease unwanted and costly turnover.

Processes of Involuntary Exit

Involuntary exits are caused either by performance issues or changing company requirements. Downsizing is a common occurrence as firms change strategic directions or react to economic conditions, and it can lead to performance concerns and terminations.

6) Alumni Network

Alumni are a valuable source of referrals for new hires and customers, as well as a marketing army and a sales force. An organization cannot provide a complete end-to-end employee experience without an active alumni group of former employees. Alumni must be included in the conversation if companies want to build a strong and forward-thinking culture.

Today, talent comes in a variety of forms, including traditional full-time and part-time positions, as well as the more recent addition of contingent or contract workers. Regardless of employment status, what matters is finding the right person with the right skills at the right time for the right role.

When an organization has an alumni network, it signifies that the organization employs with a long-term relationship in mind. Employees understand that they will always be valued members of the business, not only during their employment. This can be achieved through an alumni program.

Creating an alumni network is a significant milestone for any organization. It demonstrates that the organization has made a significant transition from saying goodbye at offboarding to welcoming new changes that come with keeping alumni involved over time. It also affords many benefits to the organization. For example, members stay active and connected to the organization and have access to company updates, networking opportunities and more while giving back through events and mentoring or coaching opportunities.

Chapter 20: Human Resource Management and Organizational Values

Organizational Values

Organizational values refer to the core ethics or principles that an organization abides by no matter what. These organizational values are necessary for all organizations and give birth to the organization's culture. Some organizational values include high performance, integrity and innovation.

To understand the process of HR management, we must first understand what we mean by HR. It is a department in any organization that is responsible for searching, screening, recruiting and retaining employees. Hence, the definition of HR management is the process that is involved in employing candidates, training them to hone their skills and traits, creating policies for them that keep employees satisfied and motivated and dealing with their compensation and rewards.

Roles of HR Management

The roles of HR management are as follows:

Staffing

Even with profound technological advancements in the recent era, humans are still needed for the effective and smooth running of all the operations in an organization. Staffing refers to the complete process of hiring employees, from posting ads to negotiating a salary package. The four main steps involved in staffing are:

1. **Staffing plan development**

The advancement of a staffing plan helps in deciding the number of individuals to be employed in light of income assumptions. The advancement of arrangements supports multiculturalism at work. Due to global shrinkage, many companies now have employees from all cultures. Hence, it is necessary to create an environment that is welcoming and inclusive for all groups.

2. **Recruitment**

Recruitment entails locating candidates to fill vacant positions.

3. **Selection**

The recruited candidates go through interviews in this stage, and a salary package is negotiated with the selected employees.

4. **Development of workplace policies**

Every organization needs to have policies on important matters, like dress codes, diversity and inclusion, ethics, sexual harassment, discipline processes, vacations and discipline process policies. These policies are crucial, as they serve as guidelines that allow the smooth running of operations and the avoidance of subjectivity. Managers need to be free of bias and impartial when devising these policies.

Compensation and Benefits Administration

Compensation and benefits administration is another crucial role performed by HR managers. They are responsible for coming up with payment systems that reward employees for their services. These rewards/compensation packages can be monetary or nonmonetary.

It is important for managers to devise salary packages that are market competitive to retain and motivate employees. A few examples of worker remuneration include medical benefits, retirement plans, stock buy choices, rewards, sick leave, vacation time, etc.

Retention

Retention policies ensure that employees are motivated enough to stay with the organization. Employees may be tempted to leave the organization due to a number of reasons, such as poor compensation packages, poor fit with the organization's culture and challenges/issues with a manager. Hence, managers need to find out the reason(s) employees are leaving the organization and rectify the problems to ensure the retention of employees.

Training and Development

Once employees have been hired, managers need to provide them with the right training programs that polish their old skills and equip them with any new skills needed to perform their jobs effectively. Some of the training programs that can be provided to workers incorporate work expertise, teamwork, legal responsibilities and ethics related to behavior in the workplace.

Dealing With Laws Affecting Employment

Managers should know about every law that can influence the work environment, such as separation law, remuneration law (minimum wage), worker security law, work law and medical care law. If managers are unaware of laws pertaining to these important matters, they are likely to run into many challenges and problems. Additionally, managers need to stay up-to-date with any changes in these laws.

Worker Protection

It is crucial for an HR manager to create an environment that ensures employee safety. Some of the dangers HR managers must pay attention to in the workplace include chemical hazards, ventilation and heating requirements, protection of private information and the use of no-fragrance zones.

An organization that does not take worker protection seriously cannot operate for long, as it is impossible for employees to perform their jobs smoothly if their safety is at stake.

Communication

Managers cannot solve employees' problems if they are unaware of them. Hence, managers need to establish good communication channels with their employees to ensure they are aware of employee needs and progress.

Awareness of External Factors

Besides an organization's internal factors, it is important for HR managers to also be aware of the external factors in an organization's environment, as they may impact the company positively or negatively.

Some of the external factors that managers should be aware of include globalization and offshoring, changes in laws pertaining to employment, health care costs, changing workforce demographics, relevant technologies being used, layoffs and downsizing, diversity in the workforce and using social networking to keep employees informed and aware.

Skills Needed to Be a Successful HR Manager

Taking care of employees' needs is not an easy task. HR managers need to possess certain skills to fulfill their role optimally. Some of these skills include:

Ability to Multitask

An organization is made up of many departments and different employees with different needs. An HR manager must know how to simultaneously deal with different tasks and be able to organize and prioritize them.

Specific Job Skills

HR managers must possess specific skills—like computer skills, knowledge of laws pertaining to employment, the ability to draft short-term and long-term strategic plans, good decision-making and robust critical thinking skills—to fulfill their job requirements.

Sense of Fairness and Good Ethics

A manager has to make important decisions for all kinds of employees, whether they are from a minority or a majority, as well as other crucial decisions regarding employee compensation packages, benefits, etc. Hence, managers need to be unbiased in their approach and follow impartial standards when making critical decisions like hiring or firing employees.

Critical Thinking, Writing and Communication Skills

It is important for managers to have critical thinking skills, as they have to make complex decisions regarding recruitment and termination, be able to align the strategic business plan with one proposed by HR and ensure employee satisfaction and retention. They also need good writing skills to be able to communicate effectively with employees.

Different Management Styles Used by Managers

Effective HR management is the key to the success of every organization. To manage employees effectively, there are different techniques that managers can adopt, but they are mainly divided into types. Those managing types are:

Task-Oriented Management

Managers following the task-oriented management style are mainly concerned about the tasks of the job. They ensure employees understand what is generally expected of them and have the tools they need to do their work.

People-Oriented Management

Managers who adopt the people-oriented management style are more concerned with interpersonal relations in the workplace. Instead of heavily focusing on the tasks present in a certain job, these managers prioritize the welfare of employees and are usually trusting and friendly.

Participatory Management

Participatory management incorporates both task-oriented and people-oriented management. Managers following this approach provide support and input when needed and help with the task when required; hence, the focus is on both the task and the employee performing the task.

Directing Management

Directing management is appropriate when more hands-on management is necessary. It focuses on the task and does not allow room for employee participation. The manager delegates what the employees must do within strict deadlines and employees have to follow the guidelines, as they do not have much autonomy in the matter.

Teamwork Style Management

Teamwork management is a people-oriented style. It focuses on encouraging teamwork and taking input from all the team members. An advantage of this style is that a manager is likely to be provided with many different creative solutions for a particular problem, as different people approach the same problem in a unique way.

Autocratic Style Management

Autocratic management is a task-oriented management style. Managers using this style focus strictly on completing all tasks and do not give relationships any significant priority. Managers are also likely to adopt the "my way or the highway" approach.

This style of management is also known as the taskmaster style. The person in charge uses his or her authority to make all the relevant decisions about who will do what, how it will be done and when it will be done.

Free-Rein Style Management

The free-rein style is the complete opposite of autocratic style management. It gives complete freedom to employees and allows them to decide how to go about things. The manager may set a direction by delegating a few objectives, but employees have complete autonomy over how those goals will be achieved. As a result, managers are mostly detached from day-to-day activities but are available and will show up to help if needed.

How to Determine the Best Management Style

There are different leadership models aimed at determining the best management style in different situations. One of these is the path-goal model. According to this model, the manager's job is to define the goals to be achieved and lay down the path to achieving them, providing clarification if necessary.

Another much more approved model for determining the best management style is the situational leadership model. This model works through the observance of three key regions: the errand conduct of the supervisor, the relationship conduct of the manager and the availability of the employees.

Relationship conduct implies how steady a manager ought to be while overseeing employees; task conduct alludes to the style that managers ought to take on while keeping in mind employee readiness; and readiness refers to the willingness and skills of the employees in performing the task.

The gist of the situational leadership model is that managers should switch to an autocratic style of leadership when the readiness of employees is low. In other words, when employees do not have much expertise and/or relevant skills needed to finish the job on their own, managers should lay out the guidelines and delegate all the tasks, making all the important decisions themselves.

However, when employee readiness improves, they acquire expertise in the jobs to be performed and gain the motivation to do them. Managers should then shift to participative style management, which allows much more autonomy to the employees.

There is no one perfect management style for every situation. Most real-time situations demand a mix between autocratic style and participative style management. It is important for managers to be able to change their styles and be flexible according to the situation in order to manage effectively.

Chapter 21: Diversity and Inclusion

Employers utilize diversity and inclusion efforts to meet regulatory requirements and improve the bottom line by having a more varied, equitable and inclusive workforce.

Diversity

There are various meanings of diversity, as organizations often change the idea to suit their own needs. As a general rule, diversity alludes to the likenesses and differences among individuals, considering all parts of their characters and levels of self-appreciation.

Different Types of Diversity

The following are the most frequently discussed categories of diversity:

- Age
- Physical disability
- Ethnicity
- Family status
- Sex
- Gender identity
- Language
- Life experiences
- Neurodiversity
- Organizational function and level
- Physical characteristics
- Race
- Religion, belief and spirituality
- Veteran status

Designing Diversity Programs

Viable diversity programs should start, plan, talk and act based on basic business matters. The ideas below should be followed during the planning and execution process of a diversity program:

- Keep the CEO, upper management and other key partners informed throughout the process
- Focus on accomplishing organizational objectives
- Start with the organization's motivation and remain focused on it
- Encourage a feeling of possession and responsibility
- Plan interior and outer correspondence to keep workers informed and engaged and expectations under control

Additionally, metrics and diversity training should be addressed during the design process. Metrics can be collected after all the changes have been finalized, while diversity training should be addressed before the diversity initiative is implemented.

Sourcing and Recruitment for Diversity

Organizations recruit individuals with an assorted set of differences and shared traits, like individual characteristics, perspectives, attitudes, histories and experiences. Diversity recruitment is a basic step toward building a comprehensive work environment that reflects the clients it serves and which is well prepared to contend in a changing economy and marketplace.

The circumstances are fundamentally more complicated on a worldwide scale. Although countries characterize diversity in various ways, most organizations look for diverse workforces to stay competitive and innovative.

Diversity recruitment can be broad (advertisements on job boards) or tightly focused (interviews or sites that find résumés of people who may not be searching for positions yet but who match a set of criteria).

Questions to Consider

- Are there diversity and recruitment targets in place at the company? If so, are these objectives self-imposed or compelled by law?
- With which organizations/agencies might the company collaborate to find a wide pool of candidates?
- Have job descriptions been revised recently for open positions? Are they still accurate representations of the talents required to do the job well?

- Have the hiring goals been communicated to the hiring manager, double-checked for comprehension and agreed upon to increase the chances of a successful hire?
- Are there current job descriptions and defined performance requirements for positions so that any new recruits can be evaluated honestly and without bias?
- Where should the business publicize opportunities to draw in a different pool of capable applicants?
- Is the organization using strategies and advantages to draw in an assorted workforce (adaptable hours, work sharing and so on)?
- What sort of preparation has the organization given enlisting supervisors to ensure that the best applicants are selected?
- Has the organization amended its onboarding cycle to guarantee that newcomers get the proper data and receive a warm welcome that will prompt a long-term partnership?
- How might HR guarantee new employees are the right fit by following up with the hiring manager and the new employees?

Inclusion

Employees of all ages, genders, ethnicities, languages, physical abilities, cultures, religions, education, sexual orientations and other qualities are welcomed and supported in an inclusive workplace. How much every individual in an association feels invited, regarded, upheld and appreciated as a colleague is part of inclusion.

Inclusion is a two-way road; all individuals must acknowledge each other with consideration. This necessitates communication and collaboration of people from various backgrounds, as well as an understanding of one another's needs and viewpoints.

Creating an Inclusive Workplace

Employing a different pool of individuals is not enough to accomplish inclusion. Here are the four principles that organizations need to take into account when forming an effective inclusion strategy:

1) Leadership participation

Leadership participation is essential when creating an inclusion strategy, as it will be the leaders who will welcome the new hires and set the tone for other employees. Here are a few ways through which leader participation could be used to set inclusion programs in motion:

- Allocate a senior leader to support the organization's drive for diversity
- Create a chief diversity/equality officer role
- Structure a diversity committee

2) Training and education

All employees should be provided with training and schooling that will help them handle inclusion. This can be done by:

- Creating inclusion awareness workshops and dealing with oblivious inclinations or responsiveness preparations
- Providing conflict resolution training

3) Methodology and policies

Methodology and policies protect employee rights, clear up confusion regarding regulations and provide employees with a behavioral guide. So, when instituting an inclusion program, HR or upper management should:

- Incorporate inclusion into the organization's fundamental beliefs
- Include inclusion in the organization's mission and vision statements
- Create antidiscrimination policies and put them in place
- Devise a statement about diversity and inclusion

4) Keeping and developing a diverse workforce

The search for a diverse workforce does not end after hiring. In fact, HR managers have to work continuously to help new hires assimilate into the workforce, understand business objectives, learn new skills and reach their maximum potential. They can use the following strategies to retain and assist in the development of new hires:

- Execute preparation programs for employees
- Initiate tutoring programs focusing on workplace assimilation
- Monitor the promotional paces of different groups of new hires

Characteristics of Diversity and Inclusion Initiatives

Effective diversity initiatives share various characteristics. For example, they:

- Line up with the organization's most significant business objectives
- Focus on making explicit adjustments to the staff and work environment that will help with accomplishing desired business results
- Decide on the number of intercultural skills and the organization's capacity to accept social change
- Understand that communication between and with employees ought to be approached in an active and effective manner, instead of passive communication.

Developing a Diversity and Inclusion Initiative

Employers can take the following steps to develop a diversity and inclusion initiative:

Step 1: Gather Information

Employers should initially observe how their labor force thinks about the work market, regardless of whether there are any segment disparities. By gathering information on employee socioeconomics, a business can more readily comprehend the variety of its workers and recognize any patterns or areas of concern. This work generally covers government and state-protected information.

Organizations should use data collected by analytics to gather information about workforce behavioral patterns.

Step 2: Determine Areas of Concern

Underrepresented or problematic areas can be perceived once information has been gathered. Employers should begin by conducting a socioeconomic assessment that factors in the age, sex and racial representation of the assorted workforce and then start observing the minutiae (location, division, position, etc.).

Employers can also determine areas of concern or problems points by asking questions like:

- Is the management dominated by White males?
- Is it true that Black women earn less than White women?
- Is it normal for the bookkeeping division to employ only females?
- Have people who communicate in English as a second language had their chances limited?

Step 3: Addressing Policies or Practices That Have a Negative Impact on Diversity and Inclusion

Businesses should analyze whether there are any obstacles to work, opportunity or incorporation for individuals from different populations. If they find any policies or practices that have a negative impact on diversity and inclusion, they should consider changing or removing them entirely.

Organizations can conduct a policy and practice analysis by focusing on the following:

- Employee referral programs
- Company culture
- Unconscious biases
- Political preferences

Step 4: Define Business Goals

At this stage, organizations have to decide how a comprehensive labor force can help with achieving business goals that are consistent with their current system.

They should also make explicit diversity and inclusion targets based on their goals.

For example, say a business's goal is to develop new products/services that allow it to outperform its competition, but its research and development (R&D) team is scattered and non-communicative. The business can solve this problem by creating a centralized communication system that allows everybody in the R&D team to share their insights and ideas with each other.

Step 5: Obtain Support and Buy-In

The case for diversity and inclusion exercises should be understood by the senior administration with direct connections to the organization's essential objectives. It is smart to pick a senior-level supporter who will be responsible for helping keep inclusion programs alive.

Step 6: Put Initiatives into Action

Changes in approaches and practices, staff preparation, centered enrolling and manager-supported diversity and incorporation of mindfulness events for workers are generally examples of diversity and inclusion drives.

Step 7: Make the Initiatives Public

Businesses should distinguish different partners and create messaging for them to teach, draw in and engage them as needed. Individuals interpret messages in an unexpected way; therefore, it is critical that each person be consistently appraised of business efforts.

Impediments to Setting Variety and Consideration Endeavors Into Action

Most organizations define three impediments with regards to planning and executing a variety of work environments and inclusion techniques. These impediments include:

1) Middle management that is haphazard about carrying out various programs
2) Monetary limitations that impede broad deployment strategies

3) Individuals who are excessively focused on surviving, not contributing

Chapter 22: Workplace Safety and Emergency Response

Occupational Safety and Health Act of 1970

The Occupational Safety and Health Act of 1970 is federal legislation that was created because of many incidents in America related to workplace safety—or the lack thereof. Employers found it easier to fight lawsuits against employees than to implement safety protocols. Many work-related injuries and diseases were common, with some large-scale tragic incidents occurring in the railroad and coal mines industries.

The act is intended to ensure safe and healthful working conditions for American workers. It stresses three major requirements for employers:

1. Employers must provide every employee with a place to work that is "free from recognized hazards that are causing or are likely to cause death or serious physical harm."
2. Employers must comply with all safety and health standards outlined in the act.
3. Employees are required to comply with occupational safety and health standards, rules and regulations that impact their actions and behavior.

Employer Responsibilities

Along with the three major rules mentioned above, OSHA contains several other requirements that employers need to comply with under the law. These are:

- Employers need to take steps to minimize hazards and ensure the availability, usage and maintenance of safe tools, equipment and personal protective equipment (PPE).
- Employers need to inform their employees about OSHA, display posters in prominent locations, make the worksite standards clear and provide employees with a copy of said standards.

- When it comes to potential hazards, appropriate warning signs must be displayed that adhere to OSHA standards for color-coding, posting or labels.
- Employers need to educate and train their employees on safety operations and procedures that need to be followed.
- Any business with 11 or more employees must maintain a record of all workplace injuries and illnesses. This record needs to be posted from February 1 to April 30 every year.
- If a serious hospitalization or a fatal accident occurs that involves three or more employees, a report must be filed with OSHA within eight hours.
- An accident report log must be maintained and made available upon reasonable request by employees, former employees or employee representatives.

Employer Rights

Employers have the right to seek advice from OSHA and play an active role in the health and safety issues in their industries. They can participate in the OSHA Standard Advisory Committee process.

The National Institute of Occupational Safety and Health (NIOSH) was established by OSHA as a part of the Department of Health and Human Services. NIOSH is responsible for researching and evaluating workplace hazards and recommending ways to reduce the effect of those hazards on employees. NIOSH also supports education and training in occupational safety and health by developing and providing educational materials and training aids and sponsoring conferences on workplace safety and health issues. Employers can reach out to NIOSH for assistance.

Some specific industry operations may become impossible to be done following OSHA standards. Employers can apply for temporary or permanent waivers with proof of adequate protection being implemented by the organization.

Employee Rights and Responsibilities

OSHA aims to give employees basic health and safety rights. When it comes to dealing with hazards, employees and employers are encouraged to work collaboratively. Employees must also comply with OSHA standards in their workplace and follow the appropriate protocols.

OSHA gives employees the following rights:

- Employees can seek safety and health in the workplace without fear of punishment.
- Employees can have access to knowledge of potential hazards on the job through reviewing OSHA resources made available by the employer.
- Employees must be provided with a hazard communication plan that has information regarding potential hazards and preventive measures. Appropriate training also needs to be provided.
- Employers must keep employee-accessible medical and exposure records related to safety and health issues.
- Employees can request OSHA inspections, speak privately with the inspector, accompany the inspector during the inspection and respond to the inspector's questions during the inspection.
- Employees can observe steps taken by the employer to monitor and measure hazardous materials in the workplace and access related records.
- Employees can request information from NIOSH about potentially toxic substances being used in the workplace.
- Employees can file complaints about workplace safety or health hazards with OSHA anonymously.

OSHA Assistance

OSHA is always available to aid employers and employees regarding workplace safety. They have all the laws, regulations and standards available on their website (www.osha.gov), along with other relevant information and prevention strategies. OSHA also regularly prepares informative brochures, pamphlets and training programs on workplace safety.

OSHA actively trains safety consultants who go out in the industry to educate employers on the related safety and health standards that they need to be aware of and maintain. Employers can take on free consultants to correct any violations they might be involved in without penalties. Once the consultation is completed, employers must take corrective action or face liability for violations.

The Safety and Health Achievement Recognition Program (SHARP)

The SHARP program recognizes small-scale employers that deal with high-hazard situations. They request comprehension consultation, correct violations and have developed ongoing safety management programs. To participate in the program, businesses need to take on additional consultations as their operations evolve and change.

Partnerships and Voluntary Programs

OSHA offers different programs that allow businesses to be actively involved in the process of setting standards and solving safety problems related to their industries.

1. **OSHA Strategic Partnership Program** – The Strategic Partnership Program (SPP) allows both employers and employees to solve health and safety problems in collaboration with OSHA. Partnerships currently exist in 15 industries—including construction, food processing, logging and health care—to develop solutions specific to their businesses.

2. **OSHA Alliance Program** – The OSHA Alliance Program allows organizations to be involved in the promotion of workplace health and safety issues. This platform is open to all professions, businesses, organizations, institutions and government agencies.

3. **Voluntary Protection Program** – The Voluntary Protection Program (VPP) allows employers to be removed from the list of routine inspections. To meet VPP criteria, employers must implement tough safety programs in their workplace. This program helps motivate businesses to operate in safe environments, avoid unnecessary damages and compensation costs and encourage further safety development. To be accepted into the VPP program

means official recognition of a company's exemplary health and safety practices.

Inspections

Both OSHA and NIOSH can investigate health and safety hazards in workplaces. Most inspections are focused on larger industries that operate with higher hazard risks. Injury and illness rates in the industry are also considered. Employers and employees can also request inspections of their organizations.

OSHA has an Enhanced Enforcement Program (EEP) that inspects and monitors employers that have a repeated history of violations or reported willful violations. The inspections that are carried out under this program make up less than 1% of the total OSHA inspections. Health hazard evaluations are carried out by NIOSH and conducted at the request of an employer, employee or government agency.

Employees who request an inspection of their workplace or participate in the inspection process are protected from any form of retaliation or adverse employment actions (that can come from the employer).

OSHA inspections are carried out by compliance safety and health officers, who have been trained on the standards and protocols needing to be assessed. During inspections, these officers can recognize safety and health hazards in workplaces. There is a hierarchy set up by OSHA regarding the priorities of inspections.

OSHA inspections follow the following hierarchy:

1. Imminent danger
2. Catastrophes and fatal accidents
3. Complaints and referrals
4. Programmed high-hazard inspections
5. Follow-up inspections

Mine Safety and Health Act of 1977 (MSH Act)

The MSH Act was established to ensure the safety of workers in coal and other mines. This act requires mine operators to follow mandatory safety and health standards. MSHA has a detailed website (www.msha.gov/) that can be accessed by miners and mine operations for information related to prevention, fatalities and hazard guidance.

Environmental Health Hazards

Environmental hazards can range from physical hazards like noise and extreme temperatures to potentially toxic chemicals being used in various operations and biological hazards, such as bacteria and virus outbreaks.

These hazards can exist on different levels for individual employees, and it is the employers' job to take appropriate steps to prevent any serious health consequences as a result of workplace operations.

Hazard Assessment

OSHA requires organizations to conduct specific hazard assessments appropriate for their operations. For example, in a factory setting, determining what safety equipment is accessible and what protective equipment is required for each worker is necessary.

Potential hazards need to be identified before injuries are caused as well. OSHA regularly updates the most common hazards for all industries on its website for awareness and training.

Injury and Illness Prevention Programs (IIPPs)

OSHA has outlined some common elements and protocols that all organizations need to adapt in their IIPPs. These protocols can differ on a state level, but all must meet federal requirements. These common elements include management leadership, worker participation, hazard identification, hazard prevention and control, education and training and program evaluation and improvement.

Disaster Preparedness and Emergency Response

Emergency preparedness is a requirement of plans and protocols by OSHA that focus on disaster response and recovery. According to some standards, OSHA requires any company with more than 10 employees to have emergency plans in writing.

Creating Preparedness Plans

The Federal Emergency Management Agency (FEMA), along with OSHA's publications, provides excellent resources for employers to successfully learn disaster preparedness and create emergency plans. The HR department needs to develop thorough, comprehensive and easily accessible plans that employees can follow to be prepared for any potential emergencies.

In creating an emergency response plan, FEMA suggests the following steps:

1. **Resource management** –HR needs to have the support of leadership and make sure that the organizational bodies are on the same page when it comes to resource planning. Disaster management requires efforts and resources, and the executive management needs to be ensured of the importance of these efforts as well as the satisfaction of getting a return on investment. This step includes communicating customer and financial impacts to organizational leaders and identifying mitigation efforts, such as insurance coverage.

2. **Needs assessment and business impact analysis** – At this stage, the OSHA direct hazard identifying process can take place after getting approval from the upper management. Hazard assessment is particularly important regarding physical realities, such as the potential of earthquakes. Natural and operation-specific threats need to be assessed before an active situation occurs.

3. **Practical implementations** – After assessing threats, practical plans need to be meticulously prepared from every angle. Safety protocols, communication plans, data recovery, medical assistance and more need to be thought of beforehand to elicit a smooth response in the middle of an actual crisis.

4. **Testing phase** – After the plans have been written and approved, training employees is an important step in making sure that threat plans can be followed in active situations. It is also important for employees to have some practice with simulations and drills, all of which can be done during this phase.

5. **Maintenance and improvements** – After threat plan testing and practice runs, updates can be made to the plans, and improvements can be made as more operations are added or more hazards are identified.

Chapter 23: The Collective Bargaining Process

Collective Bargaining

Collective bargaining refers to the negotiation process between employees and employers in an organization. Workers assemble in unions to effectively discuss and compromise with employers or their workplace settings.

Collective bargaining has a legal standing of its own when it comes to labor and employment laws. The goal of collective bargaining is to collectively fight for terms and conditions of employment and come to an agreement with the employers. The representatives of the union approach the employers to start a negotiation process that concludes in a labor contract agreeable to both parties. The subject of this negotiation can be the wages, work hours, working conditions, grievances or rights and responsibilities of both parties.

When an agreement is reached, a legal contract is signed by both parties, which is referred to as a collective bargaining agreement (CBA) or a collective employment agreement (CEA).

Labor Unions

There are labor unions in organizations that initiate the process of collective bargaining. Employees need to be a part of a recognized union and abide by the rules and regulations of said union. Union representatives are elected by union members for negotiating the bargaining process.

The union works together to first form a draft that covers employees' demands. This draft is presented to the company management, after which meetings are held between the union representatives and the employer representatives.

It can take a long time for the meetings and negotiations to reach an agreeable point between both parties. The ideal situation is cooperativeness from both sides in the negotiation process. The final agreement usually contains some compromise from both the employees and the employers, who need to make their bounds more flexible to defuse the situation. Sometimes these meetings can go sour and result in union strikes and lockouts that are aimed at forcing the company's hand in accepting the union workers' demands.

General Outlook

Generally, collective bargaining is seen as an excellent tool that helps both employees and employers. It gives power to unions to collectively assert and demand their rights as employees. It helps employers evolve the workplace while maintaining employee loyalties. Making decisions that are agreed upon or demanded by the workers helps maintain a smooth work environment that ultimately benefits the company.

Collective bargaining agreements also clarify expectations for both parties, helping get rid of ambiguities and confusion of roles that might have been present before. The discussion process can help decrease communication gaps between employees and employers.

Collective bargaining is also a symbol of democracy in the occupational setting. The joint decision-making process is aimed at a positive outcome, even if the process of negotiation becomes difficult in high-tension scenarios. Ultimately, mutually agreeable conditions are reached that facilitate the collective group.

Essential Features

The International Labor Organization (ILO) defines collective bargaining as a "negotiation about working conditions and terms of employment between an employer and a group of employees or one or more employee or an organization to reach an agreement wherein the terms serve as a code of defining the rights and obligations of each party in their employment/industrial relations with one another."

Collective bargaining should have the following features:

1. The process should have active participation from the representatives of management and employees.
2. The process should be aimed primarily at bringing stability to the working relationship between the parties.
3. The process should conclude with the implementation of the agreement.
4. Both parties should maintain a flexible attitude toward the process of negotiation.

Collective Bargaining and Bad Faith

The National Labor Relations Act (NLRA) holds the employers and unions to their duty to bargain over workplace matters. The bargain subject matter can range from wages to employee treatment. However, actions from both parties during the process can show some bad faith. These can include a lack of concessions on issues, refusing to advance proposals or bargain, stall tactics or withholding information that is important to the process.

Bad faith on behalf of management can be evidenced by an attempt to bypass the union representatives and go directly to the employees with their proposal. Management can also impose unilateral changes in the work environment that have not been brought to the unions for consent or discussion.

Unions can show bad faith in the process if they fail to notify management about their plans or intent to renegotiate the contract 60 to 90 days before the contract expires.

Collective Bargaining Positions

Different bargaining approaches can be adopted by involved parties, and all approaches have different effects on the bargaining process. There are two basic approaches to negotiation:

Positional Bargaining

This refers to the strategy where both parties are focused on their demands. The representatives of each party intend to win for their side. This is a competitive approach to bargaining and is also called hard bargaining or distributive bargaining. The underlying mechanism is a zero-sum game where one party comes out as the winner of the process and the other party loses.

Principled Bargaining

This is aimed more toward solving a problem in the workplace than it is about winning the argument. In the principled bargaining approach, both parties are open to negotiations, brainstorming and compromising to tackle the issues. The agreement then is focused on a solution that is unique and generated as a result of the bargaining process.

There are two types of principled bargaining:

- **Integrative bargaining** – Integrative bargaining is a type of principled bargaining where both parties focus on the issues and come to a mutual agreement on trade-offs to reach a final decision.
- **Interest-based bargaining** – Interest-based bargaining is also a form of principled bargaining where negotiations are made with the underlying understanding that both parties have harmonious interests in the matter.

Collective Bargaining Strategies

In all approaches and positions of the collective bargaining process, the involved parties adopt different negotiation strategies. These are four basic negotiating strategies that are used in union settings:

1. **Single-unit bargaining** – One union meets with one employer to negotiate on a singular matter.
2. **Parallel bargaining** – The union starts negotiating with one employer and utilizes the results to negotiate with the next. This strategy is also known as pattern bargaining, whipsawing or leapfrogging.
3. **Multi-employer bargaining** – The union negotiates with multiple employers in the same industry or working region simultaneously.
4. **Multi-unit bargaining** – Also known as conditional bargaining, this strategy involves many unions representing different bargaining units in the organization. For example, in the airline industry, an issue can involve different unions for pilots, engineers and the attending staff. This allows for interunion communication and collaboration on collective issues that union members are facing.

Collective Bargaining Subjects

There are four major negotiation subjects related to the bargaining process:

Mandatory Subjects

These subjects are deemed mandatory by the NLRA and include wages, hours, other terms and conditions of employment, the negotiation of the agreement and bargaining related to questions that arise from the agreement. These subjects must be negotiated and are the only ones that can become subjects of strikes and lockouts if not resolved.

Illegal Subjects

The NLRA prohibits topics such as hot cargo clauses and closed shop security agreements from being made a part of the collective bargaining process.

Voluntary Subjects

Voluntary subjects are permissible subjects that can be brought into the negotiating process but are not deemed mandatory by the NLRA. Usually, these refer to management rights, scheduling, operations, supervisor responsibilities, etc.

Reserved Rights Doctrine

Usually, in the signed agreements, the management includes a clause that states any rights not covered in the agreement are under the sole responsibility of the management.

Collective Bargaining Agreement (CBA)

The CBA is a legal contract between the employer and the employees for a specified time. The contract states the agreed-upon terms that were concluded after the negotiating process. These terms differ for each process and company.

Wages, Hours, Terms and Conditions of Employment

Usually, all CBAs contain a clause on the wages, hours, terms and conditions of employment. This clause describes the medical and other benefits along with overtime, total working hours and specific conditions of the job. This clause is generally thought of as the backbone of the CBA.

Other Clauses

Union Security Clauses

A union security clause ensures that the union as a whole can financially carry out its bargaining duties. This clause requires the union members to financially support the union.

A union shop clause gives all employees a grace period within which they need to join the union. This period is specified in the contract, but often it is no fewer than 30 days or seven days for the construction industry.

Agency Shop Clause

The agency shop clause requires all employees to join a union or pay union dues if not joining.

Closed Shop Clause

The closed shop clause requires that new employees be members of a union before they can be hired. This clause is legal only for the construction industry.

Maintenance of Membership Clause

The maintenance of membership clause gives the employees the choice of joining or not joining a union, but once they opt to join, they must maintain their membership until the current contract expires. Employees must also notify the union that they plan to discontinue their membership within 30 days of the expiration date.

No Strike/Lockout Clause

These clauses are significant both for employees and employers. They are aimed at providing economic protection due to the possible stoppage of work for both sides. Economic protection covers strikes, lockouts and any other barriers in the work that can lead to economic losses for either side.

Contract Administration Clause

The contract administration clause specifies how the various terms of the contract will be administered over its duration. It includes the procedures for disciplinary actions, grievance resolution and arbitration. The clause can also include the possibility and procedure of modifying the stated terms during the contract term.

Dues Check-Off Clause

Dues check-off clauses refer to the permission given to unions to automatically deduct union dues from employees and are used to take written authorization from employees.

The Totality of Agreement/Zipper Clause

This clause specifies that anything not included in the agreed-upon CBA is not part of this agreement. This prevents either party from opening up the contract for renegotiation during the term.

Process of Collective Bargaining

The process of collective bargaining can be carried out in five major steps:

Preparation

At this stage, negotiation teams are formed, and representatives for both the workers union and management are elected. These representatives must have the appropriate knowledge and negotiation skills. After the selection, first drafts of the argument and proposals are made after intensive discussions on each side. For example, union representatives sit down with the employees to draft specific demands regarding wages or working hours.

Discussion

At the second stage, the representatives of both parties try to establish a mutual ground to start the process of negotiating. Rules and general limitations can be set at this time before grievances are shared. After a platform is established, both parties can present their demands and views.

Proposal

These are the opening statements made by both parties. To reach a mutually agreed upon and mutually beneficial decision, both parties present their arguments, starting the process of bargaining.

Bargaining

If both parties are coming to the table with the goal of problem-solving, the bargaining process can be smooth without much tension. Both parties should ideally possess enough flexibility to hear the other side and rethink their demands to a reasonable extent.

Settlement

At the final stage, the agreement is reached after a fruitful bargaining process. Here the collective bargaining agreement is formulated and officially signed by the parties. When a settlement is reached, both parties agree to the implantation of the terms stated by the CBA.

Chapter 24: The Process of Termination

Exits and Offboarding

When it comes to ending employment with an organization, employees' exits can happen in two ways: either employees choose to leave their position in the form of resignation or retirement or the organization can ask employees to leave due to terminations or layoffs.

These exits are not easy for either employees or management. Even when employees choose to leave without resentment, the company still must deal with finding a replacement and delegating the vacant job's tasks.

Exits and terminations are important areas for HR to work on because developing efficient processes can help reduce the stress that is put on the organization and employees in these situations. A well-thought-out exit process also enables a smooth transition that adds to the positive atmosphere of the workplace and the remaining employees' trust in management.

Voluntary Exits

Voluntary exits from an organization are carried out through resignation or retirement. Whenever employees choose to part ways with the company due to other opportunities or personal reasons, they give their resignation.

Usually, resignations are not complicated and are straightforward to process; however, there are important matters around the resignation that need appropriate attention. HR needs to have a replacement plan for the position that is now open and the reassignment of the ex-employee's tasks to current employees. The position can be filled either through promotions within the company or a recruitment process, depending on the requirement.

With resignations, HR also needs to assess the employee's history and dues. Any outstanding loans and advances need to be repaid to the company. If the employee provides a 72-hour notice, the person needs to be paid a final wage, including any unused accrued vacation or PTO at the time of departure.

In addition, Consolidated Omnibus Budget Reconciliation Act (COBRA) and Health Insurance Portability and Accountability Act (HIPAA) notices must be provided for departing employees.

Planned retirements can be opted for by employees when they transition from full-time work to focusing on other avenues. HR can develop pre-retirement counseling programs to help prepare employees for this change. These programs are valuable in helping employees transition from one stage of life to another in a fulfilling way while maintaining a positive relationship between the employees and the company.

Exit interviews are recommended as part of the exit process before an employee departs the company. These interviews provide relevant feedback and valuable insight into the company's organizational process and impression. The interview can gather information regarding the employee's decision to leave the company, the factors that contributed to the decision and what improvements can be made in the organization to improve employees' experience. These interviews can produce candid results from employees, as they have more opportunities to be truthful with their feedback.

Exit interviews can highlight major problems in the management or the general work environment that might not have been visible before. Exit interviews also help maintain a positive rapport with employees in case the employer is looking to recruit them again in the future. In ideal situations, third parties are brought in to conduct exit interviews so that there is no pressure on the employees to censor themselves.

Involuntary Exits

Involuntary exits are decisions according to which employers ask employees to leave a position due to a changing business structure or employee performance issues.

Disciplinary Terminations

When disciplinary issues arise, the first line of action is not termination. Management takes steps to help the employee resolve these problems through coaching that can be informal or even a structured formal program, depending on the situation.

However, if coaching and other disciplinary actions do not resolve the performance problems, then management does have to move toward terminating the employee. HR needs to work with the employee's manager to cover all bases and ensure that appropriate procedure has been followed for the termination process. Otherwise, it can open up the organization for legal action by the employee.

In situations where an employee's actions are extreme, posing a threat to the employer or becoming a danger to the workplace, the employer should immediately move toward termination. Such conduct can include physical threats, theft or violence.

In these scenarios, employers are encouraged to suspend the employee and initiate an investigation into their misconduct. Fair investigations should be ensured, and upon appropriate evidence, if termination is justified, it should be initiated.

The process of termination is never easy, and the HR team needs to provide support to managers who are taking charge of the situation. The two areas of concern for HR in this matter are providing counseling to the supervisors regarding the termination and giving them information that helps them avoid any claims of wrongful termination.

Termination Meeting

Supervisors must conduct meetings with the employees being terminated, and these are some of the toughest duties they have to perform for the organization. HR needs to provide supervisors with all appropriate documentation that contains the necessary evidence for the termination decision before the termination meeting.

However, documentation is not enough on its own. HR also needs to counsel supervisors on how to handle such meetings and the possible situations they could face. Employees, at this point, should be aware of what is coming because the process before the termination decision should have been transparent.

Supervisors are advised to present the necessary information in the meeting without letting it be turned into an argument over the termination decision. They are also advised to keep the meeting long enough to go over the process and the needed documentation while making sure to conclude as quickly as possible after those requirements are met.

Even though the termination decision is made after due process and because of an employee's actions or performance issues, HR still needs to ensure that the person's dignity is not affected. An appropriate place and time should be decided for the termination meeting to make the difficult process as easy as possible.

After the meeting, depending on individual cases and company policy, the employer can have the employee escorted off the property. Usually, if the situation is not too tense, employees are allowed some time to pack up any personal belongings from the workplace and leave on their own accord. Supervisors can also oversee the cleanup process, especially if employees handled sensitive materials or data.

If the situation becomes volatile and there is a risk of violence, HR should keep security personnel on standby to intervene when necessary. In very extreme cases, the local police might also be involved.

Wrongful Termination

If an employer chooses to terminate an employee for a reason that breaches the contract or goes against a statute, it is considered wrongful termination (such as a case where the reason for the termination is that they belong to a protected class).

This can happen in occupational settings, and employers may try to justify their decision by citing some other "valid" reasons. If an employee can prove that termination was a result of discrimination rather than a performance issue, the termination would be considered wrongful. Wrongful terminations also apply to any retaliatory actions taken against whistleblowers or complainants.

Worker Adjustment and Retraining Notification Act of 1988 (WARN)

In 1988, Congress passed the WARN Act to counter mass layoffs and plant closings. The act protects workers and requires a 60-day advance notice from employers in the event of termination. The advance notice is to be given to every individual employee or union representative and is intended to buy workers some time to look for other employment or training avenues before they lose their positions.

Companies with 100 or more full- and part-time employees who work in the aggregate of 4,000 hours (40 x 100) or more per week are subject to the provisions of the WARN Act. These numbers include the employees on temporary leave or even ones expected to be recalled after a layoff.

Under the WARN Act, a mass layoff refers to a situation where 500 employees or a total of 33% of the workforce have been laid off. A plant closing refers to 50 or more full-time employees losing their job because of a single facility shutting down either temporarily or permanently.

The WARN Act also requires specific notice requirements in case of layoffs and plant closings. These requirements vary for each group of workers and can depend on the reason for the layoff.

There are situations in which the 60-day notice is not required to be given out to each employee. These include:

- A faltering company exception
- Unforeseeable business circumstances exception
- Natural disaster exception

Reduction in force or layoff decisions are made after determining the legality of the situation. The organization needs to ensure where it stands under the WARN Act and handle the communication and notices accordingly. This is an especially stressful time for managers tasked with deciding which employees need to be let go.

At this stage, the workplace atmosphere is challenging for employees, as it is a period of uncertainty for them. Employees may be fearful of losing their jobs soon and anticipating the worst.

It is HR's responsibility to work with managers and counsel them in dealing with employees. Honest communication should be maintained in the workplace, and the layoff process should be made as transparent as possible. Employees should not be kept in the dark or lied to about upcoming decisions. This is also important for maintaining the respect and loyalty of the remaining employees who may be struggling with survivor guilt and who could possibly be tasked with more work due to the layoffs.

Layoff Process

Layoff decisions need to be made while keeping the company's benefit in mind. Appropriate documents also need to be maintained regarding these decisions so that the company can avoid any future legal battles that relate to discrimination or other violations.

Performance appraisals can be used in the documentation as well. Managers can use this event to first lay off employees who have consistently low performance value.

Severance

A severance package can be offered to the employees being laid off, which helps mitigate the effects of their unemployment. However, severance packages need to maintain equity across all departing employees. Employee seniority and employment class can be considered when deciding on severance packages for individual employees.

Outplacement

Outplacement services are aimed at helping employees with transition tasks after the loss of employment, such as assistance in resume updating, interview preparation and job searching. These services are often provided in the form of group events after a mass layoff. Some of these services can include individual or group counseling to ease employees' loss and transition.

Unemployment Insurance

HR should thoroughly check individual employment status and records to check eligibility for unemployment insurance. This information can benefit many employees being laid off. If the company is required to produce early notices under the WARN Act, then the state unemployment office will be aware of the upcoming layoffs. HR can also help people apply for unemployment insurance.

Test 1: Questions

Functional Area 01 | Business Management

(1) Data collection that helps HR determine and track operations and performance is known as ____________.

(A) HR diagnosis.

(B) HR analytics.

(C) HR metrics.

(D) HR data.

(2) ____________ is a way to reduce the negative effects of strategy risk.

(A) Establishing a healthy cash flow

(B) Diversifying projects

(C) Developing projects that support high-risk projects

(D) All of the above

(3) Insurance moves risk from the purchasing entity to the insurance-issuing entity. Insuring for financial protection can help a company remove the burden of risk from itself.

This process is called __________.

(A) Risk transfer

(B) Risk protection

(C) Risk avoidance

(D) Risk reduction

(4) The implementation of a certain management plan is usually carried out by teams assigned roles for this purpose.

Generally, risk assessment protocols are made by ___________.

(A) Accounting and finance

(B) Leadership and HR

(C) HR and management

(D) Management and production

(5) Hiring discrimination is any sort of prejudice held against a candidate due to race, sex, religion, color, national origin, age or disability during the hiring process. This discrimination, in itself, is ___________.

(A) Unacceptable

(B) Prohibited

(C) Illegal

(D) Punishable

(6) Cross-functional stakeholders are usually responsible for a company's broader and long-term objectives. They include ______________.

(A) People from different departments collaborating to achieve a common goal

(B) The owners of the company

(C) Several owners of a company working toward one goal

(D) People affected by the running business

(7) Mr. Williams has been working very hard for the past few months, and his efforts are being rewarded by his company in the form of paid leaves and commissions. HR is responsible for making sure Mr. Williams receives the rewards to ensure that he keeps working hard.

Which of the following is not the responsibility of the HR department?

(A) Labor law compliance

(B) Commission planning

(C) Training and development

(D) Accounting

(8) HR provides a number of services to employees. Which of the following is not a service provided by HR?

(A) Equal opportunity tasks

(B) Purchasing

(C) Training programs

(D) Employee selection programs

(9) Determining the performance of employees based on their experience and needs, and employee engagement and motivation toward the growth of the company are _________ activities.

(A) Translational

(B) Transactional

(C) Transformational

(D) Strategic

(10) Principles that represent the beliefs, priorities and driving forces of an organization are known as ______________.

(A) Vision mission

(B) Core competencies

(C) Vision statements

(D) Core values

(11) The SMART model is used to develop effective corporate goals. The acronym SMART stands for:

(A) Specific, measurable, active, realistic, tactful

(B) Special, measurable, adaptive, realistic, tactful

(C) Specific, measurable, action, realistic, time-based

(D) Special, motivational, adaptive, realistic, time-based

(12) Once corporate goals are identified, the SMART model should be compiled in a strategic document called a ____________.

(A) Strategic plan

(B) Business scheme

(C) Business plan

(D) Strategic approach

(13) A certain manufacturing company has been offered two choices: select low-quality raw material in greater amounts or high-quality materials in lower quantities. The price point for both options is about the same, but the company chooses quality over quantity.

Which of the following helped the company make this unbiased decision?

(A) Vision strategy

(B) Vision mission

(C) Core competencies

(D) Core values

(14) An organization that lives by its vision and core values has a higher competitive advantage over businesses with less transparency.

Which of the following is not an advantage of core values?

(A) They help build trust.

(B) They prevent conflict among coworkers.

(C) They help promote the business.

(D) They make recruitment easier.

(15) Core competencies are just as important to a company as its core values. Which of the following is an example of competence?

(A) Generally fair quality

(B) Generally comparable value

(C) Average marketing strategy

(D) Exceptional customer service

(16) “We aim to bring consumers safe, healthy and high-quality foods that provide the best nutrition.” This is an example of a ____________.

(A) Vision statement

(B) Mission statement

(C) Core value

(D) Vision mission

(17) The role of stakeholders includes ____________.

(A) Improving organizational performance

(B) Developing new products

(C) Enhancing customer relationships

(D) All of the above

(18) A group of people from different departments of a single organization working together is known as ____________.

(A) A team

(B) Teamwork

(C) A cross-functional team

(D) A committee

(19) The percentage of employees leaving the organization in relation to the total number of employees is known as ___________.

(A) Overturn

(B) Turnover

(C) Retention

(D) Risk

(20) Cross-functional teamwork helps achieve ___________.

(A) Diversity in skill sets

(B) Employee engagement

(C) Innovation

(D) All of the above

(21) Which of the following best describes risk?

(A) The probability of an unlikely event happening

(B) The probability of any harm or loss occurring

(C) Uncertainty when looking at the past

(D) Uncertainty when looking into the future

(22) Which option best describes a strategic risk?

(A) Lack of production per market demand

(B) Flooding

(C) Injury to employees due to a certain assessment

(D) None of the above

(23) Data makes training and development more successful. An effective training program also increases ___________.

(A) Productivity

(B) Retention

(C) Both (A) and (B)

(D) Turnover

(24) HR metrics help with ___________.

(A) Performance tracking

(B) Tracking the effectiveness of HR policies

(C) Improving payroll management

(D) All of the above

(25) Low employee engagement can be measured with the help of ______________.

(A) Absenteeism

(B) Turnover

(C) Retention

(D) Both (A) and (B)

(26) Employers are obligated by law to provide their employees with __________.

(A) A relaxed work environment

(B) Safe working conditions

(C) Commissions

(D) None of the above

(27) When a store keeps its goods locked up, it is practicing ____________.

(A) Risk avoidance

(B) Risk transfer

(C) Risk shifting

(D) Risk reduction

(28) Which of the following reviews challenges and issues that may arise during a project?

(A) Cost risk analysis

(B) Decision analysis

(C) Reliability analysis

(D) Schedule analysis

(29) Installing fire and smoke alarms in a facility is an example of ____________.

(A) Risk transfer

(B) Risk avoidance

(C) Risk reduction

(D) Risk prevention

(30) Which of the following is not a step of risk resolution?

(A) Research

(B) Reduce

(C) Adapt

(D) Eliminate

(31) A statement describing the aim of a business is part of ____________.

(A) HR strategy

(B) A vision statement

(C) A mission statement

(D) Strategic goals

(32) The mission statement provides direction to __________.

(A) Employees

(B) Stakeholders

(C) Customers

(D) All of the above

(33) The HR strategy aligns with which of HR management's goals?

(A) Organizational

(B) Economic

(C) Marketing

(D) None of the above

(34) A partially ordered sequence of activities (routine tasks, including recruitment, payroll administration, performance management, maintaining records) is called a ___________.

(A) Translational activity

(B) Transformational activity

(C) Transformable activity

(D) Transactional activity

(35) What are key performance indicators (KPIs)?

(A) Performance measurement tools

(B) Business objectives stated in measurable values

(C) Performance-tracking tools

(D) All of the above

Functional Area 02 | Talent Planning and Acquisition

(36) Which act applies to private employers with 15 or more employees?

(A) Title V of the Civil Rights Act

(B) Title VI of the Civil Rights Act

(C) Title VII of the Civil Rights Act

(D) Title VIII of the Civil Rights Act

(37) The 1964 Civil Rights Act prohibits _____________.

(A) Discrimination in employment

(B) Discriminatory voting tactics

(C) Discrimination against patrons of commercial business

(D) Discrimination in federally funded programs

(38) The 1964 Civil Rights Act also established ___________.

(A) Crosscutting requirements

(B) US Commission on Civil Rights

(C) Desegregation of Public Schools Act

(D) Equal Employment Opportunity Commission

(39) When it comes to the functions of a workplace, which act prohibits discrimination against protected classes?

(A) Title IV of the Civil Rights Act

(B) Title V of the Civil Rights Act

(C) Title IV of the Civil Rights Act

(D) Title VII of the Civil Rights Act

(40) The Uniform Guidelines on Employee Selection Procedures, 1978, aimed to bring uniformity in the employment process to deal with the concept of "disparate impact," which refers to __________.

(A) A policy or practice in the workplace that has a negative influence

(B) Unintentional discrimination against protected groups as a result of the procedure

(C) Employment practices that appear to be neutral but discriminate against a protected group

(D) None of the above

(41) Reliability refers to ____________.

(A) The consistency of a measure

(B) Whether an instrument is measuring what it is intended to measure

(C) The quality of being able to be used or obtained

(D) The action of extending the period of validity of a license, subscription or contract

(42) Which of the following is an essential process for any company or organization to keep a business functional?

(A) Planning

(B) Selecting

(C) Branding

(D) Recruiting

(43) Which marketing strategy helps promote not only the business itself but employers that are looking to attract the best suitable candidates for open positions?

(A) Advertising

(B) Branding

(C) Recruiting

(D) Marketing

(44) Candidates that are not part of an organization are called ___________.

(A) External candidates

(B) Internal candidates

(C) Targeted candidates

(D) None of the above

(45) What is a good first step in the broader recruitment process for the upcoming pool of candidates?

(A) Preparing the job description

(B) Advertising the position

(C) Developing the selection criteria

(D) Planning the interview process

(46) How many types of recruiting are there?

(A) Two

(B) Three

(C) Four

(D) Five

(47) Which of the following is an advantage of internal recruitment?

(A) It provides a new perspective to the organization.

(B) It increases diversity in the organization.

(C) It allows employees to grow and progress without leaving an organization.

(D) It encourages referrals from current employees.

(48) Onboarding refers to __________.

(A) The process of determining which roles within a company are vital and generating action plans for persons to fill those positions

(B) The process of helping new hires adjust to their new work environment

(C) The ability of a company to prevent employee turnover or the number of individuals who leave their jobs either freely or involuntarily in a certain period of time

(D) The process in which employees go through professional training or pursue learning opportunities with the support of their employer in order to develop their skills, knowledge and careers

(49) The truism in the industry, which is also backed by research, suggests that new employees have __________ days to prove themselves suitable for their new job.

(A) 60

(B) 70

(C) 80

(D) 90

(50) When it comes to onboarding in the HR world, four agreed-upon elements that are distinct from each other and must be focused on to have an effective orientation program are the four C's. They include _____________.

(A) Compliance, clarification, culture, connection

(B) Compliance, convenience, culture, connection

(C) Compliance, clarification, culture, communication

(D) Compliance, clarification, content, connection

(51) In which onboarding strategy are compliance and clarification covered, but both culture and connection are not?

(A) Proactive onboarding

(B) High-potential onboarding

(C) Passive onboarding

(D) None of the above

(52) The third level of a successful onboarding process is __________.

(A) Role clarity

(B) Social integration

(C) The knowledge of and fit within an organizational culture

(D) Self-efficacy

(53) For individual employees, the long-term effects of a successful orientation effort are ______________.

(A) Organizational commitment and reduced stress

(B) Performance and reduced employee turnover

(C) Job satisfaction and performance

(D) Job satisfaction and organizational commitment

(54) Rapidly advancing technology has paved the way for alternative staffing in the form of ______________.

(A) Technological advancements

(B) Telecommuting

(C) High technology

(D) Computing

(55) A company that works as the HR department for another organization is called a ____________.

(A) Professional employer organization

(B) Functional organization

(C) Divisional organization

(D) Flat organization

(56) Which of the following allows people to work fewer hours in the workweek and is especially beneficial for people who have home commitments?

(A) Internship programs

(B) Full-time employment

(C) Job sharing

(D) Temporary workers

(57) ______________ is a big plus when it comes to alternative staffing.

(A) Job flexibility

(B) Greater access to work

(C) Cost-effectiveness

(D) Growth of enterprise

(58) Contract workers are _____________.

(A) Two or more employees who share one full-time job

(B) Employed by professional employer organizations (PEOs) and are offered to outside companies to perform HR work

(C) Employed by a single agency that takes on the responsibility of screening and testing candidates

(D) Independent workers who work with organizations on a project or fee basis

(59) The changes made in individual units of an organization to reduce or eliminate redundancy refer to ___________.

(A) Legal restructuring

(B) Corporate restructuring

(C) Cost restructuring

(D) Turnaround restructuring

(60) The HR department also needs to be cognizant of possible legal disputes in ________ environments.

(A) Unstable

(B) Stable

(C) Internal

(D) External

(61) An essential function of the HR department in any organization is _________.

(A) Ensuring effective communication

(B) Planning ahead

(C) Supporting employees

(D) None of the above

(62) Outplacement services ____________.

(A) Offer employees flexible work schedules

(B) Help rehabilitate laid-off employees back into the workforce

(C) Provide benefits that are employer funded but employee selected

(D) None of the above

(63) HR functions that are more measurement friendly than some other functions of HR include ____________.

(A) Recruitment and management

(B) Management and employment

(C) Planning and recruitment

(D) Planning and employment

Functional Area 03 | Learning and Development

(64) ___________ is a strategy used to improve an organization's structure and processes through the implementation of policies, leadership, learning, training or job redesigning.

(A) Organizational development

(B) Management development

(C) Employee development

(D) Career development

(65) Which of the following focuses on an organization's talent needs?

(A) Career development

(B) Career management

(C) Talent management

(D) None of the above

(66) The purpose of organizational development strategy is ___________.

(A) Allowing employees to gain a better understanding of their jobs and improve their skills

(B) Motivating managers by guiding them to achieve their professional growth goals

(C) Aligning organizational and employee goals and performance

(D) Improving effectiveness and efficiency within an organization

(67) Which of the following is achieved by increasing cultural values, employee productivity, market share, margins, morale and other factors that boost organizational strength?

(A) Employee development

(B) Organizational development

(C) Career development

(D) Management development

(68) ____________ is a practice that integrates career development, organizational development and training to improve organizational and individual performance.

(A) Organizational effectiveness

(B) Career development

(C) HR development

(D) Management development

(69) The purpose of instructional HR development is __________.

(A) Improving an organization's competitive advantage in the marketplace

(B) Enhancing effectiveness within an organization

(C) Increasing employee productivity

(D) None of the above

(70) Who is responsible for developing programs and encouraging the participation of the workforce in performance management?

(A) HR professionals

(B) Managers

(C) Directors

(D) Employees

(71) Which of the following cannot be categorized as a distinct role?

(A) Performance engineers

(B) Managers

(C) Learning agents

(D) Consultants

(72) __________ develops steps that lead to education, learning, experience and professional development.

(A) Onboarding

(B) The employee development model

(C) The career development model

(D) Recruitment

(73) An organization's workforce needs to understand __________ to advance and grow.

(A) Performance benchmarks

(B) Employee benchmarks

(C) Practice benchmarks

(D) External benchmarks

(74) Which of the following should be maintained to accomplish business objectives?

(A) Extrinsic motivation

(B) Employee motivation

(C) Intrinsic motivation

(D) Identified motivation

(75) __________ can develop a career development map that allows employees to switch career paths or jobs by identifying roles that require similar skills.

(A) Employees

(B) HR professionals

(C) Managers

(D) Directors

(76) What is the process of improving and expanding employees' skills, capabilities and knowledge for a particular job?

(A) Branding

(B) Making performance appraisals consistent

(C) Multitasking

(D) Training

(77) Training takes place at ________ levels.

(A) Three

(B) Four

(C) Five

(D) Six

(78) Training that occurs at a single job process or category is known as __________.

(A) Organizational level training

(B) Individual-level training

(C) Task-level training

(D) None of the above

(79) _____________ is defined as the employee training system under which an expert or highly experienced person is assigned as an advisor or guide to relatively less experienced employees to guide and nurture their development.

(A) Benchmarking

(B) Mentoring

(C) Development

(D) Employee engagement

(80) Which of the following programs helps create a pathway that allows employees to navigate on-the-job challenges?

(A) Formal mentorship

(B) Informal mentorship

(C) Distance mentoring

(D) Group mentoring

(81) A mentor or a coach who strives for their protégé's best interests can be considered a/an ________.

(A) Sub-partner

(B) Active partner

(C) Nominal partner

(D) Accountability partner

Functional Area 04 | Total Rewards

(82) ____________ is a systematic methodology used to provide employees with monetary and nonmonetary resources in return for their services.

(A) Employee compensation

(B) A compensation package

(C) Monetary compensation

(D) Empowerment compensation

(83) What is the goal of a compensation package?

(A) Recruiting, training, detainment

(B) Motivation, goal appreciation, incentive

(C) Training, motivation, detainment

(D) Motivation, training, recruitment

(84) The most critical compensation for motivating employees and improving job performance is ___________.

(A) Monetary compensation

(B) Nonmonetary compensation

(C) Short-term incentives

(D) Long-term incentives

(85) All types of cash compensation—including insurance, medical care premiums, retirement plans and paid vacations—are a form of ____________.

(A) Costs incurred

(B) Monetary compensation

(C) Nonmonetary compensation

(D) Short-term incentives

(86) Flexible time, time off, mentorship programs, gym membership, day care facilities, tuition assistance, free parking and short Fridays are examples of ____________.

(A) Monetary compensation

(B) Nonmonetary compensation

(C) Short-term incentives

(D) Long-term incentives

(87) Which of the following statements correctly defines "cost incurred"?

(A) Cost incurred is an accrual accounting concept that involves the recording of time.

(B) Cost incurred is an accrual accounting concept that covers the records of consumption of time and resources of the company.

(C) Cost incurred is an accrual accounting concept that records when a resource or asset is consumed along with the expenses.

(D) Cost incurred is an accrual accounting concept that records when a resource or asset is consumed along with the nonmonetary compensation.

(88) What is the key difference between compensation and reward?

(A) Compensation and reward are the same.

(B) Compensation is the incentive given to employees in appreciation of their job performance, while a reward is given in recognition of achievement.

(C) Compensation is an incentive given on the basis of achievement, while a reward is given as a bonus.

(D) None of the above.

(89) Mr. Larson has been working very hard on a project for his company for the past two months. A week ago, he completed the project, and the company acknowledged his effort and dedication by giving him an award.

What is this award an example of?

(A) Compensation

(B) Reward

(C) Total rewards philosophy

(D) Pay theories

(90) Tangible awards, such as salaries, bonuses, medals, and certificates given to employees for meeting certain goals or accomplishments, are an example of ___________.

(A) Extrinsic rewards

(B) Intrinsic rewards

(C) Ambivalent rewards

(D) Non-financial rewards

(91) Mr. John trained a team of 40 employees within 30 days. The team ended up working in the field 10 days before they were scheduled to do so. The company appreciated Mr. John's efforts and provided him with a bonus.

Mr. John was given ___________.

(A) An extrinsic reward

(B) An intrinsic reward

(C) Nonmonetary compensation

(D) Short-term incentives

(92) Which of the following statements best describes an intrinsic reward?

(A) An intrinsic reward is something intangible.

(B) An intrinsic reward comes with a sense of accomplishment.

(C) An intrinsic reward is the positive feeling associated with being recognized or acknowledged.

(D) All of the above.

(93) Which question is not suitable for developing a compensation package?

(A) What is considered a fair wage by the employees?

(B) Are the wages high enough to hinder the company from achieving its financial objectives?

(C) Does the compensation philosophy follow the labor market, industry and organizational changes?

(D) What should be included in a reward?

(94) After asking employees some general questions, a company devised a total rewards philosophy plan on the basis of __________.

(A) External factors

(B) Internal factors

(C) External and internal factors

(D) Pseudo factors

(95) A mission statement that helps in the development and implementation of compensation packages that attract, motivate, retain and reward employees is termed ____________.

(A) Total compensation philosophy

(B) Total rewards philosophy

(C) Equity compensation philosophy

(D) Reward and compensation philosophy

(96) Which of the following is/are not an internal factor of the total rewards philosophy?

(A) Financial constraints

(B) Pecking order

(C) Economic conditions

(D) Organizational structure and culture

(97) Line of sight happens when employees are aware that their performance impacts both monetary and nonmonetary payments. As a result, good performance is correlated with better rewards, and a merit/high-performance culture is created in which employees are motivated to perform their best.

This definition best describes _______________.

(A) Performance-based philosophy

(B) Total rewards philosophy

(C) Compensation philosophy

(D) Entitlement philosophy

(98) Mr. O'Toole is working as a department head for Trade Export Center. However, his overall performance has not been good for the past few months. Despite his poor performance, he is receiving compensation, as he is a senior member of the company and has been serving the company for more than two decades.

What is this an example of?

(A) Entitlement philosophy

(B) Market compensation philosophy

(C) Market minus philosophy

(D) Market plus philosophy

(99) Alexa is working as an HR executive in the corporate sector, but her salary is quite low, even lower than market rates. And the company she is working for is not providing her with any compensation or rewards. She is quite frustrated and thinking of resigning.

This is an example of __________.

(A) Entitlement philosophy

(B) Market compensation philosophy

(C) Market plus philosophy

(D) Market minus philosophy

(100) Jasmine is thinking of joining Oracle, as the company offers high salaries to employees in comparison to the average market.

This example explains __________.

(A) The market plus philosophy

(B) The market minus philosophy

(C) The entitlement philosophy

(D) The market compensation philosophy

(101) David is working for an organization at a low wage. He is considering whether he will get any benefits. The environment of the company is quite appreciative.

This example best matches ______________.

(A) The market plus philosophy

(B) The market minus philosophy

(C) The entitlement philosophy

(D) The market compensation philosophy

(102) When designing compensation package plans, companies consider economic conditions like __________.

(A) Recession

(B) Inflation

(C) Both (A) and (B)

(D) None of the above

(103) The pay system that determines compensation according to the industry compensation standards or the going rate is known as ___________.

(A) Going grade system

(B) Pay grade system

(C) Pay going system

(D) Broadbanding

(104) A university student named Erik is working in an organization as a freelance graphic designer. He is very skilled, so the company compensates him very well.

This organization's pay system will be ___________.

(A) Skill-based

(B) Pay-grade

(C) Going grade

(D) Variable

(105) Which of the following statements best describes the equity theory?

(A) People associate their level of satisfaction with their payment as compared with that of others.

(B) People associate external satisfaction with internal happiness.

(C) People constantly need to compare themselves with others.

(D) People achieve satisfaction by earning a six-figure salary.

(106) A company in South Carolina is well-known for its compensation packages and other benefits. According to a recent study, the employees of the company scored higher on the self-esteem scale and are self-driven.

Which theory best explains this effect?

(A) Equity theory

(B) Expectancy theory

(C) Reinforcement theory

(D) None of the above

(107) If high performance is rewarded, then individuals are more likely to work with the same potential.

Which of the following theories explains this concept?

(A) Reinforcement theory

(B) Equity theory

(C) Expectancy theory

(D) Compensation theory

Functional Area 05 | Employee and Labor Relations

(108) An HR team's role is very important in a business. What is this role?

(A) Keeping track of employees' attendance and making sure they arrive in the office on time

(B) Taking care of the whole employee process and ensuring that the transition into each organizational level is visible and well organized

(C) Making sure the right employees are hired for the business and that their needs are met

(D) Handling all direct customer needs

(109) What are the first four stages of the employee life cycle model (in the right order)?

(A) Retention, development, hiring, training

(B) Advertisement of employee requirements, hiring, training, onboarding

(C) Onboarding, advertisement, hiring, training

(D) Hiring, onboarding, development, retention

(110) How is hiring best done?

(A) Hiring is best done by ensuring the company hires and retains the best talent.

(B) Hiring is best done by ensuring the position is met with the right applicants.

(C) Hiring is best done by ensuring the required number of employees are hired.

(D) Hiring is best done by ensuring every department accepts the hired employees.

(111) What should professional managers not do during the hiring stage?

(A) Hire employees who seem desperate

(B) Examine the benefits provided to employees

(C) Prefer employees that they know, such as friends and relatives

(D) Make a timeline for the hiring procedure

(112) What is one disadvantage of being broad in the search for the right employees?

(A) It can lead to the hiring of employees who may not be a good fit for the organization's needs.

(B) It can attract unnecessary attention from competitors.

(C) Businesses can end up hiring more than the required number of employees.

(D) All of the above.

(113) What is employee onboarding?

(A) Bringing new staff up to speed

(B) Introducing employees to other staff members

(C) Letting the hired employees know about the company's rules and regulations

(D) Completing the final step of the hiring stage

(114) What is a crucial part of the onboarding process?

(A) Introducing the company's rules and regulations

(B) Paying attention to the compensation and benefits offered and the level of qualifications and credentials being sought

(C) Lengthy job requirements in a job description

(D) Laying out the corporate strategy, explaining what it means to new hires and clarifying any confusion

(115) Why is the retention stage critical in the employee life cycle?

(A) Some managers may prefer some employees in the workplace over others, and this can create bias.

(B) Employees may get stronger because of trade unions, etc.

(C) Employees may want to be paid more, and that can create issues.

(D) Employees may be taken for granted by their managers.

(116) A good company will always make sure to gain its employees' trust. Which stage makes sure of this?

(A) Onboarding

(B) Development

(C) Retention

(D) Alumni program

(117) What does the development stage include?

(A) A valuable source of referrals for new hires and customers

(B) Keeping staff informed about current trends while allowing them to deepen their skills

(C) Strengthening employees' present abilities and introducing them to new abilities for growth

(D) Training employees

(118) What is the role of onboarding digital technologies?

(A) It makes it easier for new hires to fit in and is thus essential for increasing employee productivity.

(B) It helps in gaining employee trust.

(C) It makes the need for further training redundant.

(D) All of the above.

(119) What is a learning management system?

(A) A program that is designed to increase the technical skills, knowledge, efficiency and value creation to do any specific job

(B) A platform that can be used to manage and deliver online training content in various formats

(C) A program that managers use to train and develop employees

(D) A platform that is accessible to all employees and where they are updated on their regular tasks and duties

(120) How can HR increase employee retention?

(A) By paying employees more

(B) By training employees better

(C) By hiring fewer employees

(D) By building better relationships with employees

Test 1: Answers and Explanations

Functional Area 01 | Business Management

(1) (C) HR metrics.

HR metrics are different data measurements that demonstrate how effective the HR department's efforts are to the organization's overall success.

(2) (D) All of the above.

The negative effects of strategy risks can be mitigated by developing and maintaining processes that support high-risk projects. For instance, establishing healthy cash flow and adding diversification in projects can mitigate financial damage if a venture fails.

(3) (A) Risk transfer.

Risk transfer is the process of moving the burden of risks to a third party. Risk transfer is usually done by purchasing insurance policies or including an indemnification clause in contracts.

(4) (B) Leadership and HR.

Generally, HR and the leadership are responsible for developing risk assessment protocols, but designated teams may carry out implementation. Risk assessment is a technique for actively assessing risks; its objective is to remove or minimize the consequence of a risk.

(5) (C) Illegal.

According to the EEOC, hiring discrimination is illegal. Companies are not allowed to discriminate against job applicants based on their sex, color, race, sexual orientation, age and more.

(6) (A) People from different departments collaborating to achieve a common goal.

Cross-functional stakeholders refers to a team of people from different departments of an organization working toward a common goal.

(7) (D) Accounting.

HR is not responsible for accounting. It is responsible for seven main tasks: strategic management, employment and workforce planning, HR development, total rewards, policy development, labor and employee relations and risk management.

(8) (B) Purchasing.

HR is responsible for talent acquisition, employee training, administering total rewards programs and developing organizational policies, but it is not responsible for purchasing products.

(9) (C) Transformational.

Employee engagement and motivation toward the growth of the company are the key transformational responsibilities of an HR department. Transformational activities aim to reconstruct the organizational structure by making organizational policies more focused on the future. Transformational activities include determining the performance of employees based on their experience and needs.

(10) (D) Core values.

Core values are guiding principles that represent an organization's beliefs, priorities and driving forces. Core values set the standard for how the organization interacts with stakeholders, partners and customers.

(11) (C) Specific, measurable, action, realistic, time-based.

The SMART model is used to develop effective corporate goals. It stands for specific, measurable, action, realistic and time-based. It allows HR to streamline goals to make them easier to accomplish, create performance and goal-tracking methods, define the appropriate course of action needed to achieve a goal, determine the capacity of the workforce to achieve said goal and set guidelines for goal achievement.

(12) (C) Business plan.

Once identified, the SMART model should be compiled in a strategic document called a business plan. A business plan should meet the organization's purpose established in the strategic planning process.

(13) (D) Core values.

Core values set guiding principles that eliminate biased choices. For example, if an organization's core value is to sell the highest-quality sustainable cotton, the operation team will automatically eliminate the choice of obtaining unsustainable cotton.

(14) (C) They help promote the business.

Promoting the business is not an advantage of core values. Strong corporate core values support smart decision-making and conflict prevention, lead to easier talent acquisition and clear communication, and increase trust between employees and managers.

(15) (D) Exceptional customer service.

Exceptional customer service is an example of competence. Core competencies are the defining products, services, skills and capabilities that give a business advantages over its competitors. In other words, they are the competitive advantages that distinguish a company from others in its field.

(16) (A) Vision statement.

This is a vision statement. An organization's vision statement informs the shareholders, partners and customers about the driving force of the organization and the best practices necessary to accomplish it. A vision statement should communicate what the organization wants to become and its long-term goals.

(17) (D) All of the above.

Cross-functional group members have complementary skills and the responsibility to develop new products, reevaluate different organizational processes, enhance customer relationships and improve organizational performance.

(18) (C) Cross-functional team.

In a cross-functional collaboration, different teams from different departments work together on large or modest projects. They collaborate and communicate regularly to accomplish short- and long-term organizational goals.

(19) (B) Turnover.

The turnover rate measures the percentage of employees leaving the organization in relation to the total number of employees. A data-driven HR department can analyze turnover to identify why employees leave and create model scenarios in advance to boost retention and reduce turnover.

(20) (D) All of the above.

Cross-functional teamwork builds buy-in and trust by promoting camaraderie and eliminating misconceptions within organizations. It enhances employees' engagement as well as their capacity to innovate. A cross-functional setting provides an excellent opportunity to promote learning and knowledge sharing, adding diversity to skill sets.

(21) (D) Uncertainty when looking into the future.

Risk is any unexpected event that can affect a project for better or worse. It can affect anything: people, processes, technology and resources. The key element of this definition is that the effect of the uncertainty—if it occurs—may be positive or negative on the plan's objectives.

(22) (A) Lack of production per market demand.

Strategic risk refers to the internal and external events that may make it difficult or impossible for an organization to achieve its objectives and strategic goals. It occurs when an organization is unable to perform according to market standards.

(23) (C) Both (A) and (B).

Predictive analytics helps identify weak points during a training program, such as when an employee loses focus, to make changes in the right direction. Therefore, data makes training and development more successful. An effective training program also increases retention and productivity.

(24) (D) All of the above.

HR metrics help determine how appropriate a decision is based on the organization's existing and future staffing needs, while HR data provides essential information about an employee's performance and contribution to the organization. HR data helps HR track and report payroll expenses by documenting department, location and position costs.

(25) (D) Both (A) and (B).

HR can run reports to measure low engagement based on turnover and absenteeism.

(26) (B) Safe working conditions.

Employee safety is one of an employer's key responsibilities. Business owners are legally obligated to provide a safe work environment to their employees.

(27) (A) Risk avoidance.

Risk avoidance is the process of eliminating potential hazards that may damage a project or disrupt an operation.

(28) (D) Schedule analysis.

A schedule analysis reviews challenges and issues that may arise during a project. It is also used to identify facts, anomalies and issues that can exist throughout the project duration due to intentional or unintentional actions.

(29) (C) Risk reduction.

The process of minimizing risk within an organization is called risk reduction. Examples of risk reduction include medical care, fire departments, night security guards, sprinkler systems and burglar alarms.

(30) (C) Adapt.

Risk resolution does not involve adapting to risk. It is conducted in four steps: research, accept, reduce and eliminate. Risk resolution aims to study and assess threats and minimize them to prevent the company from being severely impacted by a crisis.

(31) (C) A mission statement.

A mission statement is a precise explanation of a business's reason for existence. It describes the organization's purpose and intention.

(32) (D) All of the above.

The mission statement supports the vision of the company and serves to communicate purpose and direction to employees, customers, vendors and other stakeholders.

(33) (A) Organizational.

The HR strategy aligns the organizational goals with HR management, and HR objectives set the foundation for various organizational goals, including business reputation, profitability, ethics and principles.

(34) (D) Transactional activity.

A transactional process is a partially ordered sequence of activities. Transactional activities refer to routine tasks, including recruitment, payroll administration, performance management, maintaining records, etc.

(35) (D) All of the above.

KPIs help organizations keep track of performance in cross-cultural collaborations. They are business objectives stated in measurable values.

Functional Area 02 | Talent Planning and Acquisition

(36) (C) Title VII of the Civil Rights Act.

Title VII of the Civil Rights Act is the only title that applies to private employers that have 15 or more employees.

(37) (A) Discrimination in employment.

The 1964 Civil Rights Act prohibits private sector and federal government employers from discriminating against any employee in the workforce based on race, color, religion, sex or national origin.

(38) (D) Equal Employment Opportunity Commission.

The Civil Rights Act of 1964 established the EEOC, which strives "to promote equal opportunity in employment through administrative and judicial enforcement of the federal civil rights laws and education and technical assistance."

(39) (D) Title VII of the Civil Rights Act.

Under Title VII of the Civil Rights Act, all discrimination against protected classes is prohibited when it comes to workplace functions. These functions include hiring and firing, compensation and fringe benefits, recruitment, testing, training and more.

(40) (B) Unintentional discrimination against protected groups as a result of the procedure.

The concept of disparate impact refers to unintentional discrimination against protected groups during the recruitment procedure.

(41) (A) The consistency of a measure.

Reliability relates to the consistency of a measure. It ensures that the final result of an assessment will be stable and trustworthy.

(42) (D) Recruiting.

Recruiting is the process of attracting, engaging and assessing qualified candidates for open positions and persuading them to work for the company. It is essential for any company or organization to keep a business functional.

(43) (B) Branding.

Branding can help an employer ascertain an organization's unique value proposition, create a persona that attracts talent and increase employees' productivity. Being part of a successful brand makes employees feel proud, which, in turn, increases referrals.

(44) (A) External candidates.

An external employee has applied for the job but has not been accepted yet. This employee is recruited from outside the company, not through internal promotion.

(45) (C) Developing the selection criteria.

Developing the selection criteria for the upcoming pool of candidates is a good first step in the broader recruitment process. These criteria could be looked at as a checklist that details the must-haves in the candidates on the KSAs, job specifications and competencies for the job.

(46) (A) Two.

When HR has a position to fill in the company, it has two options: recruiting internally or externally. Internal candidates are employees who are already working in the organization. The new position is essentially a promotion for these employees. In comparison, external recruits are new hires from outside the organization.

(47) (C) It allows employees to grow and progress without leaving an organization.

There are many advantages when it comes to recruiting internally. For example, employees get a chance to grow without leaving one organization, and employers can save a lot of manpower and money that would otherwise be spent on job advertisements, selection, etc.

(48) (B) The process of helping new hires adjust to their new work environment.

Employee orientation or onboarding refers to the process of helping new hires adjust to their new work environment. This involves them being able to adjust socially in their workplace and becoming familiar with the performance expectations for the new position.

(49) (D) 90.

A truism in the industry suggests that new employees have about 90 days to prove themselves suitable for a new job.

(50) (A) Compliance, clarification, culture, connection.

The four C's are compliance, clarification, culture and connection. They aim to provide employees with relevant information and an immersed understanding of organizational culture.

(51) (C) Passive onboarding.

Only compliance and some clarification are covered in the first level of passive onboarding, but both culture and connection are not included.

(52) (B) Social integration.

Social integration is the third level of a successful onboarding process. It is achieved by having current employees help new hires learn about the organization.

(53) (D) Job satisfaction and organizational commitment.

The long-term effects of a successful orientation effort for individual employees are job satisfaction and organizational commitment, resulting in new employees helping the organization focus on specific goals.

(54) (B) Telecommuting.

Telecommuting makes it possible for people to work from home while being connected to the workplace electronically. It makes work accessible to people who might have issues commuting.

(55) (A) Professional employer organization.

A company that works as the HR department for another organization is known as a professional employer organization. When employed by an organization, a PEO employs candidates and "leases" them to the original organization.

(56) (C) Job sharing.

Job sharing allows people to work fewer hours in the workweek and maintain a better work-life balance. This flexible work arrangement also works in favor of the organization, as fewer work hours require the company to spend less on benefits.

(57) (C) Cost-effectiveness.

Most of the methods used in alternative staffing cost employers less time and money than traditional means of handling the same situation. Alternative staff also does not require the usual benefits packages or payroll taxes, so payouts are decreased.

(58) (D) Independent workers who work with organizations on a project or fee basis.

A contract worker is an individual a company employs for a specific period or on a project or fee basis. These workers do not receive any benefits like paid time off and health insurance. They provide organizations with a staffing alternative, especially during a time of crisis when immediate work is required.

(59) (B) Corporate restructuring.

Corporate restructuring is a process in which changes are made in individual units of an organization to reduce or eliminate redundancy, modify operations or increase profitability. For example, in mergers and acquisitions, one company incorporates another company into itself to increase profitability.

(60) (A) Unstable.

In an unstable environment, the HR department needs to handle sensitive material carefully because if one party is displeased, the organization can be at risk of a legal battle.

(61) (C) Supporting employees.

Supporting employees is an essential function of the HR department in any organization, but it should not be superficial.

(62) (B) Help rehabilitate laid-off employees back into the workforce.

Outplacement services allow laid-off employees to be rehabilitated back into the workforce. These services offer both practical and mental support for employees and help them successfully transition into new jobs.

(63) (D) Planning and employment.

Planning and employment are HR functions that are measurement friendly because data for these functions can be collected by looking at HR metrics and different types of analyses.

Functional Area 03 | Learning and Development

(64) (A) Organizational development.

Organizational development enhances an organization's structure and operations through policies, leadership, learning, training or job redesign. It aims to increase an organization's effectiveness and efficiency.

(65) (B) Career management.

Career management is concerned with an organization's talent needs, whereas career development is concerned with employees' desires and interests. Career management enables people to move into roles that are best suited to their skills and aspirations. In contrast, talent management links these two worlds, locating the sweet spot that represents the organization and its employees' shared goals and bringing the two worlds together to promote mutual happiness and organizational strength.

(66) (D) Improve effectiveness and efficiency within an organization.

An organizational development strategy aims to increase an organization's effectiveness and efficiency.

(67) (B) Organizational development.

Organizational development aims to increase a company's competitive edge in the marketplace. It is achieved by enhancing organizational strength, which is done by improving cultural values, employee productivity, market share, margins, morale and other factors.

(68) (C) HR development.

HR development improves organizational and individual performance by combining career development, organizational development and training.

(69) (C) Increasing employee productivity.

HR development aims to boost employee productivity and performance, which directly impacts an organization's revenue and success.

(70) (A) HR professionals.

HR professionals are in charge of developing programs and encouraging employee participation in performance management. Business objectives, specified competencies and expected project outputs contribute to the effectiveness of this approach.

(71) (D) Consultants.

The HR department is divided into several sublevels with different tasks and duties, such as learning agents, managers and performance engineers. Consultants cannot be categorized into these levels.

(72) (C) The career development model.

A career development model develops education, learning, experience and professional development. It also pinpoints the crucial *what* and *when* in employees' professional lives.

(73) (A) Performance benchmarks.

To improve and grow, an organization's workforce must comprehend performance benchmarks. Activities should be created to deepen and maintain interest in present roles for employees who do not aim to rise to supervisory roles or take on more responsibilities.

(74) (B) Employee motivation.

Employee motivation needs to be maintained to achieve business objectives. If it is not maintained, then employees may lose interest in their work, which will decrease profitability, productivity and efficiency.

(75) (B) HR professionals.

By identifying tasks that require similar skills, an HR professional can create a career development map that makes transferring career paths or jobs easier.

(76) (D) Training.

Employee training is the process of enhancing and increasing employees' skills, abilities and knowledge to help them perform a specific job. Training is a powerful tool that many businesses utilize to boost production and efficiency.

(77) (A) Three.

There are three stages of training: organizational, task and individual levels.

At the organizational level, the entire organization or simply one department within it focuses on preparing personnel for anticipated future needs and/or goals via organizational-level training. In contrast, training focuses on a single employment procedure/category at the task level. As the name implies, individual-level training takes place on a personal level.

(78) (C) Task-level training.

Task-level training focuses on a single employment procedure or category. Low performance in a certain task/process may suggest that task-level training is required.

(79) (B) Mentoring.

Mentoring is an employee training approach in which an expert or highly experienced person is assigned to relatively less experienced employees as an advisor or guide to encourage their development.

(80) (A) Formal mentorship.

A formal mentorship program can help employees navigate on-the-job obstacles and annoyances. Employees learn how to navigate tough workplace situations with the help of their mentors, case studies or real-time experiences.

(81) (D) Accountability partner.

A mentor or coach can be thought of as an accountability partner who looks out for the best interests of protégés. By asking the proper questions, accountability partners empower trainees to become more self-aware and develop critical thinking skills.

Functional Area 04 | Total Rewards

(82) (B) A compensation package.

A compensation package is a systematic methodology of providing employees with financial and/or non-financial rewards in return for services performed. Compensation packages can take the form of day care facilities, flexible time or membership programs.

(83) (D) Motivation, training, recruitment.

The ultimate goal of a compensation package is motivation, recruitment and training of employees. These financial or non-financial compensation packages motivate employees and help them feel like their services are being acknowledged by the company and that they are adding great value to the company's reputation.

(84) (B) Nonmonetary compensation.

Nonmonetary compensation plays a significant role in improving job performance and employee motivation. It includes flexible time, time off, mentorship programs, gym membership, day care facilities, tuition assistance, free parking and short Fridays.

(85) (B) Monetary compensation.

Monetary compensation is the cost incurred compensation used to benefit company employees. This compensation can be in the form of free health care, retirement compensation and more. Monetary compensation adds value to the company's reputation.

(86) (B) Nonmonetary compensation.

Nonmonetary compensation adds value to an employee's job performance and motivation. Furthermore, it shows that a company or the organization is significantly concerned with the needs of its employees.

(87) (C) Cost incurred is an accrual accounting concept that records when a resource or asset is consumed along with the expenses.

The cost incurred increases the value of every business. It adds potential value to the business reputation and falls under the concept of monetary compensation, where an employee is compensated with financial benefits that the company officially documents.

(88) (B) Compensation is the incentive given to employees in appreciation of their job performance, while a reward is given in recognition of achievement.

Compensation and rewards are different concepts. An employee is compensated on the basis of job performance, such as how much input a person invested in the company in the past days or weeks. Compensation can be monetary or nonmonetary.

In comparison, a reward is the appreciation of achievement, such as when a hard worker achieves a goal and is rewarded for it.

(89) (B) Reward.

Rewards are generally given as an acknowledgment of an employee's efforts. The company values the extra efforts of its employees and builds a sense of trust and admiration.

(90) (A) Extrinsic rewards.

Extrinsic rewards are physical entities, such as salaries, bonuses, medals, and certificates. These rewards are given when an employee meets certain goals. Other than bonuses and salaries, rewards can take any shape, but they must have a tangible quality.

(91) (A) An extrinsic reward.

The company admired Mr. John's efforts; therefore, he received a bonus. And since the reward is tangible, it is extrinsic.

(92) (D) All of the above.

An intrinsic reward is intangible, and it can be in the form of a sense of accomplishment, a general satisfaction or any positive feeling associated with the acknowledgment.

(93) (D) What should be included in a reward?

This statement is not included in compensation package planning. The questions in the options revolve around equity compensation, benefits, variable pay and guaranteed pay. These are the components of an ideal compensation package plan. Businesses prepare surveys and ask their employees to come up with the best possible answers. The collcted information lays the basic foundation of the compensation package plan.

(94) (C) External and internal factors.

The total rewards philosophy is an excellent concept for devising a compensation package plan. Here, internal factors (financial constraints and pecking order) and external factors (economic conditions) are equally considered. This consideration helps policymakers develop the best compensation package plan.

(95) (B) Total rewards philosophy.

Total rewards philosophy is a mission statement that helps develop and implement compensation packages by considering the internal and external factors. Total compensation policy refers to making compensation decisions with respect to internal equity, scope variation, position authority and a need to develop compatible changes according to the external market.

(96) (C) Economic condition.

Economic conditions are the external factors of the total rewards philosophy, while financial constraints, pecking order and organization structure and culture are the internal factors.

(97) (A) Performance-based philosophy.

The key feature of the performance-based philosophy is the line of sight that compensates employees' performance with positive rewards.

(98) (A) Entitlement philosophy.

The example states that despite Mr. O'Toole's poor performance, he is still preferred as he is a senior member. This is an example of entitlement philosophy.

(99) (B) Market compensation philosophy.

This example depicts market compensation philosophy, as Alexa is not getting paid according to the market rate. Market compensation philosophy states that the offered salary should be compatible with market rates.

(100) (A) The market plus philosophy.

Oracle offers higher wages to new employees; therefore, Jasmine is attracted to the employment opportunity. This is an example of market plus philosophy, and it explains the impact of high wages on the labor force.

(101) (B) The market minus philosophy.

The example highlights the low wages and that the company is compensating by increasing effective compensation package plans. Therefore, this example fits the market minus philosophy.

(102) (C) Both (A) and (B).

Whenever an organization plans a compensation package, it considers inflation-recession statistics. Inflation-recession is a state where the graph of economic growth drops while the unemployment rate increases.

(103) (A) Going grade system.

The company pays salaries according to market rates, so it follows the going grade system.

(104) (A) Skill-based.

Erik is earning a higher salary based on his skills, so the company's pay system will be skill-based. The system values a person's skills, regardless of educational history.

(105) (A) People associate their level of satisfaction with their payment as compared with that of others.

According to the equity theory, people are constantly comparing their salaries with others. This comparison can be positive or negative.

(106) (B) Expectancy theory.

The company is providing its employees with the best facilities and compensation packages; therefore, the employees are investing their maximum input into the company's reputation. This is an example of expectancy theory.

(107) (A) Reinforcement theory.

According to reinforcement theory, a reward increases the expectancy of similar behaviors. Companies use this theory to maximize employee input by rewarding high performance.

Functional Area 05 | Employee and Labor Relations

(108) (B) Taking care of the whole employee process and ensuring that the transition into each organizational level is visible and well organized.

HR takes care of employee-related matters from recruitment to exit. It is also the responsibility of HR to ensure that the transition into each organizational level is visible and well organized.

(109) (D) Hiring, onboarding, development, retention.

The first four stages of the employee life cycle model are hiring, onboarding, development and retention.

(110) (A) Hiring is best done by ensuring the company hires and retains the best talent.

The hiring and selection process is the first step of the employee life cycle model. This requires ensuring the best talent is hired and retained by the company.

(111) (C) Prefer employees that they know, such as friends and relatives.

Managers should avoid hiring friends, as this could lead to complications, including an unfair work environment.

(112) (A) It can lead to the hiring of employees who may not be a good fit for the organization's needs.

To make sure an organization hires the right individual with the relevant skills and traits, an organization needs to be specific in its ads and posts, as being too broad would lead to hiring unfit employees

(113) (A) Bringing new staff up to speed.

Employee onboarding is the process of integrating new employees into a company and its culture and providing new hires with the tools and information they need to become productive members of the team.

(114) (D) Laying out the corporate strategy, explaining what it means to new hires and clarifying any confusion.

A crucial part of any onboarding process is laying out the corporate strategy, explaining what it means to new hires and clarifying any confusion. This can prevent workplace confusion.

(115) (D) Employees may be taken for granted by their managers.

The retention stage is critical in the employee life cycle because once employees have been with a company for a time, there's a real danger that they may be taken for granted by their managers. Managers should focus their energies on keeping top employees and ensuring they are happy and sufficiently challenged in their respective roles within the team.

(116) (C) Retention.

It is a company's job to earn the trust of its personnel and demonstrate daily that it is deserving of their continued loyalty. Improving the retention stage is a fantastic way to lower the risk of losing employees while increasing employee satisfaction and retention.

(117) (C) Strengthening employees' present abilities and introducing them to new abilities for growth.

During the development stage, a manager consistently encourages professional growth within the team to help employees advance.

(118) (A) It makes it easier for new hires to fit in and is thus essential for increasing employee productivity.

Onboarding digital technologies help new hires fit into the workplace and understand the workplace culture. This integration decreases workplace confusion and increases employee productivity.

(119) (B) A platform that can be used to manage and deliver online training content in various formats.

A learning management system is a software program or web-based technology that is used to design, implement and evaluate the learning process via various formats.

(120) (D) By building better relationships with employees.

The best way to increase employee retention and reduce labor turnover is to build better relationships with employees. Managers can do this by meeting employee needs, remaining fair with employees, offering them job perks, etc.

Test 2: Questions

Functional Area 01 | Business Management

(1) The reason for the existence of any company/organization is defined by __________.

(A) A vision statement

(B) A mission statement

(C) Core values

(D) None of the above

(2) A vision statement is a statement made by an organization that conveys what it would like to achieve. It describes ______________.

(A) The company's long-term goals

(B) The company's aim

(C) The ambitions of the employees

(D) Both (A) and (B)

(3) A cosmetics brand believes that "Everyone can be glamorous." This slogan is not only embossed on the brand's catalogs and products but also displayed everywhere within its offices.

What does this slogan signify?

(A) The brand's vision

(B) The brand's core values

(C) The brand's mission

(D) A catchy phrase

(4) Cross-functional collaboration usually proves to be very useful for organizations at all levels.

Which of the following is not an advantage of cross-functional collaboration?

(A) Prioritizing normal routine tasks

(B) Diversity in thought

(C) Smart decision-making

(D) Greater informational scope

(5) Which of the following attributes, when missing, causes a cross-functional team to fail?

(A) Lack of leadership

(B) Lack of trust

(C) Lack of communication

(D) All of the above

(6) An effectively performing cross-functional team includes personalities with motivation and open minds. In such a collaboration, it is important to maintain a balance between high achievers and big personalities.

A person with which of the following traits will most likely be accepted as a part of a cross-functional team?

(A) Someone who does whatever he or she wants

(B) Someone assertive and dominating

(C) Both (A) and (B)

(D) Someone willing to change and adapt when needed

(7) A/an ___________ solution helps organizations centralize data and access it through mobile or desktop devices.

(A) Online

(B) Live

(C) Virtual

(D) Software

(8) In the modern business world, companies often use virtual offices to their benefit.

___________ is an advantage of a virtual office.

(A) Increased productivity

(B) Remote planning

(C) Low technology costs

(D) All of the above

(9) Which of the following strategies should a company use to encourage employees to perform their best?

(A) Reward its employees

(B) Provide critical feedback to its employees

(C) Both (A) and (B)

(D) None of the above

(10) HR is an important asset when it comes to managing businesses. The role of HR includes ___________.

(A) Employee recruitment

(B) Employee training

(C) Organizational policy development

(D) All of the above

(11) The acronym *HRM* stands for ______________.

(A) Human resource management

(B) Human resourceful management

(C) Human relation management

(D) Humane resource management

(12) Which department is responsible for developing risk management plans?

(A) Research and development

(B) HR

(C) Accounts and finance

(D) Marketing

(13) Risk management is also known as _____________.

(A) Duty of care

(B) Responsibility of care

(C) Obligation to care

(D) None of the above

(14) Areas that require risk management include ___________.

(A) Compensation

(B) Recruitment

(C) Health and safety

(D) All of the above

(15) Cash embezzlement is a common occurrence in businesses. Which of the following practices can successfully mitigate embezzlement?

(A) Requiring multiple signatures on all financial documents

(B) Identifying authority for financial transactions

(C) Stringent accounting procedures

(D) All of the above

(16) The focus of HR management revolves around ___________.

(A) Employees

(B) Training

(C) Machine learning

(D) Financial analysis

(17) Storm damage, earthquakes, fires, hurricanes, floods and other natural disasters are considered _______________.

(A) Location risks

(B) Strategic risks

(C) Human risks

(D) Natural risks

(18) Human risk can be mitigated by ____________.

(A) Making discipline policies

(B) Urging employees to seek treatment

(C) Keeping a check on employees

(D) All of the above

(19) It is important to evaluate the impact of strategic risks to develop an effective strategy. Which of the following is derived from an organization's target debt rating?

(A) Per capita income

(B) Risk-adjusted return

(C) Gross capital

(D) Economic capital

(20) "Risk-adjusted return on capital" measures ____________.

(A) The risk taken against the expected return

(B) The organization's target debt rating

(C) The amount needed to bear the impact of unexpected losses

(D) None of the above

(21) "Creativity, loyalty and integrity" are all ____________.

(A) Core values

(B) Vision statements

(C) Mission statements

(D) A part of HR policy

(22) “Our purpose as an organization is helping to support the health, well-being and healing of both people—customers, team members and business organizations in general—and the planet.”

This statement is an example of ____________.

(A) A vision statement

(B) A mission statement

(C) Core values

(D) Core competencies

(23) “We aim to provide the best customer service.” This statement is an example of ________________.

(A) Core values

(B) A mission statement

(C) A vision statement

(D) Core competencies

(24) In most companies, which of the following is defined as the core competency that helps streamline the organization’s processes?

(A) Accounts and finance

(B) Marketing

(C) HR

(D) All of the above

(25) There are many effective risk analysis techniques that can help organizations identify potential risks.

A cost risk analysis ______________.

(A) Reviews challenges and issues that may arise during a project

(B) Measures different options in business decisions

(C) Measures the effectiveness of a project with the help of statistics

(D) Reviews uncertainties that may impact an organization's expenditures

(26) Which department is responsible for tracking and monitoring risk by following up with parties involved?

(A) HR

(B) Security

(C) Accounts and finance

(D) Marketing

(27) Each risk is assessed based on the level of risk it poses and the probability of its occurrence.

Which of the following risks is most likely to occur?

(A) A risk with moderate probability

(B) A risk with extreme probability

(C) A risk with minor probability

(D) All of the above

(28) A ___________ measures the effectiveness of a project with the help of statistics.

(A) Reliability analysis

(B) Cost risk analysis

(C) Decision analysis

(D) None of the above

(29) The failure to report to work is known as ___________.

(A) Turnover

(B) Absenteeism

(C) Retention

(D) None of the above

(30) The percentage of employees leaving a company over a certain period of time is known as _____________.

(A) Turnover

(B) Absenteeism

(C) Retention

(D) None of the above

(31) If a company buys insurance, it is practicing ________________.

(A) Risk avoidance

(B) Risk reduction

(C) Risk prevention

(D) Risk transfer

(32) ____________ helps HR personnel identify reasons for exits, positions worked and types of employees who are most likely to leave.

(A) Cumulative data

(B) Analytical data

(C) Attrition data

(D) None of the above

(33) Strategic management usually consists of ______ steps.

(A) Seven

(B) Three

(C) Two

(D) Five

(34) The HR department maintains what kind of records?

(A) Sales record

(B) Data

(C) Employee records

(D) Storage records

(35) Which of the following is not a core competency?

(A) Knowledge management

(B) Manufacturing processes

(C) HR

(D) Cognitive abilities

Functional Area 02 | Talent Planning and Acquisition

(36) Along with the acquisition, Title VII of the Civil Rights Act also ________________.

(A) Applies to any possible retaliation against an employee who acts against discrimination

(B) Authorizes the attorney general to address certain equal-protection violations based on sex

(C) Prohibits state and local governments from denying access to public property

(D) Creates a community relations service that will assist employees in disputes involving discrimination claims

(37) Whether an instrument is measuring what it is intended to measure refers to ______________.

(A) Dependability

(B) Accessibility

(C) Reliability

(D) Validity

(38) When it comes to recruiting talent, the selection process needs to be ______________.

(A) Consistent

(B) Valid

(C) Appropriate

(D) None of the above

(39) Which of the following is not a subtype of validity?

(A) Content validity

(B) Legal validity

(C) Criterion-related validity

(D) Predictive validity

(40) Which act prohibits discrimination against people with disabilities and applies to all private employers, as well as state and local governments?

(A) Title I of the Age Discrimination Act

(B) Title I of the Employment Act

(C) Title I of the Americans with Disabilities Act

(D) None of the above

(41) The Fair Credit Reporting Act ______________.

(A) Prohibits age discrimination in the workplace concerning any term, condition or privilege of employment

(B) Notifies employers about the circumstances in which they can require a medical examination for applicants and employees

(C) Intends to ensure fair and accurate consumer reporting

(D) Prohibits employers from using neutral tests or selection procedures that can have an unintentionally discriminatory impact on people

(42) What is a straightforward method of announcing a job opening to the current employees working within an organization?

(A) Job bidding

(B) Job posting

(C) Succession planning

(D) Branding

(43) Which candidates can be recruited by advertising a job position using various available mediums?

(A) External candidates

(B) Internal candidates

(C) Targeted candidates

(D) None of the above

(44) There are multitudes of platforms on social media—both professional and casual—where employers can find __________.

(A) Part-time employees

(B) Temporary candidates

(C) Professional employees

(D) Potential candidates

(45) Which of the following is a dedicated platform where employers can connect with the labor market and vice versa?

(A) Instagram

(B) LinkedIn

(C) YouTube

(D) Pinterest

(46) How many types of employment applications are there?

(A) Two

(B) Three

(C) Four

(D) Five

(47) Which of the following tests are used to evaluate candidates' level of knowledge or skill when it comes to the jobs they have applied for?

(A) Aptitude tests

(B) Agility tests

(C) Cognitive ability tests

(D) Medical tests

(48) The goal of an effective orientation plan is to _____________.

(A) Reduce stress in the workplace

(B) Motivate employees

(C) Retain employees

(D) Make the adjustment process for the new employees as smooth as possible

(49) Which level of onboarding has all the four C's formally addressed within its orientation programs?

(A) First

(B) Second

(C) Third

(D) Fourth

(50) __________ is the lowest level of the onboarding process and refers to providing newly hired employees with basic knowledge about the organization.

(A) Clarification

(B) Compliance

(C) Culture

(D) Connection

(51) The fourth and final level of short-term outcomes is __________.

(A) Social integration

(B) Role clarity

(C) The knowledge of and fit within an organizational culture

(D) Self-efficacy

(52) Which of the following is/are a kind of onboarding outcome?

(A) Short-term outcomes and long-term outcomes

(B) Short-term outcomes and organizational outcomes

(C) Long-term outcomes

(D) Organizational outcomes

(53) It is essential that new employees feel welcomed and taken care of in their new workplace. The HR department should try to strategize tasks and meetings in a way that the new employees do not feel left out or isolated.

How can HR achieve this goal?

(A) By ensuring the presence of clear communication

(B) By putting employee assistance in writing

(C) By conducting regular check-ins

(D) By providing employees with appropriate attention

(54) When an organization needs to complete a project that is proving to be difficult or needs a side project done in relatively less time, ________ provides a great alternative.

(A) Job sharing

(B) Outsourcing

(C) Telecommuting

(D) Temporary workers

(55) Who is employed by a single agency that takes on the responsibility of screening and testing candidates before sending them to other organizations for a specific time?

(A) Contract worker

(B) Full-time worker

(C) Part-time worker

(D) Temporary worker

(56) Employment agencies and brokers assist ________ in finding jobs and managing payroll.

(A) Contract workers

(B) Temporary workers

(C) Interns

(D) Part-time workers

(57) With booming gig platforms and freelancing markets, organizations can benefit a lot by reaching out to __________.

(A) Temporary workers

(B) Part-time workers

(C) Independent contractors

(D) None of the above

(58) Which of the following programs are mostly targeted toward students or fresh graduates to give them experience in the field?

(A) Learning programs

(B) Training programs

(C) Internship programs

(D) Refresher programs

(59) It is the responsibility of __________ to work for the benefit of an organization and its brand but also be thoughtful in their approach to individual employees who have been loyal to their jobs.

(A) Managers

(B) HR professionals

(C) Employers

(D) Directors

(60) HR professionals need to be cautious because of the intricacies involved in __________.

(A) Cost management

(B) Autocratic management

(C) Democratic management

(D) Change management

(61) Which of the following is not a key point in successful change management?

(A) Recruitment

(B) Effective communication

(C) Administrative tasks

(D) Supporting employees

(62) Corporate restructuring is an intricate process that involves a lot of __________.

(A) Pay slips

(B) Printing

(C) Paperwork

(D) Reports

(63) __________ helps rehabilitate laid-off employees back into the workforce.

(A) Employee support

(B) Outplacement services

(C) Planning ahead

(D) Branding

Functional Area 03 | Learning and Development

(64) Meeting specific objectives or skills within a given period is the focus of ____________.

(A) Coaching

(B) Mentoring

(C) Training

(D) Testing

(65) The goals of mentoring and coaching are ____________.

(A) Mandatory

(B) Rigid

(C) Flexible

(D) None of the above

(66) Mentoring can help ____________.

(A) Individuals according to their specific needs

(B) Employees in their professional development

(C) Individuals gaining specific new skills

(D) Create flexibility in the learning process

(67) Coaching cannot __________.

(A) Increase both individual and team commitment to the organization

(B) Implement changes unless clear and measurable goals have been set beforehand

(C) Aid individuals in gaining specific skills

(D) Give individuals the freedom to learn what they want and teach them how to go about it

(68) ____________ familiarizes employees with the tools needed to generate a high-quality product.

(A) Team training

(B) Professional training

(C) Soft skills training

(D) Quality training

(69) Which of the following involves a formalized program and teams up recruits with an experienced employee to help new hires learn specific skills?

(A) Mentoring

(B) Employee orientation

(C) In-house training program

(D) Exterior training

(70) In which approach is a test used to see how effectively employees have recalled the material?

(A) The behavior evaluation method

(B) The reaction evaluation method

(C) The learning evaluation method

(D) The results evaluation method

(71) Which seating is best suited for small-group discussions?

(A) Classroom-style seating

(B) Banquet-style seating

(C) Chevron-style seating

(D) Conference-style seating

(72) __________ help inexperienced employees learn new skills in a scenario that is not dangerous for workers or the public.

(A) Socratic seminars

(B) Facilitations

(C) Case studies

(D) Simulations

(73) Which of the following makes HR professionals responsible for performing functions critical to an organization's success?

(A) The functional area

(B) Training and development

(C) Performance management

(D) Organizational structure

(74) Informing managers and supervisors about the evaluation process is the responsibility of __________.

(A) Managers

(B) Employees

(C) HR personnel

(D) None of the above

(75) ______________ is conducted by senior HR personnel.

(A) Career mapping

(B) Succession planning

(C) Training

(D) Organizational development

(76) A performance objective has _______ key components.

(A) Five

(B) Six

(C) Three

(D) Four

(77) What does ABCD stand for?

(A) Audience, behavior, condition, development

(B) Audience, behavior, consistency, degree

(C) Audience, behavior, context, degree

(D) Awareness, behavior, condition, development

(78) "According to the adult learning theory, adults are more independent and prefer self-directed methods of learning compared to instructor-led learning techniques."

Which assumption about adult learning theory does the quote refer to?

(A) Self-concept

(B) Individual-level training

(C) Experience

(D) Orientation and readiness to learn

(79) The HR department can provide development opportunities to current employees by ____________.

(A) Mapping tasks to competencies and establishing assessment metrics and standards of performance

(B) Evaluating career development opportunities, including employee interest in advancement and nontraditional careers

(C) Comparing an employee's formal and informal skill sets to selected competencies

(D) None of the above

(80) "Problems with materials, information and technology used to complete tasks or conduct work can lead to performance inefficiencies."

This quote refers to which category of productivity and performance dysfunction?

(A) Technological

(B) Behavioral

(C) Skills and knowledge

(D) Process-related

(81) What is the framework around which an organization operates, designs its goals and performs functions?

(A) Organizational development

(B) Organizational culture

(C) Organizational structure

(D) Organizational behavior

Functional Area 04 | Total Rewards

(82) Which of the following statements defines the concept of job evaluation?

(A) Job evaluation is the process used to determine the relative importance or worth of a job in an organization.

(B) Job evaluation is the process used to determine the compatibility of the employees in an organization.

(C) Job evaluation is the process used to determine the average salary of the employees within an organization.

(D) Job evaluation is the process used to measure monetary and nonmonetary compensation in an organization.

(83) Which of the following components is essential for setting the goals of a job evaluation?

(A) Systematic pay rate scale

(B) Comparative pay rate scale

(C) Average pay rate scales

(D) None of the above

(84) How many types of job evaluations are there?

(A) Three

(B) Two

(C) One

(D) Five

(85) Mr. Alex is working as an HR specialist in the corporate sector in Southern California. He is analyzing all the jobs in the area by considering specific sets of skills, traits, certificates, experiences and knowledge.

Which technique is Mr. Alex using for his job analysis?

(A) The analytical approach

(B) The nonanalytical approach

(C) The comprehensive approach

(D) The collective approach

(86) Mrs. Smith is working as an HR specialist in South Florida. She is evaluating the new job vacancies that will increase the employment rate in their office. After narrowing down the specific skills required for each job, she conducts a detailed analysis of the pay rates of each job.

What do you understand from this example?

(A) Mrs. Smith is using a nonanalytical approach for job evaluation.

(B) Mrs. Smith is using an analytical approach for job evaluation.

(C) Mrs. Smith is using both the analytical and the nonanalytical approaches for job evaluation.

(D) Mrs. Smith is using the comparative analytic approach for job evaluation.

(87) Job evaluation is only concerned with determining the ________ worth of the job within the organization compared to the _______ worth or the impact it has on the labor market.

(A) External, internal

(B) Internal, external

(C) Introvert, extrovert

(D) Extrovert, introvert

(88) Which of the following factors are relative to job worth?

(A) Duty, responsibility, salary

(B) Duty, responsibility, job accountability

(C) Responsibility, duty, pay rates

(D) Monetary compensation, responsibility, job accountability

(89) ______________ is the main motivation or purpose behind a job evaluation.

(A) Determining fair and equitable pay

(B) Determining the advantages of pay rates

(C) Measuring the credibility of pay rates

(D) Comparing pay rates

(90) Which of the following is not an objective of a job evaluation?

(A) Ranking jobs within the organization

(B) Developing an efficient and consistent/uniform system for assigning pay grades to each job

(C) Determining the internal worth of the job within the organization, as compared to the external worth or the impact it has on the labor market

(D) Ensuring there are no biases and prejudices in determining the pay grade system

(91) Identify the first step of the job evaluation process.

(A) Gathering relevant information about the job

(B) Determining job ranking

(C) Identifying jobs to be evaluated

(D) Selecting benchmark jobs

(92) Factors like mental and physical effort, time consumption, pressure, communication and concentration, leadership skills, educational qualifications, experience and job complexity are considered essential for job evaluation.

All of the above tie into ____________.

(A) Gathering relevant information about the job

(B) Determining job ranking

(C) Identifying jobs to be evaluated

(D) Selecting benchmark jobs

(93) David is working as an evaluator for Microsoft in California. During the first quarter of the year, he asks all the employees at Microsoft to fill out surveys. The collective information is much more detailed than he expects. He outlines the markers for a job evaluation and presents his findings in the next meeting. His boss is not impressed by the information and asks David to improve his working standards.

Imagine you are David. What is your reaction going to be?

(A) I will revise the collected information and prepare a new presentation.

(B) I will revise the survey and prepare a new presentation.

(C) Besides the survey, I will consider job descriptions, interviews and job description statements for the new presentation.

(D) I will redo my evaluation.

(94) After evaluating the credentials of a job, the next phase is to _________.

(A) Rank the job

(B) Rank the pay rates

(C) Rank the total rewards

(D) Rank the compensation benefits

(95) Zachariah is working as a job evaluator specialist at a multinational company. His boss asks him to evaluate the jobs within the organization; however, this is not possible. So, to make his life easier, Zachariah selects the common jobs within a single department and evaluates them.

In this situation, Zachariah is ____________.

(A) Gathering relevant information about the job

(B) Determining job ranking

(C) Identifying jobs to be evaluated

(D) Selecting benchmark jobs

(96) Most organizations consider ________ to collect information about salaries or wages.

(A) Job description statements

(B) Surveys

(C) Prerequisite information

(D) Newspaper or global newsfeed

(97) A survey is conducted using telephones, the Internet and newspapers. It collects information about wages and salaries.

This method of collecting information is known as a/an __________.

(A) Formal survey

(B) Informal survey

(C) Virtual survey

(D) Electronic survey

(98) Madison is the HR specialist of a construction business in Los Angeles. Her boss asks her to prepare a presentation on monetary and nonmonetary compensation for a new policy. He also asks her to conduct an evaluation of the company's eight departments. In total, the eight departments consist of 500+ employees.

Which of the following methods will be appropriate for collecting information from every employee?

(A) Preparing an electronic survey

(B) Asking each employee to fill out traditional printed surveys

(C) Conducting an informal survey

(D) Sending an email to everyone

(99) Companies must consider the external and internal environment of other organizations for ___________.

(A) Periodic reviews

(B) Feedback

(C) Job evaluations

(D) Pay grades

(100) External changes in the environment cause changes in the internal environment of the organization and affect ___________.

(A) Pay grades

(B) Compensation policy

(C) Total rewards

(D) Benefits

(101) Which of the following statements is not a true description of a formal survey?

(A) It is cost-effective.

(B) It provides detailed information.

(C) It allows HR to target various categories.

(D) It involves unstructured questions.

(102) The analytical method includes valuing a job on the basis of certain factors. This method is known as ________.

(A) Point ranking

(B) Factor comparison

(C) Pay-rate ranking

(D) Ranking

(103) In point ranking, there are certain points that are assigned to every job on the basis of the presence of factors such as pressure, education, experience and complexity.

Based upon these points, the jobs are ________.

(A) Ranked

(B) Disseminated

(C) Considered

(D) None of the above

(104) Mr. Chang is ranking each job by comparing it with other jobs using five universal factors common to all jobs.

He is using the ________ technique.

(A) Point ranking

(B) Factor comparison

(C) Pay rate ranking

(D) Ranking

(105) Which of the following is a nonanalytical method with low cost and higher subjectivity?

(A) Point ranking

(B) Factor comparison

(C) Pay-rate ranking

(D) Ranking

(106) In which of the following approaches is each job compared with every other job and assigned award points if found to be more valuable?

(A) Paired comparison

(B) Job grading

(C) Market pricing

(D) Ranking

(107) __________ is a technique in which similar categories of jobs are grouped together under one umbrella and paid equally.

(A) Paired comparison

(B) Job grading

(C) Market pricing

(D) Ranking

Functional Area 05 | Employee and Labor Relations

(108) Why are organizational values important?

(A) To understand the process of HR management

(B) To follow the organization's mission

(C) To lay a foundation for the company's objective

(D) To give birth to the organization's culture

(109) What is the definition of HR management?

(A) It is the process that is involved with hiring employees, training them, creating policies for them and dealing with their rewards.

(B) It is the process that is involved with training employees and keeping them satisfied.

(C) It is the process that is involved with advertising the need for new employees, choosing the right candidates and employing them.

(D) It is the process that is involved with hiring employees, negotiating with them and creating policies for them.

(110) What are the four main steps of staffing?

(A) Staffing plan development, recruitment, selection and policy creation

(B) Locating candidates, recruitment, retaining and creating policies

(C) Listing the recruits, developing a plan for staff, assigning duties to the staff and creating policies

(D) Interviewing, selecting, developing an organizational plan and creating policies

(111) What should managers consider when developing workplace policies?

(A) Dividing the workers according to their skills

(B) Including all workers together in a single group

(C) Being free of bias

(D) Deciding if there is a need for policies or not

(112) What does compensation and benefits administration involve?

(A) Rewarding and providing benefits to employees if they have contributed a great deal to the company above what was expected

(B) Compensating employees if there has been some sort of mistreatment

(C) Providing nonmonetary benefits to employees when needed

(D) Devising payment systems that reward employees for their services

(113) How can managers retain employees?

(A) By introducing more benefits for them

(B) By increasing salary packages

(C) By finding out why employees are leaving and rectifying the reasons

(D) By providing employees with a better work environment (air conditioners, childcare facilities, etc.)

(114) Why is dealing with employment laws important for employers?

(A) To ensure employee safety

(B) To stay up-to-date

(C) To retain employees

(D) To increase efficiency

(115) Besides an organization's internal factors, it is important for HR managers to also be aware of the external factors in an organization's environment.

What are some of these external factors?

(A) Globalization, health care costs, offshoring

(B) Offshoring, weather conditions, worker supply

(C) Government laws, diversity, business competition

(D) Demand for company's goods and services, market size, globalization

(116) Why is it necessary for an HR manager to have good communication skills?

(A) They allow HR managers to tackle threats and concerns from third parties.

(B) They allow HR managers to recruit the best talents for the company.

(C) They allow HR managers to help employees.

(D) They allow HR managers to set an example for employees.

(117) What is one skill that a manager must have in order to communicate properly?

(A) Flexibility

(B) Professionality

(C) Fairness

(D) Good writing skills

(118) Participatory management is one approach used to manage employees effectively.

In this approach, what do managers focus on?

(A) The task and the employees performing the task

(B) Encouraging teamwork and taking input from everyone

(C) Delegating tasks to employees

(D) Using a more people-oriented approach

(119) There are several ways managers can determine the best management style for the department.

Which of the following is not one of these ways?

(A) Following the situational leadership model

(B) Laying out guidelines and delegating tasks

(C) Using the autocratic style of management for a greater number of employees

(D) Utilizing the path-goal model

(120) Which of the following should an HR manager have?

(A) Links with stakeholders

(B) Accounting experience

(C) Quick responses

(D) Robust critical thinking skills

Test 2: Answers and Explanations

Functional Area 01 | Business Management

(1) (B) A mission statement.

A mission statement defines an organization's motivation and purpose. It states the contribution an organization aims to make in society and what differentiates it from competitors in the same industry.

(2) (D) Both (A) and (B).

A vision statement informs shareholders, partners and customers about the organization's long-term goals and aims.

(3) (A) The brand's vision.

"Everyone can be glamorous" is the vision the brand in question is working toward.

(4) (A) Prioritizing normal, routine tasks.

Cross-functional teams have the advantage of a systematic approach to smart decision-making, diversity in thought and a greater informational scope. Prioritizing normal, routine tasks is not necessarily an advantage of cross-functional teams because this can be done in non-cross-functional teams as well.

(5) (D) All of the above.

If leadership is missing and business objectives are poorly communicated, team members lose interest in the cross-functional project and continue to prioritize routine tasks, resulting in a performance-killing lack of accountability and commitment to the task. Lack of guidance and leadership may prevent teams from stepping out of their comfort zones and delivering expertise. Poor communication and interest in team building can cause problems between coworkers who may see each other as rivals instead of partners.

(6) (D) Someone willing to change and adapt when needed.

When approaching the task of team building, consider members who have the questioning skills to understand the unfamiliar area and the willingness to learn with an open mind, the ability to break down complex ideas and communicate them to other team members simply, the ability to teach and motivate people who do not belong to their team or department, and the capacity to accept mistakes and make improvements.

(7) (D) Software.

The availability of different communication tools can allow members of a group to establish a virtual office where all plans, progress and problems are shared. A software solution helps centralize data and allows team members to access it through mobile or desktop devices.

(8) (D) All of the above.

A virtual office can increase productivity, allow teams to collaborate without delays, strategize and plan remotely, and incur low technology costs as the need for servers and desktops declines.

(9) (C) Both (A) and (B).

Compensation and rewards are effective HR practices that help increase employee motivation and engagement. Similarly, critical feedback pushes employees to perform better as well. So organizations should ensure that employees understand both the incentives and the repercussions of their actions to deliver the highest performance standard.

(10) (D) All of the above.

The role of HR is to conduct recruiting, develop proactive plans that meet the organization's long- and short-term business objectives, provide training to new hires, administer benefit and compensation packages and ensure the implementation of the organization's policies and procedures.

(11) (A) Human resource management.

The acronym *HRM* stands for "human resource management."

(12) (B) HR.

The HR department is responsible for developing risk management plans aligned with company policies. Risk management is the process of identifying and preventing potential threats in a workplace.

(13) (A) Duty of care.

Risk management is also known as duty of care. Although no business can fully escape threats, organizations have a legal and moral obligation to develop risk management strategies to limit the extent of damage, ensuring the well-being and safety of those who perform for the organization.

(14) (D) All of the above.

Risk can affect any aspect of a business, such as recruitment, employee health and safety and compensation. So, HR needs to develop a strategy that covers all organizational bases and limits the effects of the risk on performance and organizational profitability.

(15) (D) All of the above.

HR and the business administration should develop various protocols to mitigate the risk of financial abuse, including multiple signatures on all financial documents, identifying authority for final financial transactions, etc. Stringent accounting procedures should also be established to identify fraud or theft.

(16) (A) Employees.

HR management is primarily concerned with the management of employees within organizations, focusing on policies and systems.

(17) (A) Location risks.

Location risks that threaten corporations include storm damage, earthquakes, fires, hurricanes, floods and other natural disasters.

(18) (D) All of the above.

Drug and alcohol abuse is a common human risk in the workplace. Keeping a check, developing behavior policies and urging employees to seek treatment are important to mitigate human risk. Furthermore, various insurance policies provide coverage for injury and drug abuse. Health-related delays can cause a loss of productivity and may hamper operations at the workplace. So, training backup personnel is critical to prevent loss of work when employees are absent due to illness.

(19) (D) Economic capital.

Economic capital is the financial amount needed to bear the impact of unexpected losses. It is derived from the organization's target debt rating.

(20) (A) The risk taken against the expected return.

Risk-adjusted return on capital evaluates the ROI according to the risk involved.

(21) (A) Core values.

Core values are guiding principles that represent an organization's beliefs, priorities and driving forces. These include creativity, loyalty and integrity. Core values set the standard for how the organization interacts with stakeholders, partners and customers.

(22) (B) A mission statement.

A mission statement describes the motivation and purpose of the business. It states the contribution an organization aims to make in society and what differentiates it from competitors in the same industry.

(23) (C) A vision statement.

An organization's vision statement informs the shareholders, partners and customers about what the organization wants to achieve as well as its long-term goals. It also guides the organization's efforts.

(24) (C) HR.

In most companies, HR is defined as the core competency that helps streamline the organization's processes.

(25) (D) Reviews uncertainties that may impact an organization's expenditures.

A cost risk analysis reviews uncertainties and risks that may impact a company's expenditures. It considers the different costs associated with a project (labor, materials, equipment, administration, etc.) and focuses on the uncertainties and risks that may affect these costs.

(26) (A) HR.

The HR department is responsible for tracking and monitoring risk by following up with parties involved to mitigate risks. It also identifies risks that may threaten business goals. It is the responsibility of the HR department to provide safety information and training to decrease risk.

(27) (B) A risk with extreme probability.

The four different risk levels are extreme probability, moderate probability, minor probability and minimal probability. A risk with the most extreme probability is most likely to occur.

(28) (A) Reliability analysis.

A reliability analysis measures the reliability and effectiveness of a project with the help of statistics. It studies the properties of measurement scales and the items that compose the scales.

(29) (B) Absenteeism.

The term *absenteeism* refers to failure to report to work. The definition itself hints at the failure of the organizational process.

(30) (A) Turnover.

Turnover rate is defined as the percentage of employees leaving a company over a certain period.

(31) (D) Risk transfer.

Risk transfer is moving the burden of risks, such as transferring the financial burden to the insurance company.

(32) (C) Attrition data.

A company's attrition rate is the rate at which people leave. Attrition data helps HR personnel identify reasons for leaving, positions worked and types of employees who are more likely to leave.

(33) (D) Five.

Strategic management usually consists of five steps: job analysis, staffing, training, performance management and employee rights.

(34) (C) Employee records.

The HR strategy pertains to managing human capital and performance to meet an organization's mission, values and goals. Thus, employee records are kept up to date. This strategy is critical to the success of a business, as employee behavior and performance largely impact business goals.

(35) (D) Cognitive abilities.

Core competencies do not include cognitive abilities. Core competencies help organizations focus on expanding their revenue through various methods. These competencies may include the use of technology in operation, manufacturing processes, the organization's culture, product characteristics, management of customer relationships, knowledge management and other aspects of an organization that are difficult to replicate.

Functional Area 02 | Talent Planning and Acquisition

(36) (A) Applies to any possible retaliation against an employee who acts against discrimination.

Title VII prohibits employment discrimination on the basis of race, color, sex, religion or sexual orientation. It also applies to any possible retaliation against an employee who acts against discrimination and wants to participate in an investigation or oppose any discriminatory practices.

(37) (D) Validity.

Validity refers to whether an instrument is measuring what it is intended to measure. It assesses whether a test is reliable and will allow a person to draw valid conclusions.

(38) (A) Consistent.

The recruitment process should be consistent, because if the process is biased or unfairly favors a specific demographic, it will violate Title VII of the Civil Rights Act and lead to HR missing the chance to employ talented individuals.

(39) (B) Legal validity.

Validity is a measure of whether a test accurately predicts performance. There are various subtypes of validity, including content validity, criterion-related validity and predictive validity, but legal validity is not a subtype.

(40) (C) Title I of the Americans with Disabilities Act.

Title I of the Americans with Disabilities Act does not allow any discrimination against people who have disabilities and applies to all private employers, as well as state and local governments.

(41) (C) Intends to ensure fair and accurate consumer reporting.

The purpose of the Fair Credit Reporting Act is to ensure that all information in consumer credit reports is accurate, fair and private. The act regulates how credit reporting agencies collect, access, use and share data.

(42) (B) Job posting.

Job posting is a straightforward method of announcing an opening to current employees working within an organization because it allows eligible employees to apply for a position as they would for any other job. To assess potential within the company, this method is often used before an external recruitment campaign is started.

(43) (A) External candidates.

External candidates can be recruited by advertising a job position using various available mediums, such as newspaper and radio advertisements, getting referrals from current employees or industry network colleagues, alumni network advertisements and walk-ins.

Internal and targeted candidates do not need to be advertised to, as they are already made aware of the openings in the organization through direct contact with recruiters.

(44) (D) Potential candidates.

Due to the vast access to information provided by social media, employers can now find potential candidates without conducting extensive recruitment campaigns.

(45) (B) LinkedIn.

LinkedIn is a platform where employers can connect with the labor market, attract new talent and share knowledge.

(46) (C) Four.

There are four types of employment applications: short-form, long-form, job-specific and weighted. Short-form employment applications provide a concise version of an organization's standard application for employment, while long-form employment applications require more detailed information from the candidates.

Job-specific employment applications are used when a large candidate pool is needed to be narrowed down for a particular position. Weighted employment applications allow employers to evaluate the candidates objectively by allotting relative weights to different sections of the applications.

(47) (A) Aptitude tests.

Aptitude tests are written or skill-based tests used to evaluate the level of knowledge or skill candidates possess regarding the jobs they have applied for.

(48) (D) Make the adjustment process for the new employees as smooth as possible.

The goal of an effective orientation plan is to make the adjustment process as smooth as possible for new employees. It aims to provide new employees with all the information they need to succeed. After recruitment, the orientation period is crucial because many employees may decide to leave the organization if they cannot adjust to the workplace.

(49) (C) Third.

Orientation programs at the third level of onboarding, compliance, clarification, culture and connection are all given their due importance and strategized accordingly.

(50) (B) Compliance.

Compliance is the lowest level of the onboarding process and refers to providing newly hired employees with basic knowledge about the organization, such as essential legal information and policy-related rules and regulations.

(51) (C) The knowledge of and fit within an organizational culture.

The final level of a short-term outcome is knowing and fitting within an organizational culture. It is related to employee loyalty as well as commitment, satisfaction and turnover.

(52) (A) Short-term outcomes and long-term outcomes.

Both short-term and long-term outcomes are a kind of onboarding process. Short-term outcomes aim to help new employees adjust to their job, while long-term outcomes are focused on the organization's bottom line.

(53) (D) By providing employees with appropriate attention.

By providing appropriate attention, HR can ensure that employees are not isolated or left out and feel welcomed and cared for in their new workplace.

(54) (B) Outsourcing.

Outsourcing is a great alternative for organizations that are facing project-related difficulties. For example, if a company needs to have a project done in less time, outsourcing the work is a more efficient option than doing it in-house.

(55) (D) Temporary worker.

An organization employs a contract worker on a project or fee basis. A full-time worker is employed by an organization to work standard hours, and a part-time worker is hired to work half of the standard hours in a day. None of these workers are hired by a third-party organization or single agency.

In comparison, a temporary worker is employed by a single agency that takes on the responsibility of screening and testing these candidates before sending them to other organizations for a specific time.

(56) (A) Contract workers.

Employment agencies and brokers help contract workers market their skills, find jobs and negotiate contracts with clients.

(57) (C) Independent contractors.

Organizations can reduce expenditures and uncertainty by reaching out to independent contractors for specific projects.

(58) (C) Internship programs.

Internship programs are mostly targeted toward students or fresh graduates to provide them with experience in a particular field. These programs are beneficial to trainees, young professionals and organizations, as they provide low-cost access to creative minds.

(59) (B) HR professionals.

HR professionals are responsible for working for the benefit of the company and its brand and for being considerate toward employees who have been loyal to their jobs.

(60) (D) Change management.

HR professionals need to be careful with their approach to change management because any new changes they introduce could lead to customer or revenue losses if not carefully considered. This is especially true when corporate restructuring involves significant cuts in the workforce or moves to other markets to serve some strategic need.

(61) (A) Recruitment.

Recruitment is not an aspect of business that influences change management. Effective communication, administrative tasks and employee support are important key points of successful change management.

(62) (C) Paperwork.

Paperwork is an integral part of the process of corporate restructuring. So, HR professionals need to make sure they are doing their due diligence when it comes to tying up any loose ends, as even a slight error could lead to severe repercussions.

(63) (B) Outplacement services.

Only outplacement services can help rehabilitate laid-off employees back into the workforce. These services offer both practical and mental support for employees and help them transition into their new jobs.

Functional Area 03 | Learning and Development

(64) (A) Coaching.

The goal of coaching is to achieve particular goals or learn new skills in a set amount of time. In contrast to mentoring, which is usually considerably more informal, a coaching session normally follows an already set plan with listed outcomes.

(65) (C) Flexible.

Mentoring and coaching goals are fluid and might vary over time if the protégé achieves particular objectives or learns new skills. For example, mentoring and coaching can be provided to top executives, entry-level employees, employees who have changed careers and other mentors or coaches.

(66) (B) Employees in their professional development.

Mentoring can help employees increase their understanding of the organizational structure and culture, improve their communication abilities, and assist them with networking and meeting new people. This all improves employees' personal development.

(67) (B) Implement changes unless clear and measurable goals have been set beforehand.

The goal of coaching is to ensure that particular objectives are met. However, coaching cannot induce changes unless clear and measurable goals have been established ahead of time.

(68) (D) Quality training.

Quality training familiarizes employees with the tools required to produce a high-quality product. For example, employees who are already familiar with CAD programs find it easier to render an image.

(69) (A) Mentoring.

Mentoring is a formalized program that pairs up recruits with an experienced employee to help them master specific skills. In contrast, exterior training is conducted in a seminar or conference and usually goes over the macro perspective of the job and organizational structure. It does not facilitate in-depth learning.

(70) (C) The learning evaluation method.

A test is utilized to see how well employees remembered the subject in the learning evaluation approach. A pretest/post-test comparative experimental design is used in this method. The test results of two groups, only one of which received training, are compared in this technique to determine effectiveness.

(71) (B) Banquet-style seating.

Banquet-style seating is ideal for small-group discussions, as it allows the audience members to interact with each other freely. Conference-style seating is ideal for presentations or lectures, and classroom-style seating is best suited for circumstances in which employees will view manuals and take notes. Chevron-style seating is also ideal for a larger audience. All of these seating styles are unsuitable for small gatherings.

(72) (D) Simulation.

Simulation training allows inexperienced employees to learn new skills safely.

(73) (A) The functional area.

HR professionals are required to complete all functional area tasks—such as payroll, recordkeeping and compliance—before doing anything else because these tasks have an immediate impact and are thus critical to organizational success.

(74) (C) HR personnel.

HR personnel are responsible for informing managers and supervisors about the evaluation process/program.

(75) (B) Succession planning.

Senior HR generalists or managers usually handle succession planning because they have a better understanding of people and their abilities. However, all HR professionals are responsible for assisting with the process.

(76) (D) Four.

A performance objective states the intended learning outcomes of a specified educational experience. It has four key components: target audience, behavior, degree and condition.

(77) (C) Audience, behavior, context, degree.

ABCD stands for audience, behavior, degree and context.

(78) (A) Self-concept.

Adult learning theory is composed of five assumptions. Self-concept assumption presumes that adults are more independent and prefer to learn independently.

(79) (B) Evaluating career development opportunities, including employee interest in advancement and nontraditional careers.

The job of HR is to provide training and opportunities to current employees. It can do this by identifying existing talent for training and development; evaluating prospects for career growth, including employee interest in advancement and nontraditional careers; and allocating resources to deliver development initiatives to internal audiences.

(80) (A) Technological.

Technological productivity and performance dysfunction can cause accessibility issues and hardware malfunctions, disrupt workflow and lead to performance inefficiencies.

(81) (C) Organizational structure.

The framework around which an organization operates, designs its objectives and executes a function is known as organizational structure. The success of corporate objectives and strategies is influenced by how an organizational structure is built.

Functional Area 04 | Total Rewards

(82) (A) Job evaluation is the process used to determine the relative importance or worth of a job in an organization.

Job evaluation is a process used to determine a job's relative importance or worth. It is essential to measure the credibility of a job by analyzing the compatible salary rates. This helps the organization select the right person for the position.

(83) (A) Systematic pay rate scale.

Organizations use a systematic pay rate scale for job evaluation. This scale helps the organization come up with compatible salary rates and nonmonetary compensation. The pay rate policy increases employee motivation and satisfaction.

(84) (B) Two.

Two types of job evaluations help organizations conduct job evaluations: the analytical approach and the nonanalytical job evaluation.

(85) (A) The analytical approach.

Mr. Alex is using an analytical approach to identify the basic skills required to get a job in the area. In an analytical approach, skills that define the nature of the job are measured.

(86) (C) Mrs. Smith is using both the analytical and the nonanalytical approaches for job evaluation.

The example states that Mrs. Smith is using a collective approach that covers both the analytical and nonanalytical approaches. She first considers specific skills required for the job (analytical approach). Then she compares the job with similar jobs in the market (nonanalytical approach).

(87) (B) Internal, external.

Job evaluation is only concerned with determining the internal worth of the job within the organization compared to the external worth or the impact it has on the labor market.

(88) (B) Duty, responsibility, job accountability.

The relative worth of a job is determined by three main factors: duty, responsibility and job accountability.

(89) (A) Determining fair and equitable pay.

The main purpose of job evaluation is to determine fair and equitable pay. It helps increase employee satisfaction, as employees are fairly paid for their services.

(90) (C) Determining the internal worth of the job within the organization, as compared to the external worth or the impact it has on the labor market.

The statement is a characteristic of job evaluations, while the rest of the statements are objectives of job evaluations.

(91) (C) Identifying jobs to be evaluated.

Identifying the jobs to be evaluated is the first step in the job evaluation system.

(92) (C) Identifying jobs to be evaluated.

Mental and physical effort, time consumption, pressure, communication and concentration, leadership skills, educational qualifications, experience and job complexity are factors that describe the jobs to be evaluated.

(93) (C) Besides the survey, I will consider job descriptions, interviews and job description statements for the new presentation.

The chief rejected David's presentation because it was incomplete. David included only the suggestions and recommendations made by the employees within the organization. This means that he was considering only internal facts while ignoring the external or market compatibility. Therefore, Option C is the right choice, as it targets the information gleaned from external resources.

(94) (A) Rank the job.

After completing the detailed evaluation of the job, the next step is ranking the job. Before ranking a job, a systematic scale must be used to place jobs in order of their importance to the organization.

(95) (D) Selecting benchmark jobs.

Zachariah selected the benchmark jobs from the organization's seven departments. His decision helped him establish categories and saved time.

(96) (B) Surveys.

Surveys are the traditional method of collecting data on wages or salaries. They can be formal or informal. The information collected helps the organization build a fair compensation package plan for its employees.

(97) (B) Informal survey.

Surveys that are conducted by telephone, Internet or newspaper fall into the category of informal surveys. They are semi-structured and give thorough information about the intended topic.

(98) (A) Preparing an electronic survey.

The most suitable option will be to prepare an electronic survey via Google or other software. A survey allows HR to collect information from every employee. It is cost-effective and more helpful for data interpretation than traditional surveys.

(99) (A) Periodic reviews.

Businesses must consider making deliberate changes in their internal and external environments, as these changes will help them become aware of what their workplace culture is like. This knowledge will help these companies perform appropriate periodic reviews.

(100) (A) Pay grades.

The constant changes in an organization's internal and external environment have a direct impact on pay grades. The monetary exchange keeps fluctuating, depending upon the change or shift in the organization's environment.

(101) (D) It involves unstructured questions.

This is not a true description of a formal survey. These surveys consist of structured questions that follow a chronological pattern.

(102) (A) Point ranking.

Point ranking is an approach in which the value of each job is determined by the presence of certain factors, like time consumption, pressure, education, experience and complexity. Each of these factors is assigned certain points. High-scoring jobs are ranked higher.

(103) (A) Ranked.

The point-ranking approach helps build job rankings that define the job status.

(104) (B) Factor comparison.

Mr. Chang is using a factor comparison. This is an analytical method used to evaluate the credibility of each job.

(105) (D) Ranking.

Ranking is a nonanalytical technique that is low cost and subjective in nature.

(106) (A) Paired comparison.

In the paired comparison approach, each job is compared with every other job and assigned reward points if found to be more valuable.

(107) (B) Job grading.

Job grading is a technique in which similar categories are grouped under one umbrella and paid equally. This technique makes paying easier.

Functional Area 05 | Employee and Labor Relations

(108) (D) To give birth to the organization's culture

Organizational values refer to the core ethics or principles that an organization abides by. These organizational values are important for all companies and give birth to their culture.

(109) (A) It is the process that is involved with hiring employees, training them, creating policies for them and dealing with their rewards.

HR management is the process of employing candidates, training them to hone their skills and traits, creating policies that keep them satisfied and motivated and providing them with compensation and rewards.

(110) (A) Staffing plan development, recruitment, selection and policy creation.

Staffing is the process of hiring an employee. It has four steps: staffing plan development, which helps decide the number of individuals to be employed in light of income assumptions; recruitment, which involves locating candidates; selection, which involves interviewing and negotiating salary; and the development of workplace policies.

(111) (C) Being free of bias.

Managers need to be impartial and free of bias when designing workplace policies, as these policies are crucial. They serve as guidelines that allow the smooth running of operations and the avoidance of subjectivity.

(112) (D) Devising payment systems that reward employees for their services.

HR managers need to administer employee compensation and benefits. They are responsible for coming up with payment systems that reward employees for their services. These rewards/compensation packages can be either monetary or nonmonetary.

(113) (C) By finding out why employees are leaving and rectifying the reasons.

Employees may leave the company for several reasons. A great way an HR manager can retain employees is by finding out the reasons employees are leaving the organization and rectifying them to ensure retention. Exit interviews can help managers find out the reasons behind turnover.

(114) (B) To stay up-to-date.

If managers are unaware of laws that may influence the business, they are likely to run into many challenges. Therefore, they must stay up-to-date with these laws.

(115) (A) Globalization, health care costs, offshoring.

Some of the external factors that managers should be aware of include globalization and offshoring, changes in laws pertaining to employment, health care costs, changing workforce demographics, relevant technologies being used, layoffs and downsizing, diversity in the workforce and using social networking to keep employees informed and aware.

(116) (C) They allow HR managers to help employees.

Managers need to have good communication skills not only to address problems but also to become aware of them immediately. This way, an HR manager can efficiently help employees if needed.

(117) (D) Good writing skills.

Managers with strong writing skills are not only able to quickly document important data regularly but are also able to analyze and understand previous records. Moreover, they can keep themselves aligned with the business's strategic plan.

(118) (A) The task and the employee performing the task.

Both task-oriented and people-oriented management are incorporated into participatory management. Managers who take this approach provide support, input and task assistance as needed; as a result, the emphasis is on both the task and the worker performing it.

(119) (C) Using the autocratic style of management for a greater number of employees.

Out of all the options, only Option C does not state one of the ways managers can determine management style. Path-goal is one way managers can find a leadership style that defines the goals to be achieved. Situational leadership is one of the best ways of determining management style. It also states that if workers do not have the necessary skills to finish a job on their own, managers can lay out guidelines for them and then delegate tasks.

(120) (D) Robust critical thinking skills.

Good HR managers must possess robust critical thinking skills. They must also have knowledge of laws pertaining to employment, the ability to draft short- and long-term strategic plans, good decision-making skills and computer skills.

Test 3: Questions

Functional Area 01 | Business Management

(1) Key figures that help organizations track their human capital and measure how effective their HR initiatives are known as ___________.

(A) HR diagnostics

(B) HR analytics

(C) HR metrics

(D) HR data

(2) A company's vision statement includes its ___________.

(A) Long-term goals

(B) Ambitions

(C) Driving force

(D) All of the above

(3) Which of the following is a long-term outcome a business wants to achieve?

(A) Core competency

(B) Core values

(C) Corporate goals

(D) None of the above

(4) An example of risk avoidance would be ____________.

(A) Buying insurance

(B) Keeping possessions safely locked away

(C) Installing security alarms

(D) Both (B) and (C)

(5) Cross-functional teams usually end up a failure because ____________.

(A) Teammates see each other as rivals instead of partners

(B) Employees prioritize routine tasks over team tasks

(C) There's improper guidance about job tasks

(D) All of the above

(6) Which of the following models is used to develop effective corporate goals?

(A) 51 HR metrics

(B) 8-box

(C) SMART

(D) HR value chain

(7) The advantage of a virtual office for cross-functional teams is the ________.

(A) Ability to share work progress remotely

(B) Ability to be an alternative for communication

(C) Ability to be connected over a long distance

(D) Both (A) and (C)

(8) ______________ is a service performed by HR.

(A) Accounting

(B) Purchasing

(C) Both (A) and (B)

(D) Employment planning

(9) The process of analyzing, forecasting and planning supply and demand; assessing gaps; and determining talent management interventions to ensure that an organization has the right people is known as ______________.

(A) Workforce planning

(B) Employment planning

(C) Strategic management

(D) None of the above

(10) The HR department is responsible for which of the following?

(A) Total rewards

(B) HR development

(C) Strategic management

(D) All of the above

(11) The ___________ should meet the purpose of the organization established in the strategic planning process.

(A) Business plan

(B) Employee plan

(C) HR plan

(D) All of the above

(12) Risk mitigation, risk safety and training are the responsibilities of the _____________.

(A) Research and development department

(B) HR department

(C) Accounts and finance department

(D) IT department

(13) Workforce planning is also known as _____________.

(A) Manpower planning

(B) HR planning

(C) Both (A) and (B)

(D) None of the above

(14) Which of the following is most likely a core competency?

(A) Consistently high-quality work

(B) Incomparable value

(C) Ceaseless innovation

(D) All of the above

(15) Core competencies are the __________ in an organization.

(A) Differences

(B) Similarities

(C) Strengths

(D) None of the above

(16) What kind of data helps HR determine how long employees worked before leaving, their reasons for departure, the positions worked and the types of employees who left?

(A) Cumulative data

(B) Analytical data

(C) Attrition data

(D) None of the above

(17) Which of the following departments is responsible for making risk assessment protocols?

(A) Accounting and finance

(B) Leadership and HR

(C) HR and management

(D) Management and production

(18) An organization's ability to keep its employees is known as

___________.

(A) Turnover

(B) Retention

(C) Absenteeism

(D) None of the above

(19) A good example of a human risk is ___________.

(A) Intoxication during work hours

(B) Injury due to a work assignment

(C) Injury due to a natural disaster

(D) None of the above

(20) Which of the following examples best explains location risk?

(A) Refusal to get treated for substance abuse and then showing up to work

(B) Drug abuse during work

(C) Both (A) and (B)

(D) Building damage due to an earthquake

(21) Advising construction workers to use proper safety gear is an example of

___________.

(A) Risk transfer

(B) Risk avoidance

(C) Risk reduction

(D) Risk shifting

(22) __________ is a step of risk resolution.

(A) Rehearse

(B) Adapt

(C) Eradicate

(D) Reduce

(23) The ranking of risks on an appropriate scale, such as frequency and/or severity, is known as _____________.

(A) Risk prioritization

(B) Risk mitigation

(C) Risk assessment

(D) Risk planning

(24) Which of the following steps is a part of risk management control?

(A) Risk management planning

(B) Risk resolution

(C) Risk monitoring

(D) All of the above

(25) The _____________ direct(s) the message toward an organization's workforce, informing them about the goals and direction of the company.

(A) Mission statement

(B) Vision statement

(C) Core values

(D) Corporate goals

(26) A company's strategic plans and objectives are based on its _____________.

(A) Core values

(B) Vision statement

(C) Mission statement

(D) Core competencies

(27) Which of the following is an example of embezzlement?

(A) Fake payments

(B) Forged signatures

(C) Stolen customer data

(D) All of the above

(28) The core values of an organization ____________ with the changes in business processes or product lines.

(A) Remain constant

(B) Always change

(C) Sometimes change

(D) None of the above

(29) The members of a cross-functional team are responsible for _____________.

(A) Developing new products

(B) Enhancing customer relationships

(C) Improving organizational performance

(D) All of the above

(30) What does the acronym KPI stand for?

(A) Key performance index

(B) Key performative index

(C) Key performative indicators

(D) Key performance indicators

(31) In a cross-functional collaboration, the key to securing optimal performance and achieving goals is establishing a proactive _______________ that caters to all questions, concerns, progress, plans and strategies.

(A) System of management

(B) System of communication

(C) System of trust

(D) All of the above

(32) Which of the following groups is responsible for maintaining operations, following OSHA guidelines and providing appropriate training to the staff?

(A) The HR department

(B) Employees

(C) Management

(D) Security

(33) Cross-functional projects benefit from ____________.

(A) Decision-making and process development

(B) Regular updates to the C-suite and stakeholders to implement feedback

(C) The identification of opportunities and challenges

(D) All of the above

(34) Measuring staff sick day leaves is an example of ____________.

(A) HR diagnosis

(B) HR analytics

(C) HR metrics

(D) HR data

(35) It is common in organizations to experience promotions of underperforming peers.

Which of the following ensures deserving employees receive fair commissions?

(A) A data-centered way of promotion

(B) Traditional commissions

(C) Both (A) and (B)

(D) None of the above

Functional Area 02 | Talent Planning and Acquisition

(36) Which of the following acts prohibits an employer from asking any questions related to an applicant's disability or requesting a medical examination until a conditional job offer has been made?

(A) Title V of the Civil Rights Act

(B) Title I of the Americans with Disabilities Act

(C) Title VII of the Civil Rights Act

(D) The Age Discrimination in Employment Act

(37) When recruiting, employers must select and administer which of the following tests, with results that accurately reflect applicants' skills and aptitudes rather than their impairments?

(A) Employment

(B) Personality

(C) Physical ability

(D) Skills

(38) Under which act is it unlawful to put age limitations on apprenticeship programs unless these limitations are validated due to certain exceptions?

(A) The Age Discrimination in Employment Act

(B) Title V of the Civil Rights Act

(C) Title I of the Americans with Disabilities Act

(D) Title VII of the Civil Rights Act

(39) Employers must tell applicants that they will be using the information in their consumer report in the decision-making process. This notice must be in writing and in a stand-alone format.

Which of the following acts requires employers to provide written notices?

(A) The Age Discrimination in Employment Act

(B) The Fair Credit Reporting Act

(C) Title I of the Americans with Disabilities Act

(D) Title VI of the Civil Rights Act

(40) To attain _______________, an employer must certify to the company that the applicant has been notified and granted permission.

(A) A recruitment report

(B) A turnover report

(C) An applicant's consumer report

(D) A retention report

(41) The Age Discrimination in Employment Act prohibits employers from using ___________.

(A) Physical ability tests

(B) Personality tests

(C) Employment tests

(D) Neutral tests

(42) Employees who are already working in an organization are known as _________.

(A) External candidates

(B) Targeted candidates

(C) Internal candidates

(D) None of the above

(43) Employees are welcome to show interest in ___________ at any time.

(A) Job postings

(B) Job bidding

(C) Succession planning

(D) Job sharing

(44) Employers must keep the _____________ process streamlined and fair.

(A) Job posting

(B) Recruitment

(C) Job bidding

(D) Succession planning

(45) Which of the following is not a medium for recruiting external candidates?

(A) Unprofessional organizations

(B) Job fairs

(C) Walk-ins

(D) Radio advertisements

(46) __________ are a shorter version of an organization's standard application for employment.

(A) Job-specific employment applications

(B) Long-form employment applications

(C) Short-form employment applications

(D) Weighted employment applications

(47) Which of the following tests is conducted to ascertain a candidate's physical capabilities and must be related to the job the candidate has applied for?

(A) An aptitude test

(B) A medical test

(C) A cognitive ability test

(D) An agility test

(48) _______________ are used when a large candidate pool needs to be narrowed down for a particular position.

(A) Weighted employment applications

(B) Short-form employment applications

(C) Long-form employment applications

(D) Job-specific employment applications

(49) ______________ allow employers to evaluate candidates objectively by allotting relative weights to different sections of the application.

(A) Long-form employment applications

(B) Short-form employment applications

(C) Weighted employment applications

(D) Job-specific employment applications

(50) _______ assess candidates' intelligence or other cognitive skills that are relevant to the position they have applied for.

(A) Cognitive ability tests

(B) Aptitude tests

(C) Agility tests

(D) Medical tests

(51) Which of the following interviews is more structured and has a consistent pattern of interviewing across all candidates?

(A) Non-directive interviews

(B) Directive interviews

(C) Stress interviews

(D) None of the above

(52) A behavior-based interview is _________.

(A) Focused on candidates' behavioral characteristics, as well as their skills and knowledge.

(B) A way to put candidates in an orchestrated high-stress situation

(C) Relatively unstructured and gives candidates a chance to control the interview process

(D) More structured and has a consistent pattern of interviewing across all candidates

(53) After testing and interviews, which of the following procedures is conducted before any final candidate is selected for the position?

(A) Screening applications

(B) Medical examinations

(C) Regular check-ins

(D) Background checks

(54) Which of the following tests can be employed only when it is relevant to the job being applied for?

(A) A simulation test

(B) A medical test

(C) A personality test

(D) A work sample test

(55) Almost half of the new hires for senior positions end up failing within __________ months of taking on new positions.

(A) 16 months

(B) 17 months

(C) 18 months

(D) 19 months

(56) Different organizations have different approaches to the ____________ process.

(A) Onboarding

(B) Recruitment

(C) Placement

(D) Evaluation

(57) About half of all workers working on an hourly basis end up leaving new jobs within the __________.

(A) First 110 days

(B) First 120 days

(C) First 130 days

(D) None of the above

(58) In _____________, a new employee goes through the learning process without any explicit instruction from the organization.

(A) Social onboarding

(B) Formal onboarding

(C) Informal onboarding

(D) Talent onboarding

(59) In which of the following is level-specific job-related knowledge given to new employees?

(A) Connection

(B) Culture

(C) Compliance

(D) Clarification

(60) _____________ refers to covering the compliance and clarification elements in detail and having some culture and connection mechanisms put in place.

(A) High-potential onboarding

(B) Passive onboarding

(C) Proactive onboarding

(D) None of the above

(61) Employees' understanding of their roles and expectations within an organization refers to _____________.

(A) Social integration

(B) Knowledge of the organizational culture

(C) Self-efficacy

(D) Role clarity

(62) Which of the following methods is cost-effective and can be used by organizations when they are looking for a particular skill set needed for the time being but not regularly?

(A) Temporary workers

(B) Internship programs

(C) Part-time employment

(D) Contract workers

(63) __________ occurs when there is a change in a company's vision or strategy.

(A) Cost restructuring

(B) Corporate restructuring

(C) Repositioning restructuring

(D) None of the above

Functional Area 03 | Learning and Development

(64) Which of the following aligns different parts of a business and allows them to reach maximum performance?

(A) Organizational behavior

(B) Organizational culture

(C) Organizational structure

(D) Organizational leadership

(65) ____________ aligns employees and works according to specialization.

(A) Functional structure

(B) Divisional structure

(C) Organizational structure

(D) None of the above

(66) “It is the most complicated organizational structure because it requires employees to report to multiple leaders.”

What does this quote refer to?

(A) Functional structure

(B) Matrix structure

(C) Divisional structure

(D) Flatarchy structure

(67) The efficiency and credibility of an organization’s learning program are measured by ____________.

(A) Return on investment.

(B) Return on equity

(C) Return on asset

(D) Return on capital

(68) “Adult learners are more engaged in a learning experience that can be practically implemented. The knowledge that is implemented in the form of a task is more readily accepted than conceptual information that is not immediately required.”

Which assumption of adult learning theory does the quote refer to?

(A) Orientation and readiness to learn

(B) Self-concept

(C) Experience

(D) Motivation to learn

(69) ADDIE is an acronym for ______________.

(A) Analyze, design, develop, internal and external

(B) Analyze, develop, design, implement and evaluate

(C) Analyze, design, develop, implement and evaluate

(D) None of the above

(70) As ______________, HR professionals are responsible for identifying performance objectives and developing and ranking learning activities.

(A) Designers

(B) Writers

(C) Task analysts

(D) Program designers

(71) In which of the following phases are learners trained and given information about a product and how to use it?

(A) The evaluation phase

(B) The implementation phase

(C) The developmental phase

(D) The design phase

(72) "HR professionals are required to manage and grow organizational talent to benefit the company. Different development models should be designed to identify high performers to ensure they are given increased responsibility to maximize their potential and utility to the organization."

Which of the following concepts does this quote refer to?

(A) Implementing training

(B) Career mapping

(C) Talent management

(D) None of the above

(73) In ____________ training, the entire organization or one particular department within the organization is focused on preparing employees for expected future needs and/or goals.

(A) Task level

(B) Organizational level

(C) Individual level

(D) None of the above

(74) __________ begins by identifying the desired outcome or goal, gathering data relevant to that particular case.

(A) Design

(B) Development

(C) Implementation

(D) Analysis

(75) _______________ allow employees to gain knowledge and experience by going through real-life situations.

(A) Experiential training methods

(B) Passive training methods

(C) Active training methods

(D) Instructor-led training methods

(76) _____________ is best suited for situations where employees will be reading manuals and taking notes.

(A) Theater-style seating

(B) Conference-style seating

(C) Classroom-style seating

(D) U-shaped seating

(77) ___________ provides employees with the necessary abilities to take on management positions.

(A) Team training

(B) Managerial training

(C) Safety training

(D) Professional training

(78) __________ pairs amateur employees with a more experienced employee to help them specialize in certain skills.

(A) Vestibule training

(B) Job-swapping training

(C) Job-shadowing training

(D) On-the-job coaching

(79) GROW is an acronym for __________.

(A) Goals, realities, complete, wrap-up

(B) Goals, retention, choices, wrap-up

(C) Goals, realities, choices, wrap-up

(D) None of the above

(80) Which of the following is not a stage of the GROW model?

(A) Determining objectives

(B) Investigating reality

(C) Generating options

(D) Systems and selling

(81) __________ help improve employees' technical and soft skills.

(A) Training programs

(B) Performance appraisals

(C) Salaries and benefits

(D) Succession planning

Functional Area 04 | Total Rewards

(82)__________ is a monetary package a company gives to its employees in return for their services.

(A) Total rewards

(B) Total cost

(C) Total package

(D) Total exchange

(83) How do businesses or companies compensate for the services of their employees?

(A) By giving them medical health care facilities

(B) By appreciating their efforts

(C) By conducting monetary and nonmonetary exchanges

(D) By giving them promotions

(84) Businesses compensate their employees with ___________.

(A) Pay compensation

(B) Total rewards

(C) Monetary and nonmonetary remuneration

(D) Total package

(85) The purpose of total rewards is ________________.

(A) Recruitment, holding and persuading

(B) Recruitment, hiring and selecting

(C) Motivation, perception and persuasion

(D) Retirement, recruitment and motivation

(86) Which of the following statements is not true for a total rewards package?

(A) Companies set huge budgets for total rewards packages to improve their employees' motivation and satisfaction levels.

(B) Designing a total rewards package is one of HR's critical strategies.

(C) Total rewards can be in the form of monetary and nonmonetary remuneration.

(D) Total rewards increase employee dissatisfaction and increase trustworthiness.

(87) Non-cash compensation is closely linked to the concept of intrinsic reward, while cash compensation is closely linked to the concept of extrinsic reward.

What is the right order of intrinsic and extrinsic rewards?

(A) Self-satisfaction – Self-esteem

(B) Self-esteem – Self-satisfaction

(C) Self-confidence – Self-satisfaction

(D) Self-reliance – Self-esteem

(88) Andrea is working as an HR manager in London's corporate sector. She performed very well last year, and her career prospects were acknowledged by the company. On the basis of her extraordinary performance, she was given the "Best Employee of the Year" award.

This example defines the benefits of which type of total rewards package?

(A) Monetary compensation

(B) Nonmonetary compensation

(C) Extrinsic motivation

(D) Intrinsic motivation

(89) Which of the following theories explains the significance of nonmonetary compensation?

(A) Maslow's Hierarchy of Needs and McClelland's Acquired Needs Theory

(B) Maslow's Hierarchy of Needs and Social Needs Theory

(C) McClelland's Acquired Needs Theory and James Lang Theory of Emotions

(D) Social Need Theory and Selective Component Theory

(90) What is the aim of a compensation package plan?

(A) Satisfying company needs

(B) Satisfying employee needs

(C) Satisfying HR needs

(D) Satisfying monetary needs

(91) Telecommuting, on-site childcare and flex time are examples of nontraditional work-life benefits. These benefits are a type of

_______________.

(A) Monetary compensation

(B) Nonmonetary compensation

(C) Compensation package plan

(D) Total rewards plan

(92) Due to Maria's relentless work ethic, her company earned $1 million from the conclusion of her project. The company appreciated her efforts and offered her a bonus and a free vacation.

Which of the following kinds of compensation did Maria receive?

(A) Nonmonetary compensation

(B) Total rewards compensation

(C) Monetary compensation

(D) None of above

(93) Which of the following categories is suitable for explaining nonmonetary compensation benefits?

(A) Psychological – Medical – Emotional

(B) Psychological – Medical – Cognitive

(C) Psychological – Medical – Lifestyle

(D) Psychological – Medical – Social benefits

(94) Why are employee benefits designed by companies?

(A) Employee benefits help build a sense of community and support among employees.

(B) Employment benefit plans show that employee efforts are being rewarded either by monetary or nonmonetary compensation.

(C) Employee benefits help employees pay more attention to their work.

(D) All of the above.

(95) Health, handicap and extra security—just like educational cost repayment, schooling help and retirement benefits—are examples of ____________.

(A) Non-cash compensation

(B) Cash compensation

(C) Total rewards compensation

(D) Pay package compensation

(96) ____________ are the most common type of nonmonetary compensation.

(A) Benefits

(B) Compensation

(C) Pay tax

(D) Total rewards

(97) Siri is working as a recruitment officer in Los Angeles. She is satisfied with the job environment at her office. Her company provides its employees with fitness programs, free movie tickets, travel facilities, free lunch at the workplace and many more benefits. Siri states that as soon the company initiated these plans, there was a considerable increase in hiring.

This is an example ____________.

(A) Time off

(B) Fringe benefits

(C) Total benefits

(D) Nonmonetary benefits

(98) In France, a worker is allowed to have __________ of paid time off.

(A) Five weeks

(B) Four weeks

(C) Seven weeks

(D) One week

(99) Mr. Alex works at a rehabilitation center in Israel. Working with some of the community is always difficult for him, but he is satisfied as his manager lets him off for Christmas, Thanksgiving and New Year.

In this example, Alex's manager is providing which of the following non-compensation benefits?

(A) Paid holidays

(B) Sick leave

(C) Paid time off

(D) Paid vacation

(100) An average person in the United States is provided with how many days of paid sick leave?

(A) 8.5

(B) 8.4

(C) 8.2

(D) 8.3

(101) To design an incentive program, an HR specialist must consider two important measures. What are they?

(A) Analyze the benefits and the drawbacks of the incentives

(B) Analyze the economic status of the company

(C) Analyze the drawbacks of the incentive plan

(D) Analyze the benefits of the incentive plan

(102) Who is in charge of deciding the nature of incentives?

(A) The HR manager

(B) Upper management

(C) Both (A) and (B)

(D) Headhunters

(103) Which of the following is a feature of non-cash rewards?

(A) They are memorable and emotional in nature.

(B) They are broadly acknowledged and known to increase employees' self-esteem.

(C) They are nonmonetary compensation.

(D) Both (A) and (B).

(104) Employers provide day care facilities so that employees do not have to worry about their children's needs.

This is known as __________.

(A) Monetary compensation

(B) Nonmonetary compensation

(C) Total rewards

(D) Pay package

(105) Consider a hypothetical case of two companies named A and B. Company A provides its employees with gym memberships, and it is mandatory for all employees to make use of the gym facilities. Company B, meanwhile, does not provide its employees with gym memberships. The annual progress reports of companies A and B were analyzed, and the performance of employees from company A was higher compared to the employees of company B.

What do you understand from the following case?

(A) Gym memberships help employees earn more.

(B) Going to the gym boosts employees' physical and mental well-being.

(C) The gym does not have an overall impact on the physical health of employees.

(D) Companies should not include gym memberships in their nonmonetary compensation plan, as they're a waste of time.

(106) What are the psychological benefits of a gym membership?

(A) Improved employee satisfaction

(B) Better job performance

(C) Increased motivation

(D) None of the above

(107) Which of the following statements justifies the compulsory addition of nonmonetary compensation in a company?

(A) Nonmonetary compensation is effective at increasing employee satisfaction and motivation.

(B) Nonmonetary compensation has minimum expenses.

(C) Nonmonetary compensation does not encourage intrinsic and extrinsic motivation.

(D) Nonmonetary compensation includes cash back, bonuses and salaries.

Functional Area 05 | Employee and Labor Relations

(108) A company's goal should be to focus on ______________.

(A) Designing and encouraging

(B) Development and appraisal

(C) Selection and designing

(D) Encouraging and selection

(109) __________ empowers the employee life cycle and guarantees that the transition into each stage is obvious and organized.

(A) The board of directors

(B) HR

(C) The CEO

(D) None of the above

(110) How many stages are there in the employee life cycle?

(A) Three

(B) Four

(C) Five

(D) Six

(111) Getting referrals from experts/professionals in the field is one of the best methods of ____________.

(A) Branding

(B) Hiring

(C) Retention

(D) Onboarding

(112) Customer empathy, ownership, transparency, team spirit and social responsibility are examples of __________.

(A) Diversity

(B) Job descriptions

(C) Values

(D) None of the above

(113) The process of bringing new staff up to speed is called __________.

(A) Recruitment

(B) Branding

(C) Onboarding

(D) Development

(114) ___________ happens when a current position has opened or a new position has been created in an organization.

(A) Hiring

(B) Onboarding

(C) Development

(D) Retention

(115) Which of the following is caused by either performance issues or changing company requirements?

(A) Voluntary exits

(B) Alumni networking

(C) Downsizing

(D) Involuntary exit

(116) Which of the following stages is critical in the employee life cycle?

(A) The onboarding stage

(B) The development stage

(C) The retention stage

(D) The recruitment stage

(117) HR can increase employee retention and reduce turnover by ____________.

(A) Hiring correct personnel and creating positive work relationships with coworkers

(B) Offboarding employees

(C) Sharing profits with employees

(D) Hiring appropriate personnel and offering them retirement benefits

(118) Which of the following serves as a platform for managing and delivering online training content in various formats?

(A) The performance management system

(B) The learning management system

(C) The human resource system

(D) The training development system

(119) Conferences, seminars and lunch-and-learns are all good options for __________.

(A) Social learning

(B) External learning

(C) Logical learning

(D) Physical learning

(120) ___________ must be included in the conversation if companies want to build a strong and forward-thinking culture.

(A) Employees

(B) Managers

(C) Directors

(D) Alumni

Test 3: Answers and Explanations

Functional Area 01 | Business Management

(1) (C) HR metrics.

HR metrics are key figures that help organizations track their human capital and measure how effective their HR initiatives are.

(2) (D) All of the above.

An organization's vision statement informs the shareholders, partners and customers about the organization's driving force and the best practices to accomplish its goals. It communicates what the organization wants to become and its long-term goals.

(3) (C) Corporate goals.

Corporate goals define how an organization will achieve all that is stated in the strategic planning process in the long term. They also describe what a company wants to be in the future.

(4) (B) Keeping possessions safely locked away.

The process of eliminating potential hazards that may damage a project or disrupt an operation is called risk avoidance.

(5) (D) All of the above.

Cross-functional teams fail because of a lack of guidance, loss of interest in the task, rivalry between partners, the prioritization of routine tasks over team tasks and inadequate leadership—all of which lead to a performance-killing lack of accountability and commitment to the task.

(6) (C) SMART.

The SMART model is used to develop effective corporate goals. The acronym SMART stands for specific, measurable, achievable, realistic and time-based.

(7) (D) Both (A) and (C).

The availability of different communication tools can allow members of a group to establish a virtual office where all plans, progress and problems are shared. A software solution helps centralize data and allows employees to access it through mobile or desktop devices.

(8) (D) Employment planning.

The HR department uses employment planning to establish the best candidate criteria for different roles, conduct risk assessments and implement organizational policies.

(9) (A) Workforce planning.

Workforce planning is the process of analyzing, forecasting and planning supply and demand; assessing gaps; and determining target talent management interventions to ensure that an organization has the right people.

(10) (D) All of the above.

The HR department has seven functions. It is responsible for developing strategic plans for achieving the organization's long and short term goals, recruiting employees, training new hires, administering benefits and compensation packages, implementing policy, aligning the rights and needs of employees with the goals and objectives of the organization, and conducting risk assessments.

(11) (A) Business plan.

The business plan should outline the purpose of an organization and the goals established in the strategic planning process.

(12) (B) HR department.

The HR department in an organization is responsible for providing training to new hires, reducing the likelihood of risks and ensuring safety.

(13) (C) Both (A) and (B).

Workforce planning is also known as manpower planning or HR planning. The HR department uses it to establish the best candidate criteria for different roles.

(14) (D) All of the above.

Core competencies are an organization's strengths that set a company apart from the rest. They help organizations focus on expanding their revenue through various methods. Core competencies include consistent innovation, successful marketing, great customer service and formidable size and buying power.

(15) (C) Strengths.

Core competencies are the unique standing points of an organization; they help the organization develop a strategy that focuses on areas of particular strength.

(16) (C) Attrition data.

Attrition data helps HR determine the length of time employees work at the company before leaving, the reasons for their departure, the positions they worked in and the types of employees who left.

(17) (B) Leadership and HR.

Generally, HR and the leadership are the departments responsible for developing risk assessment protocols, but designated teams may carry out implementation.

(18) (B) Retention.

Employee retention refers to an organization's ability to retain its employees. For example, an organization may retain its employees by offering them benefits.

(19) (A) Intoxication during work hours.

Intoxication during work hours leaves employees unable to work, so it is a human risk. Human risk is any people-related factor that can cause a loss of productivity and hamper operations in the workplace.

(20) (D) Building damage due to an earthquake.

Location risks that threaten corporations include storm damage, earthquakes, fires, hurricanes, floods and other natural disasters. So, building damage caused by an earthquake is a location risk.

(21) (C) Risk reduction.

Risk reduction is the process of minimizing risk by reducing the likelihood and severity of a possible loss. So, by asking construction workers to use proper gear, an organization reduces the risk its workers face.

(22) (D) Reduce.

Risk resolution has four steps: research, accept, reduce and eliminate.

(23) (A) Risk prioritization.

Risk prioritization is the ranking of risks on an appropriate scale, such as frequency and/or severity. It allows organizations to assess which risk they should try to avert or mitigate through the use of their resources.

(24) (D) All of the above.

Risk management control is a process that involves risk resolution, risk monitoring and risk management planning.

(25) (A) Mission statement.

A mission statement informs employees about the company's goals and direction.

(26) (C) Mission statement.

The mission statement makes the workforce aware of the company's goals and direction. So, strategic plans and objectives are based on a company's mission statement.

(27) (D) All of the above.

Embezzlement can threaten employee compensation and benefits. Examples of embezzlement include cash skimming and computer or credit card embezzlement. Organizations look for signs of fake payments, forged signatures and data discrepancies to evaluate whether embezzlement has occurred.

(28) (A) Remain constant.

An organization's core values remain constant regardless of the changes in business processes or product lines. When developing an organization's core values, it is important to establish whether or not the values will hold true if focus and business processes change entirely.

(29) (D) All of the above.

Cross-functional group members have complementary skills and the responsibility to develop new products, reevaluate different organizational processes, enhance customer relationships and improve organizational performance.

(30) (D) Key performance indicators.

A key performance indicator is a quantifiable measure of performance over time for a specific objective. KPIs help organizations keep track of performance in cross-cultural collaborations.

(31) (B) System of communication.

A system of communication that caters to every question, concern, plan or strategy is key to securing optimal performance and achieving goals. This is because it increases productivity and efficiency.

(32) (A) The HR department.

HR has the responsibility for maintaining operations and following OSHA guidelines and providing appropriate training to employees.

(33) (D) All of the above.

All types of cross-functional projects benefit from establishing roles, hierarchies and expectations; decision-making and process development; accountability to minimize downtime; regular updates to the C-suite and stakeholders to implement feedback; and identifying opportunities and challenges.

(34) (C) HR metrics.

Measuring the number of sick days for staff is an example of HR metrics.

(35) (A) A data-centered way of promotions.

It is common in organizations to promote underperforming peers. Various factors, including nepotism and human bias, play a part in such decision-making. A data-based approach to salary and promotion decisions can prevent the demotivation of high-performing employees by allowing leaders to drive their decisions based on performance data. For example, a relatively new employee may have performed well on a single project, but an older peer might have delivered consistent quality performance.

Functional Area 02 | Talent Planning and Acquisition

(36) (B) Title I of the Americans with Disabilities Act.

Of all the acts listed, only Title I of the Americans with Disabilities Act forbids an employer from asking any questions related to an applicant's disability or requesting a medical examination until a conditional job offer has been made.

(37) (D) Skills.

When recruiting, employers are responsible for selecting and administering valid, reliable tests and reflecting the applicants' skills and aptitude rather than their weak points. Employers should do this to give each applicant a fair opportunity.

(38) (A) The Age Discrimination in Employment Act.

Titles V and VII of the Civil Rights Act pertain to employment discrimination, and Title I of the Americans with Disabilities Act deals with discrimination against disabled people. Neither of these acts prohibits employers from putting age limitations on apprenticeship programs, but ADEA does.

According to ADEA, it is unlawful for employers to put age limitations on apprenticeship programs unless these limitations are validated by some exceptions in ADEA or made by the EEOC. Similarly, no age limitations can be put in job notices and advertisements when recruiting new talent.

(39) (B) The Fair Credit Reporting Act.

The FCRA protects consumers by regulating how credit reporting companies collect, use, access and share their data. Under this act, employers must provide the applicants with a written notice explaining that they will be using applicants' information in their consumer reports in the decision-making process.

(40) (C) An applicant's consumer report.

If employers want to attain an applicant's consumer report, they must certify to the company that the applicant has been notified and has granted permission.

(41) (D) Neutral tests.

ADEA restricts employers from using neutral tests or selection procedures that can have an unintentional discriminatory impact on people aged 40 or older.

(42) (C) Internal candidates.

Internal candidates are employees who are already working in an organization. They are already aware of the workplace culture and their responsibilities.

(43) (B) Job bidding.

In job bidding, employees are welcome to show interest in any position at any time. This motivates employees because it allows them to set a position as a goal for themselves. It also saves time for employers who are already aware of potential candidates whenever the position opens.

(44) (D) Succession planning.

In succession planning and assessment, managers and employers must keep their eyes open and identify individuals within their teams who can take on bigger roles in the future. Employers must keep this process streamlined and fair, as identifying individuals ahead of time and making their selection known within the company can be detrimental to the morale of other employees and undermine the company's overall recruitment efforts.

(45) (A) Unprofessional organizations.

Aside from referrals given by unprofessional organizations, job fairs, walk-ins and radio advertisements are all fair mediums for recruiting external candidates.

(46) (C) Short-form employment applications.

A short-form employment application provides a more concise version of an organization's standard application for employment. It can be used as a prescreening tool or as the main application for entry-level positions in the company.

(47) (D) An agility test.

Agility tests are conducted to find out candidates' physical capabilities and must be related to the job that they have applied for. For example, if the job requires a person to move quickly from one place to another, the individual must be able to demonstrate that on an agility test.

(48) (D) Job-specific employment applications.

A job-specific employment application is used when a large candidate pool needs to be narrowed down for a particular position. This application is tailored to the position that the applicant has applied for.

(49) (C) Weighted employment applications.

A weighted employment application allows employers to evaluate candidates objectively by assigning levels of importance to different sections of the applications. In this way, all applications can be weighed following a consistent system, depending on the relevance of each section.

(50) (A) Cognitive ability tests.

Only cognitive ability tests assess a candidate's intelligence or other cognitive skills that are relevant to the position they have applied for. For example, a candidate's mathematical and problem-solving skills can be tested for a finance position.

(51) (B) Directive interviews.

In comparison to non-directive and stress interviews, directive interviews are more structured and have a consistent pattern of interviewing across all candidates. Control lies mostly with the interviewer, and structure is prioritized over circumstance.

(52) (A) Focused on the candidates' behavioral characteristics, as well as their skills and knowledge.

Interviews can be carried out in different ways. A behavior-based interview, in particular, focuses on the behavioral characteristics of candidates along with their skills and knowledge.

(53) (D) Background checks.

Once the interviews and tests have all been done, the organization conducts background checks before selecting any candidate for the position. These checks can help organizations avoid legal liability and verify claims made by the applicants.

(54) (B) A medical test.

According to federal law, medical tests can be requested only when they are relevant to the job being applied for. Employers can ask for these tests only after they have made a conditional job offer to applicants.

(55) (C) 18 months.

According to a multitude of reports, almost half of new hires for senior positions end up failing within 18 months of taking on a new position.

(56) (A) Onboarding.

Different organizations have different approaches to the onboarding process, all of which vary in terms of formality and structure.

(57) (B) First 120 days.

In the United States, about half of all workers working on an hourly basis end up leaving their new jobs within the first 120 days.

(58) (C) Informal onboarding.

In informal onboarding, new employees go through the learning process without getting any explicit instruction from the organization. In contrast, in formal onboarding, new employees are made aware of written policies and procedures designed to help them adjust to their jobs and the social culture of the workplace.

(59) (D) Clarification.

Clarification is the level at which specific job-related knowledge is provided to new hires.

(60) (A) High-potential onboarding.

At the high-potential onboarding level, organizations cover the compliance and clarification elements in detail while implementing culture and connection mechanisms.

(61) (D) Role clarity.

Role clarity refers to employees' understanding of their roles and expectations within an organization. It signifies how well adjusted new employees are and can be used as evaluation tools at regular intervals to intervene wherever intervention is needed.

(62) (C) Part-time employment.

Part-time employment allows organizations to have projects completed without having to take on more full-time employees. This type of work is favored by organizations that need expert help or are looking to cut costs.

Part-time work also allows individuals to maintain a better work-life balance.

(63) (B) Corporate restructuring.

Corporate restructuring is the result of a change in a company's vision or strategy. Depending on the organization's size and framework, this type of restructuring can have a huge impact on both the overall workplace environment and individual employees.

Functional Area 03 | Learning and Development

(64) (C) Organizational structure.

Organizational structure is the framework around which an organization operates. This structure aligns all aspects of a business and allows it to reach maximum performance.

(65) (A) Functional structure.

The functional structure aligns employees and divides work into specializations, which leads to quicker decisions, increased productivity and reduced time to execution. The specialization of work also creates a hierarchical structure that streamlines the reporting process.

(66) (B) Matrix structure.

The matrix system is the most complicated organizational system because it requires employees to report to several team leaders and division managers. This multiple-personnel chain of command creates inefficiencies and increases time to execution.

(67) (A) Return on investment.

ROI determines the effectiveness and credibility of an organization's learning program. It's a straightforward calculation that shows that the return exceeds the investment.

(68) (A) Orientation and readiness to learn.

The orientation and readiness-to-learn assumption presumes that adult learners are more engaged in learning experiences that can be practically implemented.

(69) (C) Analyze, design, develop, implement and evaluate.

ADDIE is an acronym meaning analyze, design, develop, implement and evaluate.

(70) (D) Program designer.

HR professionals often act in the capacity of program designers and are responsible for identifying performance objectives; designing and ranking learning activities required to achieve these objectives; and selecting suitable materials, media and training aids required for intervention.

(71) (B) The implementation phase.

The ADDIE approach has five phases: analyze, design, develop, implement and evaluate. In the implementation phase, learners are trained on how to use a product or service.

(72) (C) Talent management.

The quote refers to talent management. HR specialists are responsible for managing and developing organizational talent for the company's advantage. They use different development models to identify high performers and give them increasing responsibilities in order to maximize their potential and utility to the company.

(73) (B) Organizational level.

At the organizational level, the entire organization or simply one department within it focuses on preparing personnel for anticipated future needs and/or goals. A negative trend in employee happiness and productivity indicators, a shift in the company's strategic plans or direction, the debut of a new product or an increase in the number of casualties all suggest that training is required at this level.

(74) (D) Analysis.

The analysis step starts with identifying the desired outcome or goal, gathering data relevant to that case (which can be done through surveys, questionnaires and job analyses) and using that data to highlight the performance gap, identifying instructional goals, sketching out possible solutions and choosing the best solution after a thorough evaluation of each.

(75) (A) Experiential training methods.

Employees can obtain knowledge and experience by going through real-life scenarios via experiential training, commonly known as learning through experience. Demonstrations, one-on-one training sessions (in which students are paired with an experienced expert) and performance-based approaches (in which employees are instructed to build expertise in the specific abilities needed to complete the job efficiently) are all examples of this sort of training.

(76) (C) Classroom-style seating.

Classroom-style seating is ideal for situations where employees will view manuals, take notes and listen to a lecture.

(77) (B) Managerial training

Managerial training equips a worker with the skills needed to advance to a management role. It emphasizes all of the numerous soft skills that help with better teamwork and relationships.

(78) (D) On-the-job coaching.

On-the-job coaching is delivered by pairing inexperienced employees with a more experienced one, specializing in specific abilities. It is similar to the mentor-training delivery technique, except that the mentor-training method focuses more on general development than polishing specific skills.

(79) (C) Goals, realities, choices, wrap-up.

The GROW (goals, realities, choices and wrap-up) paradigm provides a structure for directing interactions with more experienced students. However, the process may be time consuming and challenging for less-experienced students.

(80) (D) Systems and selling.

This is not a stage of the GROW model. The model is divided into four distinct stages:

1) Establish your goals

2) Look into the facts

3) Generate alternatives

4) Decide on a plan of action and wrap up loose ends

(81) (A) Training programs.

Employees stay longer at organizations when they undergo training programs. These programs help them enhance their technical and soft skills and contribute to personal growth and the fulfillment of psychological demands.

Functional Area 04 | Total Rewards

(82) (A) Total rewards.

Total rewards is a monetary package that a company gives to its employees in return for their services. There are many names associated with total rewards packages, such as total compensation or pay package.

(83) (C) By conducting monetary and nonmonetary exchanges.

When employees are investing their skills, time and effort in a company, the company compensates their efforts by conducting monetary and nonmonetary exchanges.

(84) (C) Monetary and nonmonetary remuneration.

Businesses provide their employees with monetary remuneration, such as salaries, and nonmonetary remuneration, such as day care facilities. The purpose of these facilities is to maintain a certain level of motivation and encouragement among the employees.

(85) (A) Recruitment, holding and persuading.

The total rewards package aims to recruit, hold and persuade employees. Companies often set huge budgets to pay for the services of their employees either through monetary or nonmonetary compensation. These measures increase employee motivation.

(86) (D) Total rewards increase employee dissatisfaction and increase trustworthiness.

The statement violates the basic concept of the total rewards package. Pay packages improve employee motivation and increase trustworthiness. Furthermore, planning a total rewards package is an essential HR strategy, so companies allocate a huge budget for it.

(87) (B) Self-esteem – Self-satisfaction.

Nonmonetary compensation is directly linked with intrinsic motivation, such as high self-esteem. In contrast, monetary compensation is the source of extrinsic motivation, such as self-satisfaction. When employees' efforts are rewarded by a total rewards package, their level of satisfaction increases.

(88) (B) Nonmonetary compensation.

Andrea performs very well in her field, so she is being rewarded with nonmonetary compensation. This can be in the form of appreciation, day care facilities, flex time or telecommuting. These factors encourage her professional growth.

(89) (A) Maslow's Hierarchy of Needs and McClelland's Acquired Needs Theory.

Both these theories explain the significance of nonmonetary compensation. This compensation is helpful in boosting an individual's intrinsic motivation. According to these theories, nonmonetary rewards increase self-esteem, which ultimately helps a person achieve self-actualization.

(90) (B) Satisfying employee needs.

The compensation package aims to satisfy employee needs. The company rewards employees for their service through a compensation package. These packages can be in the form of monetary or nonmonetary compensation. Every employee has different needs; therefore, the compensation package plan must be fair enough to satisfy every need of every employee.

(91) (B) Nonmonetary compensation.

Telecommuting, on-site childcare and flex time are examples of nontraditional work-life benefits. They are nonmonetary compensation, as they're directly linked to an individual's intrinsic motivation.

(92) (C) Monetary compensation.

Maria received a free vacation and a bonus for her extraordinary performance. The example states that the company is indirectly rewarding her efforts through monetary compensation. The bonus is the direct monetary compensation, while the paid vacation is indirect monetary compensation.

(93) (C) Psychological – Medical – Lifestyle.

Nonmonetary compensation comes with psychological, medical and lifestyle advantages. These are the most suitable categories for understanding the significance of nonmonetary compensation.

1. Psychological advantages – Benefits that enhance an employee's emotional and psychological wellness.

2. Medical advantages – Advantages that promote an employee's physical well-being

3. Lifestyle advantages – Perks that promote an employee's way of life

(94) (D) All of the above.

Non-cash compensation creates a sense of trustworthiness among employees. Their efforts are encouraged by the company and rewarded in multiple ways. Moreover, this compensation builds a sense of community among the employees that helps them increase their concentration on their tasks.

(95) (A) Non-cash compensation.

On the whole, health, handicap and extra security—just like educational cost repayment, schooling help and retirement benefits—are all examples of non-cash compensation. There is no direct cash involvement.

(96) (A) Benefits.

Benefits are the most common type of nonmonetary compensation. They are designed to target employees' specific needs.

(97) (B) Fringe benefits.

Employees are given extra benefits in the form of fringe benefits. The nature of these benefits is purely entertaining and helps maintain employees' psychological well-being.

(98) (A) Five weeks.

The French government passed a constitutional law that managers must grant their employees five weeks of paid holidays. These holidays fall under the category of non-cash compensation benefits.

(99) (A) Paid holidays.

Mr. Alex is provided with paid holidays for New Year, Christmas and Thanksgiving. Companies offer paid holidays for national and religious occasions.

(100) (B) 8.4.

Employees in the United States are given an average of 8.4 paid sick days each year.

(101) (A) Analyze the benefits and the drawbacks of the incentives.

For incentive programs, HR specialists must consider a detailed analysis of the incentives' benefits and drawbacks before deciding on any policy. This analysis helps HR specialists identify the credibility of incentive programs, such as how productive the incentives will be.

(102) (A) The HR manager.

HR managers decide whether incentives will be monetary or nonmonetary. They plan incentive programs according to the employees' needs. An ideal incentive program addresses employees' needs and increases their motivation level.

(103) (D) Both (A) and (B).

Non-cash awards are more memorable and emotional in nature. They are also broadly acknowledged and known to increase employees' self-esteem.

(104) (B) Nonmonetary compensation.

Companies offer day care facilities to mothers or fathers during their employment tenure. This facility helps them concentrate on their tasks and not worry about their children's daily needs.

(105) (B) Going to the gym boosts employees' physical and mental well-being.

Including a gym membership in a nonmonetary compensation plan is an effective way to improve employees' job performance. Exercise boosts stamina and increases self-confidence; these two components are essential for optimal functioning. Moreover, a gym membership helps reduce stress, anxiety and even burnout.

(106) (A) Improved employee satisfaction.

One of the significant benefits of a gym membership is enhanced employee satisfaction.

(107) (A) Nonmonetary compensation is effective at increasing employee satisfaction and motivation.

Nonmonetary compensation boosts employee satisfaction and motivation. It makes employees feel that a company appreciates their work. This sense of worth leaves a positive impact on the employees' job performance. However, non-cash rewards are also essential for intrinsic and extrinsic employee motivation.

Functional Area 05 | Employee and Labor Relations

(108) (A) Designing and encouraging.

A company's mindset should be focused on designing and encouraging an atmosphere that promotes employees' achievements and long-term commitment.

(109) (B) HR.

The HR department is responsible for empowering the employee life cycle and ensuring that the transition from one step to the next is visible and well organized.

(110) (D) Six.

The employee life cycle model has six stages: hiring, onboarding, development, retention, exit process and alumni program.

(111) (B) Hiring.

One of the most effective strategies for hiring/recruiting personnel is using references from experts/professionals in the sector because it is highly likely that these people know of talented people who can fill open jobs.

(112) (C) Values.

Values include customer empathy, ownership, transparency, team spirit and social responsibility.

(113) (C) Onboarding.

The process of bringing new employees up to speed is referred to as employee onboarding. This is the path that employees take from the time they join the organization until they reach peak productivity. The procedure helps new employees adapt to a firm's culture.

(114) (A) Hiring.

Hiring happens when a current position has opened or a new position has been created in an organization. The first step in the employee life cycle model is the hiring and selection process. This stage aims to ensure that the organization hires and retains the best talent.

(115) (D) Involuntary exit.

Productivity concerns or changing company requirements can lead to involuntary exits.

(116) (C) The retention stage.

In the employee life cycle, the retention stage is crucial because once employees have worked for a company for a while, there is a significant risk that their supervisors may take them for granted. Employees may leave as a result.

(117) (A) Hiring correct personnel and creating positive work relationships with coworkers.

HR can increase employee retention and reduce turnover by attracting top talent and establishing open, fair and mindful relationships with them.

(118) (B) The learning management system.

A learning management system is a platform for organizing and providing various types of online training content. It allows employees to access information from any location and pursue development opportunities whenever and wherever it is convenient.

(119) (B) External learning.

Internal and external learning can be accomplished through conferences, seminars and lunch-and-learns. These social events keep employees up-to-date on current events while allowing them to expand their knowledge.

(120) (D) Alumni.

Alumni must be included in the conversation if companies want to build a strong and forward-thinking culture. Alumni serve as a marketing and sales force as well as a source of referrals for new hires and customers. Without an active alumni group of former employees, an organization cannot deliver a complete end-to-end employment experience.

Test 4 on Employee and Labor Relations Only

Since the largest subsection on the PHR Exam is on Employee and Labor Relations, this test is designed specifically for that topic to give maximum practice on the subject.

(1) Why is hiring the correct personnel important?

(A) If a company is careful in the recruitment process, there is a higher chance of lower labor turnover.

(B) If a company hires the correct personnel, it can meet all of its needs.

(C) If a company hires the correct personnel, it does not need to further train them. This will reduce company costs.

(D) If a company selects the right individuals in the recruitment process, it can meet the company standards.

(2) What is the exit process?

(A) When a manager exits the company

(B) When the employee life cycle is completed

(C) When an employee exits the company

(D) When the company goes into recession

(3) What are the two forms of the exit process?

(A) When an employee is terminated or chooses to leave

(B) When the manager's contract ends or when the manager has to be terminated

(C) When an employee does not meet the contract needs or when the contract itself ends due to some reason

(D) None of the above

(4) What are a few values of a company?

(A) Team spirit, corporate social responsibility, transparency

(B) Competitive pay, better working conditions, corporate social responsibility

(C) Customer empathy, corporate social responsibility, employee morale

(D) Company image, market share, corporate social responsibility

(5) The development stage of the employee life cycle model can be refined using

____________.

(A) Retention

(B) Training

(C) Internal and external learning

(D) RMS

(6) When employees exit an organization, their exit can cause problems in the functioning of the business.

Which of the following problems do managers face most frequently after employees exit?

(A) The business has to hire new employees, which can be costly.

(B) Customer relationships can be affected.

(C) Delegating responsibilities to the remaining employees becomes difficult.

(D) Labor turnover happens.

(7) What is resignation?

(A) When an employee does not perform the job well and has to be dismissed

(B) When an employee does not meet the contract requirements

(C) When an employee willingly exits one department and moves to another

(D) When an employee willingly leaves the company

(8) What is an exit interview?

(A) An exit interview allows employees to share with the company why they have decided to leave.

(B) An exit interview allows employees to join another company easily if they wish to.

(C) An exit interview allows employees to state their opinions about the company's condition.

(D) An exit interview allows the other employees to stay satisfied.

(9) Ideally, who should conduct exit interviews?

(A) Fellow employees

(B) Trade unions

(C) HR

(D) A third party

(10) How do exit interviews help the company?

(A) They attract potential employees.

(B) They reduce costly labor turnover in the future.

(C) They create a safe environment for other employees.

(D) They allow employees to easily join a new company.

(11) What are alumni?

(A) A source of referrals for new hires and customers

(B) Sponsors

(C) Groups that support the company

(D) A team that hires new employees

(12) What is HR?

(A) A department in a company that has the responsibility for hiring and retaining employees

(B) Anything that has to do with employees in a company

(C) Employees in a company

(D) A department in any organization that is responsible for searching, screening, recruiting and retaining employees

(13) What is not a role of HR management?

(A) Selecting

(B) Hiring

(C) Advertising

(D) Development

(14) Why is a staffing plan important?

(A) It helps recruit better employees.

(B) It helps in deciding the number of individuals to be employed according to incomes.

(C) It helps keep the current staff under control.

(D) None of the above.

(15) What is the selection process?

(A) Advertising the need for employees, identifying them and then choosing them

(B) Determining policies regarding dress code and timing, etc.

(C) Searching for prospective employees

(D) Interviewing and negotiating salaries with prospective employees

(16) Why are workplace policies important?

(A) Without policies, a work environment can turn chaotic.

(B) They are used as guidelines to ensure that activities run smoothly and subjectivity is avoided.

(C) They help reduce time wastage among employees.

(D) They increase employee engagement and thus improve the manager-employee relationship.

(17) Why is worker protection important?

(A) It leads to reduced costs in the future.

(B) It gives new hires a better impression.

(C) It will become impossible for employees to perform their jobs well without it.

(D) It will attract more customers to the business.

(18) What are some of the skills needed to be a successful HR manager?

(A) The ability to multitask, be fair and separate personal life from business life

(B) The ability to communicate properly, multitask, be fair and possess specific job skills

(C) The ability to be friendly with employees, be flexible and hire great talents

(D) All of the above

(19) People-oriented management and task-oriented management are two techniques that HR managers can adopt to make sure operations run smoothly.

What is the difference between these two techniques?

(A) Managers who adopt the people-oriented management style are more concerned with relationships outside the workplace.

(B) Managers who adopt the people-oriented management style are more concerned with customer relationships than employee relationships.

(C) Task-oriented managers are more concerned with job tasks than relationships.

(D) Task-oriented managers are more concerned with building relationships than focusing on tasks.

(20) What is an autocratic style of management?

(A) When managers consult with employees before deciding anything

(B) When managers and employees work together to solve problems

(C) When managers are very strict with employees and may be unfair as a result

(D) When managers focus on completing tasks and do not give much importance to maintaining relationships with employees

(21) How many styles of management are there?

(A) Four

(B) Six

(C) Nine

(D) None of the above

(22) What is a feature of the situational leadership model?

(A) Managers can switch to the autocratic style if needed.

(B) The manager's job is to define goals for the employees.

(C) The model does not focus on relationships.

(D) Managers normally prefer to remain friendly with employees, as they think of them as teammates.

(23) Why do employers have to make efforts to increase diversity and inclusion in their workplaces?

(A) To avoid cliques

(B) To meet regulatory requirements

(C) To build an easy recruitment system

(D) To maximize the market share of the business

(24) What is workplace diversity?

(A) The differences among different individuals, considering all their characters and attributes

(B) The differences in people's skills

(C) The differences in people's ethnicities

(D) All of the above

(25) Diversity plans talk about basic business matters. What is not an idea that should be followed by these plans?

(A) Focusing on accomplishing organizational objectives

(B) Focusing on informing the CEO and upper management of all the processes

(C) Focusing on maximizing output and profit

(D) Focusing on encouraging a feeling of possession and responsibility

(26) What is one positive effect of inclusion?

(A) Workers will be happy to be paid more.

(B) Employees at each level will get the desired job.

(C) Female employees will remain satisfied.

(D) Employees feel motivated to add to the business.

(27) All employees should be provided with proper training and schooling. How can this be done?

(A) By creating inclusion workshops and providing conflict resolution training

(B) Through LMS

(C) By investing in training programs

(D) By outsourcing and dealing with inclinations

(28) What steps, in the right order, should be taken by employers that want to develop a diversity and inclusion initiative?

(A) Determine areas of concern, deal with them, put initiatives into action and define business goals

(B) Conduct research, determine areas of concern and address policies

(C) Obtain support, define business goals, address policies and determine areas of concern

(D) Gather information, determine areas of concern, address policies, define business goals and obtain support

(29) How can employers implement initiatives for action and generate speed for work?

(A) Foster an activity intended specifically for these initiatives

(B) Outsource help

(C) Convince their employees and get them on their sides

(D) Invest more in the actions and tasks at hand

(30) Most organizations define three impediments with regards to planning and executing a variety of work environments and inclusion techniques.

Which of the following is not one of these three impediments?

(A) Monetary limitations

(B) Top management that uses an autocratic style of management

(C) Individuals who are excessively focused on surviving, not contributing

(D) A middle management that makes a less-than-impressive display of carrying out various programs

(31) Companies use methodologies and policies to effectively make use of inclusion strategies.

How do they do this?

(A) They provide protection to employers.

(B) They make sure employees are following rules.

(C) They provide a fair work environment.

(D) None of the above.

(32) Why is diversity in recruitment important?

(A) So all employees can have diverse skills.

(B) So employers have to spend less time on employee relations.

(C) So a comprehensive work environment can be built.

(D) So employers do not have to satisfy every employee.

(33) Exits and terminations are important areas for HR to work on because developing efficient existing processes __________.

(A) Helps reduce stress

(B) Can be costly for the company

(C) Can create a bad impression

(D) None of the above

(34) What does a well-thought-out exit process create in the workplace?

(A) A positive atmosphere

(B) A negative atmosphere

(C) A fair workplace environment

(D) Goodwill

(35) What is the major reason for voluntary exits?

(A) The manager was not happy with the employee's work.

(B) The employee reached the age of retirement.

(C) The employee was offered a better opportunity.

(D) The employee wanted to open his or her own firm.

(36) Other than recruiting new people, in what other ways can HR fill the jobs of ex-employees?

(A) By demoting managers

(B) By assigning tasks to current employees

(C) By dismissing relative projects

(D) By promoting within the company

(37) What is the deadline by which an employer needs to pay an employee's final wages?

(A) 48 hours

(B) 72 hours

(C) 2 weeks

(D) 1 month

(38) What is the purpose of COBRA and HIPAA?

(A) They both provide rules for hiring an employee.

(B) They both are employee rights protection acts.

(C) They both decide the average wage for company employees.

(D) They both provide notices for departing employees.

(39) Employees can choose planned retirements when they transition from full-time work to focusing on other avenues.

Which programs can help employees go through this phase easily?

(A) LMS

(B) Pre-retirement counseling programs

(C) Post-retirement counseling programs

(D) Any training program

(40) Why are exit interviews important during the exit process?

(A) They provide relevant feedback and valuable insight.

(B) They allow managers to know why an employee wants to leave.

(C) They are important for paperwork.

(D) They are valuable for new employees.

(41) What is the initial step taken when a disciplinary issue arises for an employee?

(A) Conducting a direct termination

(B) Investigating the reason for the problem

(C) Attempting to resolve the problem through coaching

(D) Demoting the employee rather than direct termination

(42) If a disciplinary issue is not resolved, which step can HR take to resolve this issue?

(A) Perform a direct termination

(B) Investigate the reason why the issue persists

(C) Attempt to resolve these problems through coaching

(D) Work with the employee's manager and go through the termination by taking proper steps to avoid legal actions against the firm

(43) When is immediate termination important?

(A) When financial troubles affect the company

(B) When extreme actions have been taken by the employee

(C) When the employee's non-serious attitude toward his or her responsibilities results in a loss for the company

(D) When the employee comes late to the office on a daily basis

(44) What is the purpose of termination meetings?

(A) They allow supervisors to finalize the termination decision.

(B) They provide coaching for the employee.

(C) They are a legal and formal method for termination.

(D) They give the employee another chance and reverse the decision of HR.

(45) With whom do employees attend termination meetings?

(A) The manager

(B) The CEO

(C) The supervisor

(D) The board of directors

(46) When does the supervisor have to oversee the cleanup process after termination?

(A) All the time

(B) When an employee is aggressive

(C) When an employee is dealing with sensitive data or material

(D) Only in indirect termination cases

(47) The Worker Adjustment and Retraining Notification Act was passed to counter mass layoffs and plant closings.

When was the act passed?

(A) 1999

(B) 2001

(C) 1898

(D) 1988

(48) Who passed the WARN Act?

(A) The Democrats

(B) Congress

(C) The Senate

(D) None of the above

(49) What is the main clause of the WARN Act?

(A) It protects workers and requires a 60-day advance notice for termination.

(B) It provides financial security for employees.

(C) It states the minimum annual salary for an average employee should be $15,000.

(D) It communicates that a termination decision can be taken only in public courts.

(50) Under which condition is an employee subject to the provisions of the WARN Act, if company has more than 100 employees working 40 or more hours per week each?

(A) Upon the completion of 2,000 hours per week by the 100+ employees

(B) Upon the completion of 5,000 hours per week by the 100+ employees

(C) Upon the completion of 2,500 hours per week by the 100+ employees

(D) Upon the completion of 4,000 hours per week by the 100+ employees

(51) What does plant closing refer to?

(A) 50 or more employees losing their jobs

(B) 500 or more employees losing their jobs

(C) 34% of employees losing their jobs

(D) 100% of employees losing their jobs

(52) What are some situations in which the 60-day notice is not required to be given out to each employee?

(A) A faltering company exception

(B) Unforeseeable business circumstances exception

(C) Natural disaster exception

(D) All of the above

(53) What measure should HR not take during layoffs?

(A) Initiating honest communication

(B) Making all decisions transparent

(C) Publicly advertising the events and reasons for the decision

(D) Maintaining the respect and loyalty of the remaining employees

(54) Why should a termination meeting be held at an appropriate place and time?

(A) To ensure that the employee's dignity is not affected

(B) To ensure that other employees are not aware of the meeting

(C) To avoid misconduct

(D) To formalize the process

(55) What is wrongful termination?

(A) Illegal termination

(B) Termination resulting from personal reasons

(C) Termination carried out when an employee is wrong

(D) Termination carried out when the employer is wrong

(56) In diversity designing programs, metrics should also be considered. When should they be collected for a successful result?

(A) Before hiring employees

(B) After all the changes have been made

(C) Before all the changes have been made

(D) None of the above

(57) Why do organizations around the world look for a diverse workforce?

(A) To have employees with diverse skill sets

(B) To create more flexibility in the workplace

(C) To stay innovative and competitive

(D) To benefit from already trained employees

(58) Inclusion is when all individuals are treated fairly and respectfully, have equal access to opportunities and resources and can add equally to the organization.

How is inclusion a two-way street?

(A) Employers and employees both have to satisfy each other.

(B) Every individual must reward and acknowledge coworkers.

(C) Employees must expect something in return for acknowledging someone in the workplace.

(D) Communication should be the first goal, after which inclusion can be created.

(59) HR managers must work tirelessly to help new workers assimilate into the workforce, comprehend business objectives, learn new skills and reach their full potential.

Which is not one of the strategies managers can use to reach this goal?

(A) Starting tutoring programs

(B) Monitoring different groups of new hires

(C) Executing preparation programs for employees

(D) Incorporating inclusion in every aspect of the business

(60) How can companies conduct a policy and practice analysis?

(A) By avoiding any minor obstacles

(B) By mentioning it in advertisements for potential recruits

(C) By focusing on employee referral programs

(D) By remaining focused on custom policies

(61) How does making initiatives public help companies develop a diversity and inclusion initiative?

(A) It helps companies ensure that stakeholders are properly communicated with.

(B) It helps companies ensure audit reports can be made quickly.

(C) It helps companies ensure that everyone is satisfied with business operations.

(D) It helps companies ensure that a diverse environment can be created.

(62) How can employers institute initiatives for action and generate speed for work?

(A) Convince employees and get them on their sides

(B) Outsource help

(C) Foster an activity intended specifically for these initiatives

(D) Invest more in the actions and tasks at hand

(63) Why should senior management understand diversity and inclusion exercises?

(A) To meet explicit diversity and inclusion targets

(B) To direct the organization's essential objectives

(C) To avoid managerial assumptions

(D) To obtain full support and help of upper management

(64) How can employers determine areas of concern when developing diversity and inclusion initiatives?

(A) By conducting regular meetings with the lower management

(B) By using data collected by analytics

(C) By completing a socioeconomic assessment

(D) By performing surveys

(65) Which of the following is not a way through which leader participation could be used to set inclusion programs?

(A) Allocating a senior leader to lead or support the organization's diversity drive

(B) Structuring a diversity committee

(C) Creating a chief diversity officer role

(D) Obtaining support from employees

(66) Why was OSHA formed?

(A) To safeguard employee rights

(B) To maintain workplace safety

(C) To ensure the health of employees

(D) To avoid any violent acts from occurring in the workplace

(67) A key point of the Occupational Safety and Health Act was the creation of OSHA.

What is OSHA responsible for?

(A) Setting safety standards for industries and enforcing them

(B) Minimizing hazards surrounding areas around a workplace environment

(C) Proper administration

(D) Taking care of the health and safety of employers

(68) Which of the following is not a requirement set by the OSHA Act?

(A) Employers must file a report with OSHA within 3 hours if a few employees are hospitalized or have a fatal accident.

(B) Employers need to inform their employees of OSHA policies.

(C) Employers need to take steps to minimize hazards.

(D) Employees should compensate an employee who has been a victim of an accident.

(69) NIOSH was also established by OSHA as a part of the Department of Health and Human Services.

What is NIOSH responsible for?

(A) Researching and evaluating workplace hazards and helping employees find ways to reduce the effect of those hazards

(B) Providing occupational safety and health standards rules and regulations that impact employer actions and behaviors

(C) Inspecting and monitoring employers that have a repeated history of violations or willful violations

(D) Taking care of workplace disturbances that specifically involve environmental hazards

(70) Which of the following acts supports education and training in the field of occupational safety and health?

(A) The Occupational Safety and Health Act

(B) The NIOSH Act

(C) The Training for Safety Act

(D) The MSH Act

(71) If some industry operations cannot be conducted following OSHA standards, what should the company do?

(A) Close the company

(B) Hire an attorney to discuss legal matters

(C) Apply for waivers

(D) Hand over most operations to an outsourcing business

(72) What does the OSHA alliance program do?

(A) It allows both employers and employees to solve health and safety problems in collaboration.

(B) It solves workplace health and safety problems with the help of a third party.

(C) It motivates businesses to operate in safer environments.

(D) It allows organizations to be involved in the promotion of workplace health and safety issues.

(73) The VPP allows employers to be removed from the list of routine inspections. However, there are some criteria that have to be met before an employer is allowed to participate in this program.

What are these criteria?

(A) Employers need to give proof of no previous misconduct with an employee.

(B) Employers must implement tough safety programs in their workplace.

(C) Employers have to put employee rights above business goals for a while.

(D) None of the above.

(74) What does the Enhanced Enforcement Program do?

(A) It enhances the performance of employers.

(B) It examines and monitors employers that have a repeated history of violations.

(C) It follows up on inspections.

(D) It provides proper guidelines to employers so that the number of workplace accidents is as low as possible.

(75) OSHA has outlined some common elements under the Injury and Illness Prevention Program that companies need to adapt.

What is not one of these elements?

(A) Hazard identification

(B) Education and training

(C) Exit meetings

(D) Worker participation

(76) According to OSHA, a company with _____ employees is required to have emergency plans in writing.

(A) Seven

(B) Eight

(C) Ten

(D) Fifteen

(77) According to FEMA, every company should have a preparedness plan.

What is the first step of the plan, as suggested by FEMA?

(A) Practical implementation

(B) Resource management

(C) Customer service

(D) Testing phase

(78) When creating an emergency response plan, FEMA suggests a step called "assessment and business impact analysis."

What happens during this step?

(A) Smart plans regarding every angle of the accident are carefully prepared.

(B) Customer and financial impacts are effectively communicated.

(C) An assessment of the steps being taken for the hazards is conducted.

(D) Hazards and threats are assessed.

(79) What does a preparedness plan do?

(A) It can help businesses avoid suffering from substantial future costs.

(B) It can help businesses maintain a good relationship with shareholders.

(C) It can help businesses prepare themselves for any potential threats.

(D) It can help businesses prepare for a sudden increase in the demand for goods and services.

(80) What is the last step in a preparedness plan?

(A) Testing

(B) Maintenance and improvements

(C) Monitoring

(D) Follow-up inspections.

(81) Why is the practical implementation of plans important?

(A) To make the employees feel better

(B) To ensure that a positive workplace environment can be created

(C) To elicit a smooth response in the middle of a crisis

(D) To avoid extra costs

(82) What are the first four levels in OSHA's inspection hierarchy?

(A) Inspections, complaints and referrals, imminent danger, accidents

(B) Inspections, imminent danger, follow-up inspections, complaints and referrals

(C) Imminent danger, complaints and referrals, accidents, inspections

(D) Imminent danger, accidents, complaints and referrals, inspections

(83) __________ need(s) to be thought of beforehand to elicit a smooth response during an emergency.

(A) Hospital appointments

(B) Emergency protocols

(C) Maintenance

(D) Data recovery

(84) What does it mean for a business to be inducted into the VPP program?

(A) It means that the business follows OSHA guidelines only on hiring.

(B) It is the official recognition of a business's exemplary health and safety practices.

(C) It is a symbol of the business's dedication to OSHA guidelines for hiring only.

(D) All of the above.

(85) Which of the following is an employer's right regarding workplace safety?

(A) To seek advice from OSHA

(B) To ignore any complaints

(C) To dismiss an employee who complains

(D) To answer any questions regarding allegations made against them

(86) What is collective bargaining?

(A) The negotiation process between employees and employers in an organization

(B) The negotiation process between employees and employers of different organizations

(C) The negotiation process between directors of the same organization

(D) The negotiation process between directors of different organizations

(87) What is the goal of collective bargaining?

(A) To collectively fight with the government for terms and conditions of employment

(B) To collectively fight with employers for terms and conditions of employment

(C) To collectively fight with employers for the minimum wages of employees

(D) To collectively fight with employers for the maximum number of employee working hours

(88) The representatives of the union approach employers to start a negotiation process that concludes in a contract called a/an _________.

(A) Employee contract

(B) Union contract

(C) Workers contract

(D) Labor contract

(89) CBA stands for ___________.

(A) Collective bargaining article

(B) Collective bargaining agreement

(C) Collective bargaining association

(D) Collective bargaining assurance

(90) The process of collective bargaining in an organization is initiated by a/an ___________.

(A) Public union

(B) Industrial union

(C) Labor union

(D) Worker union

(91) Which of the following does collective bargaining benefit more?

(A) Employers

(B) Employees

(C) The government

(D) Both (A) and (B)

(92) Collective bargaining is also a symbol of ___________.

(A) Democracy

(B) Monarchy

(C) Autocracy

(D) Plutocracy

(93) Which of the following is not an essential feature of collective bargaining?

(A) The process should have active participation from management and employees.

(B) The process should be aimed primarily at bringing stability to the working relationship between parties.

(C) The process should conclude with the implementation of the agreement.

(D) Both parties should work for personal gains instead of looking for mutual benefits.

(94) On what matters does the NLRA allow employers and unions to bargain?

(A) Workplace matters

(B) Employment matters

(C) Average salary

(D) None of the above

(95) What is the time duration after which unions can show bad faith in the process if they fail to notify the management about their intent to renegotiate a contract?

(A) 7 to 14 days before the contract expires

(B) 7 to 21 days before the contract expires

(C) 60 to 90 days before the contract expires

(D) 30 to 60 days before the contract expires

(96) How many types of bargaining approaches are there?

(A) Three

(B) Two

(C) Four

(D) Five

(97) Which of the following is not a type of bargaining approach?

(A) Positional bargaining

(B) Multi-party bargaining

(C) Adversarial bargaining

(D) Both (B) and (C)

(98) What is positional bargaining?

(A) It is a type of bargaining in which both parties are focused on their demands.

(B) It is a type of bargaining in which both parties are focused on solving a problem.

(C) It is a type of bargaining in which both parties are focused on acquiring a mutual benefit.

(D) All of the above.

(99) What is principled bargaining?

(A) It is a type of bargaining in which both parties are focused on their demands.

(B) It is a type of bargaining in which both parties are focused on solving a problem.

(C) It is a type of bargaining in which both parties are focused on mutual benefit.

(D) All of the above.

(100) Which of the following are type(s) of principled bargaining?

(i) Integrative bargaining

(ii) Interest-based bargaining

(A) (i) only

(B) (ii) only

(C) Both (A) and (B)

(D) None of the above

(101) Which of the following is not a collective bargaining strategy?

(A) Positional bargaining

(B) Single unit bargaining

(C) Multi-unit bargaining

(D) Parallel bargaining

(102) To which industry does the closed shop clause apply?

(A) The information industry

(B) The service industry

(C) The construction industry

(D) The material industry

(103) What is the agency shop clause?

(A) It is a clause that requires all employees to join a union or pay union dues if not joining.

(B) It is a clause that requires that the new employees be members of a union before they can be hired.

(C) It is a clause that ensures that a union as a whole can financially carry out its bargaining duties.

(D) It is a clause that gives the employees the choice of joining or not joining a union.

(104) Select the correct order for the process of collective bargaining.

(A) Proposal, discussion, preparation, bargaining, settlement

(B) Discussion, proposal, preparation, bargaining, settlement

(C) Preparation, proposal, discussion, bargaining, settlement

(D) Preparation, discussion, proposal, bargaining, settlement

(105) When a settlement is reached in the final negotiation stage, both parties have to agree to the implementation of __________.

(A) The ILO

(B) The CBA

(C) The NLRA

(D) All of the above

(106) What is the difference between single-unit bargaining and parallel bargaining?

(A) In parallel bargaining, a union negotiates with both employers and the employees.

(B) In parallel bargaining, a union negotiates with more than one employer.

(C) Parallel bargaining is a double-unit bargaining system, unlike single-unit bargaining.

(D) Parallel bargaining involves more than one union, whereas a single unit involves only one.

(107) During the process of collective bargaining, actions from both parties during the process can show bad faith.

Which of the following can be considered bad faith?

(A) A party arriving late

(B) A party withholding important information

(C) A party advancing proposals

(D) Unilateral changes

(108) Why are termination meetings one of the toughest duties HR has to perform for an organization?

(A) They can be very time consuming.

(B) HR needs to provide the supervisor with the documentation and counsel the supervisor.

(C) HR needs to outsource so that the outsourcing company investigates the business for the documentation required.

(D) HR needs to make sure the supervisor is the right person to conduct the meeting with the employee being terminated.

(109) When can termination be considered wrongful?

(A) When an employer terminates an employee because of discriminatory reasons

(B) When an employer has not completed the whole procedure of termination

(C) When a termination meeting has not been conducted

(D) When an employee has been terminated for becoming violent

(110) What is a massive layoff according to the WARN Act?

(A) 100% of the employees have been laid off.

(B) 71% of the employees have been laid off.

(C) 43% of the employees have been laid off.

(D) 33% of the employees have been laid off.

(111) ____________ refer to the core ethics or principles that an organization abides by no matter what.

(A) Organizational values

(B) Organizational culture

(C) Organizational structure

(D) Organizational environment

(112) Organizational values are necessary for all organizations, and they give birth to ____________.

(A) The organization's environment

(B) The organization's structure

(C) The organization's culture

(D) None of the above

(113) Managers cannot solve employees' problems if they are unaware of them. What do managers need to establish in order to solve employees' problems?

(A) Worker protection

(B) Good communication channels

(C) Training and development

(D) Awareness of external factors

(114) External factors that managers should be aware of include ____________.

(A) Globalization and offshoring

(B) Corporate culture and staffing

(C) Globalization and staffing

(D) Offshoring and office culture

(115) An organization is made up of many departments and employees with ___________.

(A) Different abilities

(B) Different ways of thinking

(C) Different skills

(D) Different needs

(116) It is crucial for an HR manager to create an environment that ensures _____________.

(A) Employee behavior

(B) Employee turnover

(C) Employee safety

(D) Employee autonomy

(117) Which of the following is a task-oriented management style?

(A) Teamwork-style management

(B) Autocratic management

(C) Free-rein management

(D) Directing management

(118) Teamwork management is ______________.

(A) A people-oriented management style

(B) A task-oriented management style

(C) Both (A) and (B)

(D) None of the above

(119) In ______________, managers switch to an autocratic style of leadership when employee readiness is low.

(A) The autocratic leadership model

(B) The situational leadership model

(C) The democratic leadership model

(D) The strategic leadership model

(120) Which model makes it the manager's responsibility to define goals and the path through which those goals will be achieved?

(A) The transformational model

(B) The ethical model

(C) The path-goal model

(D) None of the above

Test 4: Answers and Explanations

(1) (A) If a company is careful in the recruitment process, there is a higher chance of lower labor turnover.

Organizations must first attract and acquire top talent in order to retain employees. If firms are more attentive in their recruiting process, they will probably retain excellent employees. Lower labor turnover is better for a company.

(2) (C) When an employee exits the company.

There comes a point for employees when their employment life cycle will conclude, whether due to retirement, new employment or personal reasons. When an employee exits the company, it is called the exit process.

(3) (A) When an employee is terminated or chooses to leave.

The exit process can take one of two forms: employees choose to leave on their own (resignations and retirements) or employees are asked to depart in some fashion (termination, downsizing or layoff).

(4) (A) Team spirit, corporate social responsibility, transparency.

Customer empathy, ownership, transparency, team spirit and corporate social responsibility are examples of company values. An organization must follow these to ensure a smooth onboarding process.

(5) (C) Internal and external learning.

The development stage of the employee life cycle model can be refined either by learning management software or through conferences, seminars and lunch-and-learns, which are all good options for internal or external learning.

(6) (C) Delegating responsibilities to the remaining employees becomes difficult.

When an employee leaves, one of the most common problems managers face is delegating responsibilities. Work has to be distributed among the remaining employees until a replacement is found.

(7) (D) When an employee willingly leaves the company.

Resignation is when an employee willingly leaves a company and a job.

(8) (A) An exit interview allows employees to share with the company why they have decided to leave.

An exit interview is a conversation between a company and an employee who has decided to leave the business. It lets the company know why the employee has decided to leave.

(9) (D) A third party.

To put employees at ease and encourage honest responses, exit interviews should be performed by a neutral third party, such as an HR representative. If a departing employee's immediate supervisor performs an exit interview, the departing employee may be hesitant to be open and honest.

(10) (B) They reduce costly labor turnover in the future.

When completed in a consistent and standardized way, exit interviews can help foster positive relationships and a welcoming work environment in the future. Therefore, costly labor turnover is eventually reduced.

(11) (A) A source of referrals for new hires and customers.

Alumni serve as a marketing and sales force as well as a source of referrals for new hires and customers. Without an engaged alumni group composed of former employees, an organization cannot deliver a complete end-to-end employment experience.

(12) (D) A department in any organization that is responsible for searching, screening, recruiting and retaining employees.

The HR department in a company is a group that is responsible for managing the employee life cycle. This consists of searching, screening, recruiting and retaining employees.

(13) (C) Advertising.

The roles of HR include staffing, recruitment, selection, compensation and benefits, retention, training and development, legal issues, worker protection, communication and awareness of external factors.

(14) (B) It helps in deciding the number of individuals to be employed according to incomes.

A staffing plan is a process in which a firm (usually managed by the HR department) examines and identifies an organization's personnel needs, such as the number of individuals to be employed according to income.

(15) (D) Interviewing and negotiating salaries with prospective employees.

Selection involves choosing the most suitable candidates from those who apply for the job. It offers jobs to desired candidates by interviewing them and then negotiating further things, such as salary.

(16) (B) They are used as guidelines to ensure that activities run smoothly and subjectivity is avoided.

Policies are important in any type of workplace or business because they help enhance the standards expected of employees in all of their professional dealings and allow employers to manage their employees effectively by defining what is acceptable at the workplace. As a result, activities run smoothly and there is no subjectivity, such as bias.

(17) (C) It will become impossible for employees to perform their jobs well without it.

An organization that does not take worker protection seriously cannot succeed for long, as employees cannot perform their jobs smoothly if their safety is at stake.

(18) (B) The ability to communicate properly, multitask, be fair and possess specific job skills.

HR managers are expected to communicate properly, multitask, be fair and possess specific job skills to be able to easily take care of tasks at hand.

(19) (C) Task-oriented managers are more concerned with job tasks than relationships.

Managers following the task-oriented management style are mainly concerned about the tasks of the job; in people-oriented management, managers are more concerned with interpersonal relations in the workplace.

(20) (D) When managers focus on completing tasks and do not give much importance to maintaining relationships with employees.

Autocratic managers tend to make choices based upon their own ideas and do not listen to their team or seek input from others. Their main focus is on completing tasks.

(21) (D) None of the above.

There are seven styles of management: task-oriented, people-oriented, participatory, directing, teamwork style, autocratic style and free-rein.

(22) (A) Managers can switch to the autocratic style if needed.

This model works through the observance of three key areas: the manager's errant conduct, the manager's relationship conduct and the employees' availability. An important feature of this model is that managers can switch to an autocratic style of leadership when the readiness of employees is low.

(23) (B) To meet regulatory requirements.

Diversity and inclusion result in a positive workplace. Due to this, employers use diversity and inclusion initiatives to comply with regulations while also improving the bottom line by having a more diverse, egalitarian and inclusive workforce.

(24) (A) The differences among different individuals, considering all their characters and attributes.

Workplace diversity entails accepting the fact that each person is unique and appreciating people's differences. Languages, sex, life experiences, age, ethnicity and family status can all be considered.

(25) (C) Focusing on maximizing output and profit.

Diversity plans do not have anything to do with business output or profit; instead, they focus on accomplishing organizational objectives, including those of the CEO and upper-class management, starting with the organization's motivation and encouraging a feeling of possession and responsibility among all employees.

(26) (D) Employees feel motivated to add to the business.

As a result of the inclusion, each employee feels more valued and is more likely to contribute to the company that provided them with such an atmosphere.

(27) (A) By creating inclusion workshops and providing conflict resolution training.

Workers can be provided with proper training and schooling by being made part of inclusion awareness workshops or responsiveness preparations. Moreover, they should also be provided with conflict resolution training.

(28) (D) Gather information, determine areas of concern, address policies, define business goals and obtain support.

These are the right steps for diversity and inclusion initiatives.

(29) (A) Foster an activity intended specifically for these initiatives.

Businesses should start an activity that can help these specific initiatives. Changes in approaches and practices, staff preparation, centered enrolling, manager-supported diversity and incorporation of mindfulness events for workers are generally examples of diversity and inclusion drives.

(30) (B) Top management that uses an autocratic style of management.

Organizations define three things that can prove to be impediments: poorly performing middle management, monetary limitations that impede broad deployment strategies and individuals who are excessively focused on surviving, not contributing.

(31) (D) None of the above.

Methodologies and policies protect employee rights, clear up confusion regarding regulations and provide employees with a behavioral guide.

(32) (C) So a comprehensive work environment can be built.

Having a diverse workforce allows businesses to better understand and address the requirements of people with diverse backgrounds, which fosters strong connections and communication and thus builds a comprehensive work environment.

(33) (A) Helps reduce stress.

Exits and terminations are important areas for HR to work on because developing efficient existing processes can help reduce stress.

(34) (A) A positive atmosphere.

A well-thought-out exit process enables a smooth transition that adds to the positive atmosphere of the workplace.

(35) (C) The employee was offered a better opportunity.

A voluntary exit happens whenever an employee chooses to partner with another company for other opportunities or personal reasons.

(36) (D) By promoting within the company.

HR can fill the position of ex-employees by promoting within the company or starting a recruitment process, depending on the requirement.

(37) (B) 72 hours.

If employees provide 72-hour notice, they need to be paid their final wages, including any unused accrued vacation or PTO at the time of departure.

(38) (D) They both provide notices for departing employees.

According to COBRA and HIPAA, employers must provide notices to departing employees.

(39) (B) Pre-retirement counseling programs.

HR can develop pre-retirement counseling programs to help prepare employees for this change. These programs are valuable in helping employees transition from one stage of their life to another in a fulfilling way and in maintaining a positive relationship between employees and the company.

(40) (A) They provide relevant feedback and valuable insight.

Exit interviews are recommended as part of the exit process before an employee departs the company. These interviews provide relevant feedback and valuable insight into the company's organizational process and impression.

(41) (C) Attempting to resolve the problems through coaching.

Management takes steps to help the employee resolve the problems through coaching, which can be informal or a structured formal program, depending on the situation.

(42) (D) Work with the employee's manager and go through the termination by taking proper steps to avoid legal actions against the firm.

HR needs to work with the employee's manager to cover all bases and ensure that appropriate procedure has been followed for the termination process. Otherwise, it can open the organization up to legal action by the employee.

(43) (B) When extreme actions have been taken by the employee.

If the employee's actions are too extreme and can become a danger to the workplace, the employer should immediately terminate the employee.

(44) (A) They allow supervisors to finalize the termination decision.

Termination meetings should be about 10 to 15 minutes long and have the sole purpose of providing a simple and concise statement of the decision to terminate an employment relationship.

(45) (C) The supervisor.

Supervisors must conduct termination meetings with the employees being terminated.

(46) (C) When an employee is dealing with sensitive data or material.

Supervisors can also oversee the cleanup process, especially if the employee handles sensitive materials or data.

(47) (D) 1988.

Congress passed the WARN Act in 1988.

(48) (B) Congress.

Congress passed the WARN Act during the 1980s.

(49) (A) It protects workers and requires a 60-day advance notice for termination.

The WARN Act protects workers and requires a 60-day advance notice from employers in the event of a termination. The advance notice is to be given to every individual employee or union representative and is intended to afford the workers some time to look for other employment or training avenues before they lose their positions.

(50) (D) Upon the completion of 4,000 hours per week by the 100+ employees.

Employees who work in the aggregate of 4,000 hours or more per week are subject to the provisions of the WARN Act.

(51) (A) 50 or more employees losing their jobs.

A plant closing refers to 50 or more full-time employees losing their jobs because of a single facility shutting down either temporarily or permanently.

(52) (D) All of the above.

There are situations where a 60-day notice is not required to be given out to each employee. These include a faltering company exception, an unforeseeable business circumstances exception and a natural disaster exception.

(53) (C) Publicly advertising the events and reasons for the decision.

HR should not publicly advertise the events to other companies or to the mass media. Honest communication should be maintained in the workplace, and the layoff process should be made as transparent as possible to employees privately. Employees should not be kept in the dark or lied to about upcoming decisions. This is also important for maintaining the respect and loyalty of the remaining employees who may be struggling with survivor guilt and who could possibly be tasked with more work due to the layoffs.

(54) (A) To ensure that the employee's dignity is not affected.

HR needs to ensure that the employee's dignity is not affected during the termination process. So, an appropriate place and time should be decided for the termination meeting to make the difficult process as easy as it can be.

(55) (A) Illegal termination.

If an employer chooses to terminate an employment contract based on a reason that violates the contract or goes against a statute, the decision is considered wrongful termination.

(56) (B) After all the changes have been made.

Collecting diversity or inclusion program metrics is a challenge, and it is best to collect metrics after all the changes have been finalized.

(57) (C) To stay innovative and competitive.

A diverse workplace is a valuable asset because it recognizes each employee's unique qualities and the possibilities they provide. Diversity recruitment is a basic step toward building a comprehensive work environment, and a diverse company can stay innovative and competitive.

(58) (B) Every individual must reward and acknowledge coworkers.

Inclusion is a two-way street; everyone must reward and acknowledge one another with respect. As a result of this thoughtfulness, all employees feel more valued and are more likely to contribute to the company that provided them with such an atmosphere. This type of environment involves cross-cultural communication and collaboration, as well as an awareness of one another's requirements and perspectives.

(59) (D) Incorporating inclusion in every aspect of the business.

This is not one of the strategies HR managers can use. HR managers can use the following strategies to retain and assist in the development of new hires:

- Execute preparation programs for employees
- Initiate tutoring programs focusing on workplace assimilation
- Monitor the development paces of different groups of new hires

(60) (C) By focusing on employee referral programs.

Organizations can conduct a policy and practice analysis by focusing on employee referral programs.

(61) (A) It helps companies ensure that stakeholders are properly communicated with.

Making initiatives public means everyone is involved and communicated with. This will eventually create an inclusive work environment. Moreover, each person receives a steady stream of information or feedback about their efforts, leading to improvements.

(62) (C) Foster an activity intended specifically for these initiatives.

Businesses should start an activity that can help these initiatives. Changes in approaches and practices, staff preparation, centered enrolling, manager-supported diversity and incorporation of mindfulness events for workers are examples of diversity and inclusion drives.

(63) (B) To direct the organization's essential objectives.

For the initiative to succeed, senior management buy-in and support are vital. Senior management must understand the business case for initiatives, with clear connections to the company's strategic goals. It is a good idea to find a senior-level champion who will be responsible for providing visible support for the initiative and ultimately keep the program running.

(64) (C) By completing a socioeconomic assessment.

Employers should begin by conducting a socioeconomic assessment of factors in the age, sex and racial representation of the assorted workforce and then observe the minutiae (location, division, position, etc.).

(65) (D) Obtaining support from employees.

Obtaining support from employees is not one way leader participation can be used to set inclusion programs in motion. Leader participation can be used to set inclusion programs in motion by allocating a senior leader to lead or support the organization's diversity drive, creating an equality officer role or structuring a diversity committee.

(66) (B) To maintain workplace safety.

The Occupational Safety and Health Act of 1970 was formed to enforce safety and health standards for most of the country's workers.

(67) (A) Setting safety standards for industries and enforcing them.

A key point of the Occupational Safety and Health Act was the creation of OSHA, which is now responsible for setting safety standards for industries and enforcing them.

(68) (A) Employers must file a report with OSHA within 3 hours if a few employees are hospitalized or have a fatal accident.

This is not an OSHA requirement. If serious hospitalization or a fatal accident occurs that specifically involves three or more employees, a report must be filed with the OSHA office within eight hours.

(69) (A) Researching and evaluating workplace hazards and helping employees find ways to reduce the effect of those hazards.

NIOSH is responsible for researching and evaluating workplace hazards and recommending ways to reduce the effect of those hazards on employees.

(70) (B) The NIOSH Act.

Aside from researching and evaluating workplace hazards, NIOSH also supports education and training in the field of occupational safety and health by developing and providing educational materials and training aids and sponsoring conferences on workplace safety and health issues.

(71) (C) Apply for waivers.

Some specific company operations may become impossible to carry out in accordance with OSHA rules, in which case employers can seek temporary or permanent waivers with evidence of suitable protection.

(72) (D) It allows organizations to be involved in the promotion of workplace health and safety issues.

OSHA's Alliance Program develops formal connections with organizations dedicated to workplace safety and health and interacts with them to avoid injuries and illnesses.

(73) (B) Employers must implement tough safety programs in their workplace.

The VPP allows employers to be removed from the list of routine inspections. But to meet the criteria of the program, employers must implement tough safety programs in their workplace.

(74) (B) It examines and monitors employers that have a repeated history of violations.

OSHA has an Enhanced Enforcement Program that inspects and monitors employers that have a repeated history of violations.

(75) (C) Exit meetings.

Exit meetings are not elements of an IIPP. Under IIPPs, companies need to follow some protocols, including management leadership, worker participation, hazard identification, education and training, hazard prevention and control and program evaluation and improvement.

(76) (C) Ten.

OSHA requires any company with more than 10 employees to have emergency plans in writing.

(77) (B) Resource management.

Five steps should be followed when creating a preparedness plan that meets FEMA requirements: resource management, needs assessment and business impact analysis, practical implementations, testing and maintenance and improvements.

(78) (D) Hazards and threats are assessed.

After receiving approval from senior management, the OSHA direct hazard identification process can begin. Hazard assessment is especially crucial when dealing with physical realities, like the possibility of earthquakes. So, before entering an active scenario, both natural and operation-specific hazards must be recognized.

(79) (C) It can help businesses prepare themselves for any potential threats.

A preparedness plan refers to the precautions taken before, during and after a disaster or an emergency to ensure people's safety. It also protects the business from future threats.

(80) (B) Maintenance and improvements.

There are four steps in the emergency preparedness plans. The last one is maintenance and improvements of the work environment. In this step, updates and improvements can be made as operations are added.

(81) (C) To elicit a smooth response in the middle of a crisis.

Realistic plans must be properly established from every viewpoint following the danger assessment. This step helps in determining a project's success. Therefore, practical implementations of plans help with a smooth response in the middle of an emergency.

(82) (D) Imminent danger, accidents, complaints and referrals, inspections.

OSHA sets up a hierarchy regarding priorities of inspections: imminent danger, catastrophes and fatal accidents, complaints and referrals, programmed high-hazard inspections and follow-up inspections.

(83) (D) Data recovery.

Safety protocols, communication plans, data recovery, medical assistance and more all need to be thought of beforehand to elicit a smooth response in the middle of an actual crisis.

(84) (B) It is the official recognition of a business's exemplary health and safety practices.

VPPs are designed to improve workplace safety and health. Acceptance into a VPP is OSHA's official recognition of the efforts of employers and employees who have achieved exemplary occupational safety and health.

(85) (A) To seek advice from OSHA.

Employers have the right to obtain OSHA's assistance and participate actively in health and safety issues in their workplaces. They are welcome to join the OSHA Standard Advisory Committee as well.

(86) (A) The negotiation process between employees and employers in an organization.

Collective bargaining is the process through which employees collectively bargain with their employers via their unions to establish their employment terms, such as pay, benefits, hours, leave, occupational health and safety standards, and strategies to balance work and family life, among other things.

(87) (B) To collectively fight with employers for terms and conditions of employment.

The goal of collective bargaining is to collectively fight for terms and conditions of employment and agree with the employers.

(88) (D) Labor contract.

Union representatives approach employers to start a negotiation process that concludes with a labor contract agreeable to both parties.

(89) (B) Collective bargaining agreement.

When an agreement is reached, a legal contract is signed by both parties. It is referred to as a collective bargaining agreement.

(90) (C) Labor union.

Labor unions in organizations initiate the process of collective bargaining.

(91) (D) Both (A) and (B).

Collective bargaining is seen as an excellent tool that helps both employees and employers. It gives power to unions to collectively assert and demand their rights as employees. It also helps employers improve their workplace while maintaining employee loyalties.

(92) (A) Democracy.

Collective bargaining is a sign of democracy in a business environment. The joint decision-making process is aimed at a positive outcome, even if the process of negotiation becomes difficult in high-tension scenarios.

(93) (D) Both parties should work for personal gains instead of looking for mutual benefits.

This is not an essential feature of collective bargaining. According to the International Labor Union, collective bargaining should have active participation from management representatives and employees, be aimed primarily at bringing stability in the working relationship between the parties and conclude with the implementation of the agreement. Additionally, both parties should maintain a flexible attitude toward the negotiation process.

(94) (A) Workplace matters.

The NLRA holds employers and unions to their duty to negotiate workplace matters. The subject matter of the negotiations can range from wages to employee treatment.

(95) (C) 60 to 90 days before the contract expires.

Unions can show bad faith in the process if they fail to notify management about their plans or intent to renegotiate the contract 60 to 90 days before it expires.

(96) (B) Two.

There are two basic approaches to negotiation. Involved parties can adopt different bargaining approaches, and all approaches have different effects on the bargaining process.

(97) (D) Both (B) and (C).

There are two basic approaches to bargaining: positional bargaining and principled bargaining.

(98) (A) It is a type of bargaining in which both parties are focused on their demands.

Positional bargaining refers to the strategy where both parties are focused on their demands, and the representatives of each party intend to win for their side.

(99) (B) It is a type of bargaining in which both parties are focused on solving a problem.

Principled bargaining is aimed more at solving a problem in the workplace than winning an argument. In the principled bargaining approach, both parties are open to negotiations, brainstorming and compromising to tackle the issues quickly.

(100) (C) Both (A) and (B).

There are two types of principled bargaining: integrative and interest-based bargaining. Interactive bargaining is a type of principled bargaining in which both parties focus on the issues and agree on trade-offs to reach a final decision.

On the other hand, interest-based bargaining is also a form of principled bargaining in which negotiations are made with the underlying understanding that both parties have harmonious interests in the matter.

(101) (A) Positional bargaining.

Positional bargaining is an approach to negotiation in collective bargaining. This is a competitive approach to bargaining and not a strategy.

(102) (C) The construction industry.

A closed shop clause is an arrangement whereby an employer agrees to only hire—and retain in employment—people who are members in good standing of the trade union. This clause is legal only for the construction industry.

(103) (A) It is a clause that requires all employees to join a union or pay union dues if not joining.

The agency shop clause requires all employees to join a union or pay union dues if they are not joining.

(104) (D) Preparation, discussion, proposal, bargaining, settlement.

The process of collective bargaining can be carried out in five major steps: preparation, where negotiation teams are made; discussion, where representatives from both parties form a mutual ground; proposal, which includes the opening statements from both parties; bargaining, where parties try to solve the problem together; and settlement, where the agreement is finally reached.

(105) (B) The CBA.

Settlement is the final stage of bargaining, in which an agreement is reached and the bargaining process ends after both parties sign the papers. When a settlement is reached, both parties are required to first agree to the terms set by the CBA.

(106) (B) In parallel bargaining, a union negotiates with more than one employer.

In single-unit bargaining, a union negotiates with only one employer in a single matter, whereas in parallel bargaining, a union negotiates with more than one employer. Once the union is done negotiating with one employer, it utilizes the results to negotiate with another.

(107) (B) A party withholding important information.

Bad faith can include a lack of concessions on issues, refusing to advance proposals or bargain, stall tactics or withholding information that is important to the process.

(108) (B) HR needs to provide the supervisor with the documentation and counsel the supervisor.

Termination meetings are some of the toughest duties HR has to perform. HR needs to provide the supervisor with all appropriate documentation that contains the necessary evidence for the termination decision before the meeting. However, documentation is not enough on its own. HR also needs to counsel the supervisor on how to handle the meeting and the possible situations the meeting could entail.

(109) (A) When an employer terminates an employee because of discriminatory reasons.

An employer cannot discriminate against an employee for any reason. If an employer has terminated an employee because of any discriminatory reasons, the person's actions are termed wrongful termination and thus may be reversed.

(110) (D) 33% of the employees have been laid off.

Under the WARN Act, a mass layoff refers to a situation in which 500 employees or a total of 33% of the workforce have been laid off.

(111) (A) Organizational values.

The fundamental ethics or concepts that an organization adheres to at all times, no matter what, are referred to as organizational values.

(112) (C) The organization's culture.

Organizations require organizational values because they give birth to the culture of the organization.

(113) (B) Good communication channels.

Managers cannot solve employees' problems if they are unaware of them. Hence, managers need to establish good communication channels with their employees to ensure they are aware of employee needs and progress and, ultimately, organizational needs and progress.

(114) (A) Globalization and offshoring.

Some of the external factors that managers should be aware of are globalization and offshoring, changes in laws for employment, health care costs, changing hiring practices, relevant technologies being used, layoffs and downsizing, workplace diversity and using social networking to keep employees educated.

(115) (D) Different needs.

An organization is made up of many departments and employees with various abilities, so it is not an exaggeration to say that there is a lot happening in any organization. As a result, an HR manager must be able to shuffle or deal with multiple duties simultaneously and organize and prioritize them.

(116) (C) Employee safety.

An HR manager's job is to create an environment that ensures employee safety. Chemical risks, airflow and heating requirements, the security of personal data and the use of no-fragrance zones are just a few of the safety needs that HR managers must be aware of in the workplace.

(117) (B) Autocratic management.

Autocratic management is a task-oriented management style. It focuses solely on accomplishing all tasks and emphasizes relationships. Managers are prone to following the "my way or the highway" mentality in this management style.

(118) (A) A people-oriented management style.

Teamwork management is a people-oriented management style. It emphasizes the importance of developing teamwork and incorporating feedback from all team members. As many people approach the same problem in different ways, this style provides management with many diverse, innovative solutions to problems.

(119) (B) The situational leadership model.

According to the situational leadership paradigm, when workforce readiness is low, managers should transition to an authoritarian leadership style. To put it another way, when employees lack the experience and/or necessary abilities required to complete a job on their own, managers give out the instructions and delegate all responsibilities while making all of the key choices themselves.

(120) (C) The path-goal model.

Different leadership models exist to help determine the appropriate management style for a given situation. The path-goal model of leadership is one of them.

According to this model, the manager's responsibility is to identify the objectives, lay out the steps to attain them and clarify the tasks as needed.

Made in the USA
Coppell, TX
08 November 2024